'61

University of Pittsburgh

SERIES IN COMPARATIVE ADMINISTRATION

number 1

COMPARATIVE STUDIES IN ADMINISTRATION

COMPARATIVE STUDIES IN ADMINISTRATION

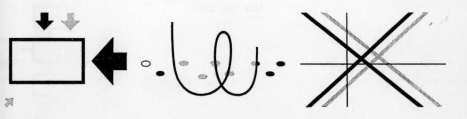

Edited by the Staff of the Administrative Science Center,

James D. Thompson

Peter B. Hammond

Robert W. Hawkes

Buford H. Junker

Arthur Tuden

Foreword by **Edward H. Litchfield**

UNIVERSITY OF PITTSBURGH PRESS

foreword

Only in recent years have we come to recognize that administration is a distinct and identifiable social process which occurs in all contemporary institutions and which becomes of increasing importance as those institutions and the environments in which they function become larger and more complex. With our recognition of the existence and importance of the process, administrative science has emerged as a distinctive field of inquiry. It is possible that it may develop ultimately into a separate discipline which will take its place beside the more traditional social and behavioral sciences.

Evidence of the new recognition of administration as a distinctive social process is steadily increasing. Schools of business and public administration which were once combined only for organizational convenience are now gradually finding common ground for teaching and research programs. Administrative science has found a professional journal devoted exclusively to its problems in the new *Administrative Science Quarterly*.[1] On a number of campuses new study centers exploring specialized aspects of administration have been established. Programs of professional societies such as the American Society for Public Administration show far more concern for the process as it occurs in other than governmental settings than they did ten or even five years ago. Schools of business administration have made significant efforts in noncorporate fields—such as Harvard's concern for university administration and Cornell's interest in hospital administration.

The University of Pittsburgh has recognized the significance of the

1. Founded in 1956 in Cornell's Graduate School of Business and Public Administration.

administrative process in modern society in a still more comprehensive way. It has established the Administrative Science Center staffed by persons from the behavioral sciences and from the applied areas of administration for the express purpose of studying the process as it occurs in many different institutional settings in a variety of contemporary cultures. This volume, *Comparative Studies in Administration,* is one of the early products of the Center's work.

It is important to understand the context in which this volume appears. While the steady progress which we have noted in administrative science is significant and encouraging, many of the shortcomings which I noted some years ago still exist and, indeed, on further examination others have come to light.[2] Three among them are particularly significant:

1. There is a grave discrepancy between our understanding of the process in different types of institutional areas. Administration in the corporation continues to be a subject of extensive investigation and one about which we are learning more with the passing of each year. Here, students are many, interest is real, knowledge is growing, and attitudes are relatively sophisticated. On the other hand, in such a field as college and university administration, knowledge of the process, *per se,* is meager, both research and training are virtually non-existent, and interest itself varies from a casual concern to outright distaste and distrust.[3] Understanding of the process in other institutional settings varies widely within these two extremes.

2. Although the situation is improving, there is still a serious lack of knowledge in any one field of the developments in the process in other applied areas. More sophisticated public administrators are now giving attention to the developments in business administration, but it has not been my observation that a great deal of interest in or knowledge of such developments has yet permeated to the working levels of public administration throughout the country. I am equally confident that workaday business management knows little of the significant developments in the field of administrative science which are taking place in the more academic aspects of the behavioral sciences. As one might expect, the transfer of knowledge from one institutional field to another is in direct proportion to the interest which the field shows in the proc-

2. See "Notes on a General Theory of Administration," *Administrative Science Quarterly,* Vol. I, No. 1, June 1956.

3. For further developments of this point, see "Organization in Large American Universities: The Administration," *The Journal of Higher Education,* Vol. XXX, No. 12, December 1959.

ess in its own setting. The more underdeveloped the area's interest in its own administrative problems, the less concern it shows in learning from others.

3. We are still without a significant body of theory which has general meaning for more than one type of institution. In relatively few cases have we succeeded in achieving a level of generalization based on cross-institutional observation. Administrative science will never fully emerge as a distinctive field of inquiry until at least the minimums of broad theory have been developed.

There are a number of reasons why our progress is not more rapid. Among the more important of them are the following:

1. In many applied fields the process finds recognition difficult because of a fundamental distrust with which administration is viewed by the predominant professional groups working in those fields. This is true of the attitudes of medical personnel in a hospital setting. It is true of the professor in many university organizations. One sees it in the attitude of the foreign service officer in the Department of State. Even in the administratively self-conscious corporation it is frequently noted in the attitudes of scientists in large research and development laboratories. The reasons for this almost universal attitude of professional people toward administration are too complex for analysis here. What is important at this point is to recognize that it is difficult to encourage scientific inquiry into a process which is viewed with distrust and even disdain by the highest status groups in the institutions in which the process occurs. Here one may pause and parenthetically observe that the emergence of administrative science as a study of the universals of the administrative process is handicapped by an almost equally universal circumstance—the distrust of the practicing professional of the process itself and of the persons who undertake it.

2. Paradoxically, while it is the large and complex institution which is most apt to develop an understanding of the process, it is the same complex institution which in its highly specialized characteristics tends to militate against the broad generalization which is essential to the understanding of the process itself. Thus, the modern corporation, while more conscious of administration than any other institution, is faced with an ever increasing difficulty in developing people in such specialized fields as manufacturing, marketing, or finance who are broad enough to understand the total administrative process as it is carried on at top-management levels. Stated somewhat differently, the institutional size and complexity which make the process important also encourage specializations which make it difficult to achieve either the breadth of

understanding, or more particularly the breadth of behavior, which the process requires.

3. In a number of instances the transfer of knowledge from one institutional field to another is discouraged by lack of understanding and even sympathy of one institution for another. Anyone who lives in more than one institutional setting encounters this at every turn. One's businessmen associates are scornful of the bureaucrats. The professor has a fundamental distrust for the corporation, and the bureaucrat shares his feeling. One's medical colleagues can seldom see the parallels between any of these institutions and the hospital or the clinic. This kind of institutional provincialism discourages the transfer of knowledge from one field to another within a given culture and makes cross-cultural and cross-institutional transferability even harder to attain.

4. We are still handicapped by the inability of people with applied interest in administration to talk effectively with those whose interest in administration begins with the academic concern of the behavioral scientist. It is true that a few business schools are beginning to bring the behavioral disciplines into their faculties. Some hospital administration programs when situated in schools of public health have been doing this for some time. The McKinsey Foundation has rendered great service in its effort to bring the applied and theoretical points of view together. But, for all of these important developments, there is still a great deal to be done to bring the two into effective relationship to one another.

5. Many of the difficulties could be corrected if we had better methods of communicating among fields and between groups within fields. Those of us who have the architect's interest in building administrative science must recognize the paucity of vehicles with which to bring these various points of view together to the end that our research in and theorizing about the process may be improved. We know that our professional societies are organized along specialized institutional interests. Our educational programs tend to fall into the same institutional patterns with schools of business administration, schools of hospital administration, programs in public administration, curricula in hotel administration, and others in school administration. There are few journals which are devoted to bringing the several institutional areas together in a consideration of the process, *per se*. One would have difficulty in mentioning a half dozen educational institutions having faculty colloquia in the field of administrative science.

It is in this context that this volume, *Comparative Studies in Administration*, appears. Like the Administrative Science Center in which it has been prepared, it is concerned with the universals of administration as they occur in many institutional settings. In it the reader will find materials drawn from extractive, manufacturing, and transportation industries; higher education; hospitals; and military and social welfare aspects of government. The authors represent several branches of the social and behavioral sciences, including anthropology, economics, industrial management, sociology, and social psychology. The reader will also observe that in addition to seeking the constants or universals in administration, this volume seeks to add to our knowledge by according a broad role to the variables in the administrative process. In its purpose it accepts the basic proposition that after we examine the variables we will have a clearer understanding of the universals of administration.

This is the first in a series of such volumes which will be published by the Center. With the passing of time, it is to be hoped that an ever wider scope of institutional interests may be included and that the contributions may come from a number of related disciplinary and applied fields which are not represented in this first volume.

EDWARD H. LITCHFIELD
Chancellor, University of Pittsburgh

Pittsburgh, Pennsylvania
September 10, 1959

preface

The education of men and women for responsible administrative roles in complex societies can become more effective only as we gain the fundamental understanding from which more powerful principles of administration may be derived. This volume, therefore, is intended as a contribution to the study of administration, rather than as a handbook for administrators.

Although the methodological bases for the selection of the materials in this volume are set forth in Chapter 1, a few more general criteria may be mentioned briefly. Within the limitations of space and topic, we sought materials from the widest possible range of publications, academic disciplines, and fields of administration. The authors in this volume represent several branches of the social and behavioral sciences, including anthropology, economics, industrial management, sociology, and social psychology. The reprinted materials are drawn from six different sources. Data for the empirical studies were gathered in Germany, Great Britain, Norway, West Africa, and in the Fox Indian society, as well as in the contemporary United States.

The types of organizations considered are even more diversified, including those in manufacturing, mining, and shipping industries; higher education; hospitals; and military and social welfare organs of government. This range of activities, together with the diversity of authors, results in an inevitable lack of uniformity in terminology. This is compensated for, we believe, by the breadth of theoretical implications of the ideas, concepts, and relationships considered.

One omission should be noted, for it reflects the state of the literature of administrative science rather than our lack of interest or appreciation. In spite of the considerable role of administration in rapidly-developing areas of the world, those who write in American journals seem preoccupied with the technical, economic, and social aspects of change to the exclusion of the administrative processes involved.

Our search for pertinent materials was limited to publications appearing during the past five years, and not easily available to our intended audience. Some of the great writings which helped to delineate administrative science thus were omitted. Nevertheless the influences of such pioneers as Chester I. Barnard and Herbert A. Simon are unmistakable and are clearly reflected not only in the footnote citations but in the basic concepts and orientations employed by the several authors. The contributions of leaders in related disciplines, including Max Weber, Talcott Parsons, and Robert K. Merton, also are reflected here. Readers familiar with Edward H. Litchfield's provocative propositions—advanced in an article dedicating the *Administrative Science Quarterly* in 1956—will recognize that they form the skeleton around which this book is built.

We will be disappointed if our audience is confined to the campus. There is a growing number of responsible administrators who find the time and energy to exercise their curiosities as well as their problem-solving abilities. We hope this volume will stimulate some of them to help extend or correct the ideas contained herein.

We are indebted to the authors who generously gave their permission to include materials reprinted here. We are equally indebted to the publishers whose permissions are acknowledged in appropriate chapters for their ready consent to the reprinting of materials. Agnes L. Starrett, director of the University of Pittsburgh Press, has been most helpful and encouraging in the publication of this volume. Judith E. Brugh and Marian M. Hatok carefully and cheerfully typed the manuscript, and the coordination and liaison performed by Augusta T. Moretti were indispensable. Jean S. Adelman exercised indexing responsibilities admirably.

Pittsburgh, Pennsylvania
June 18, 1959

JAMES D. THOMPSON
PETER B. HAMMOND
ROBERT W. HAWKES
BUFORD H. JUNKER
ARTHUR TUDEN

xiv

contents

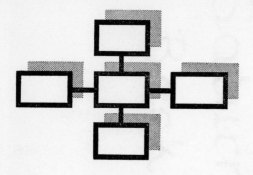

part I

INTRODUCTION

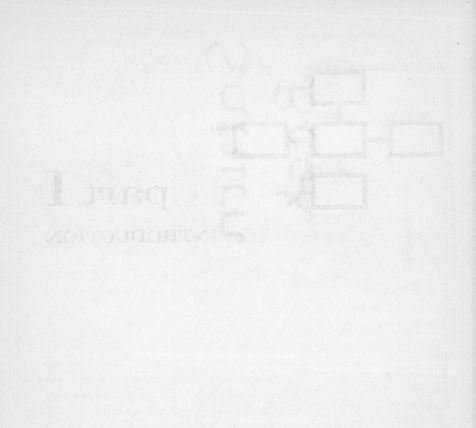

An original article prepared especially for this volume.

chapter 1

On the Study of Administration[1]

Peter B. Hammond, Robert W. Hawkes,
Buford H. Junker, James D. Thompson, and Arthur Tuden

The practicing arts—medicine, for example, or law, or engineering—appeared as action phenomena long before they were recognized as legitimate and important topics for academic, scientific appraisal. Administration also has been practiced for many generations but has emerged as a subject for higher education only during the twentieth century. Determined attempts to build a scientific understanding of administration are even more recent. The first academic journal devoted solely to this purpose—*Administrative Science Quarterly*—was established in 1956.

What we seek is a valid set of generalizations which will offer a more precise description of administration and ultimately facilitate the prediction of administrative events in unknown but conceivable circumstances. Only as this goal is approached can the science of administration make significant contributions to the art of administration, as the sciences of medicine have contributed to its practice.

Although the goal may be distant, important beginnings have been made by those who sense inadequacies in administrative law, "scientific management," human relations, and the insights of practical administrators. The useful contributions from those sources must not be overlooked, but we look to the social, behavioral, and newer sciences for basic building blocks for the future.

Now, instead of a universally valid theory, there is a growing variety of part-theories[2]—of business administration, public administration, hospital administration, educational administration, and other administrations—and many scholars insist that the similarities among

3

these are insignificant. Such theories, moreover, have typically been ethnocentric, so that in reality we have theories of business administration (American), or public administration (British), or at best, models of administration (Euro-American). It is often difficult to determine whether our theories *are* theories—or philosophies—and some students refuse to grant that such a distinction can be meaningful. Thus educational administration is not only to be understood as American but also as democratic, and business administration is not only American but "naturally" profit-centered.

The social and behavioral sciences, generally speaking, have been hesitant about studying administration. Some scholars have felt that administration is an artificial subject and not worthy of the serious attention given to such topics as the family or the human individual, which are regarded as natural and proper subjects for scientific investigation. Many fail to see a distinction between administrative processes and the specific fields within which they occur. Thus business administration is equated with economics, public administration with government, or public health administration with environmental medicine. The more "tough-minded" or "hard-headed" of the behavioral scientists even suggest that, while the small group can be studied, the hospital, the firm, and the university are too complex to be understood scientifically.

Probably every new field of study has faced these problems in breaking out of old disciplines. Despite such problems, however, administrative science is establishing an identity and is gaining momentum. We firmly believe that there is in the making a rigorous science of administration, which can account for events in particular times and places and for the ethical or normative content of those events without itself incorporating the particular conditions and values of those events. The necessary theory must take such factors into account as variables. These variables must be broad enough to include the conditions and ethics found in all fields of administration and in all cultural contexts.

In the remainder of this paper we shall present our preliminary notes toward a science of administration.

Scope and Focus of Administration

Until administration is better understood it is not likely to be defined with much agreement or confidence. On the other hand, until it is defined the organization of relevant data remains difficult. Therefore, a tentative working definition is essential. The definition presented here will focus on what administration *does* rather than what it *is*. Thus we

4

propose a tentative definition which (1) has empirical referents and (2) can be formulated in a way consistent with contemporary theory-building in the social sciences.

There seems to be reasonable consensus that administration is found in governments, armies, corporations, hospitals, prisons, school systems, universities, trade unions, churches, and philanthropic foundations. Few would insist, on the other hand, that administration is an important phenomenon in mobs, crowds, or publics.[3]

Although many societies make use of administration in certain spheres of activity such as government, it is rarely contended that societies as such are administrative organizations.[4]

If not all collectivities exhibit administration, what are the distinguishing characteristics which allow us to point to certain ones as clearly having administration and others as not having it? How does the hospital or the corporation differ from the mob? What is behind the distinction between armies and crowds? How do we differentiate a trade union from a society or a family?

In seeking to answer these questions, we have indentified four characteristics among those collectivities which clearly have administration. Their enumeration follows:

1. *Administered organizations exhibit sustained collective action.* They are not based on *ad hoc* activities, but on continued efforts having recognized results. They maintain identity long enough to become points of reference for those not physically in their presence; and if they exist only for weeks or days, they usually are considered failures.[5] Crowds or mobs, however, usually disband in a matter of hours or days. If they persist, it is through their conversion into permanent administered organizations.

2. *Administered organizations are integral parts of a larger system.* As systems they are not self-sufficient or self-maintaining. However many are the goals of administered groups, and however varied are the activities performed in them, they do not meet all of their requirements to persist as self-sufficient collectivities. Administered organizations do not depend, for example, on biological processes within the membership as the primary means of membership replacement. In this the administered organization is distinguished not only from the society but also from the family, both of which are persistent, species-maintaining collectivities.

3. *Administered organizations have specialized, delimited goals.* The objectives or purposes of the collectivity may change from time to

time, and vary in degree of explicitness, but both members and non-members understand that corporations, trade unions, hospitals, and schools have different, if occasionally overlapping,[6] roles in the society.

4. *Administered organizations are dependent upon interchange with the larger system.* Requiring sustenance but being limited in their spheres of activity, administered organizations must receive inputs from and in turn discharge outputs to the larger system.

Thus, by a process of elimination we have narrowed the search for administration to certain kinds of collectivities: those which exhibit sustained activity; are part of a larger system; have specialized purposes; and are dependent upon interchange with the larger system. This tells us *where* to look for administration, but it does not tell us *what* to look for, since by this definition any and all activity in such collectivities might be considered administrative activity. Again it is necessary, given the present state of our knowledge, to rely on "common sense" as a basis for distinguishing administrative from other kinds of activity in administered organizations.

It is rarely contended that "administrative action" is synonymous with "organizational action," but there the agreement ends. For decades American students of political science distinguished policy-making from administration, confining the latter to the middle and lower reaches of government. American students of business administration used the term to refer to their total field of study, but described activity in terms of top management, middle management, or supervision.

The problem, from our point of view, becomes one of distinguishing administrative from other kinds of activity in administered organizations—*without* declaring *a priori* that it is behavior performed by incumbents of certain kinds of fixed positions in the organization. The question of who contributes what to administration must remain an empirical question at this point.

Few would argue that the nurse's taking of a temperature is administrative behavior in the hospital, although in the vernacular, she "administers" sedatives. It is seldom said that the soldier's firing of a rifle is administrative behavior in the army. The bolt-turner on a factory assembly line is not conceived of as an administrator. But we are trapped if we attempt to describe the common characteristics of those organizational activities in terms of their *location* in a hierarchy. The fact that these activities are performed by those at the end of a chain of command, if this is so, is not the important criterion which leads to their classification as non-administrative.

The important point is that all of these activities not only are sometimes performed outside of organizational contexts, but also have meaning or significance independent of whether they are performed within organizations. Organizations grow up around such activities not because organizations are necessary to their performance, but because organization increases their convenience, economy, or significance.[7] But without an organization to be administered, administrative activity has no meaning or significance. It exists only when non-administrative activities are carried out in an organizational context.

Thus, administrative activity may be defined as activity related to the creation, maintenance, or operation of an organization as an organization.[8]

Organization Requirements and Administrative Functions

The characteristics which were posited above as distinguishing administered organizations from other types of collectivities facilitate at least a minimum statement of organizational requirements and provide the basis for hypothesising the following functions of administration:

1. *Structuring of the organization as an administrative function.* If such organizations must exhibit sustained rather than *ad hoc* activity, it follows that the actions of their component parts must be patterned and controlled, rather than random. While custom, convention and habit provide a basis for common action, administered organizations must channel and modify such activity in order to meet their specific needs.

2. *Definition of purpose as an administrative function.* If administered organizations have delimited, specialized purposes, it follows that these purposes must be selected and articulated. Organizational goals do not spring automatically out of the collective performance of non-administrative tasks. In a dynamic context goals do not remain obvious, but mechanisms for their evaluation, reflection, implementation, and periodic revision must be institutionalized. As such activities as bolt-turning, temperature taking, or rifle-firing do not in themselves define and prescribe collective goals, the definition of purposes is a function of administration.

3. *Management of the organization-environment exchange system as a function of administration.* Some of the necessary exchanges between the organizations and the environment occur in the performance of non-administrative activities; but the very essence of organi-

zation is task specialization, which calls for coordination. Hence the management of the system of exchange between an organization and its environment becomes primarily a function of administration. At a minimum this applies to the acquisition and disbursement, from and to the larger system (a) of legitimation or authority; (b) of personnel; (c) of tools, equipment or other facilities; and (d) of a medium of exchange.

In recapitulation, we have identified the administered organization by four characteristics which distinguish it from other collectivities. From those characteristics we have derived three minimum requirements of such organizations as organizations, and have said that the functions of administration are to provide for the satisfaction of those requirements.

Every science assumes that patterns can be found in its phenomena. The working definition we have adopted postulates that certain important patterns can be identified. These will be patterns of human activity which are associated with administrative functions. We turn now to strategies for gaining understanding of these patterns.

The Comparative Method and Administrative Science

Significant aspects of administration seldom lend themselves to controlled experimentation, where only the variable of interest at a particular moment is allowed to alter and everything else is held constant. The experiment, however, is only one of several valid strategies for gaining scientific knowledge. When it is practicable, experimentation is a most economic way of comparing phenomena with and phenomena without a certain treatment; but the absence of opportunities to manipulate phenomena in no way negates the possibility of gaining reliable knowledge through controlled observation of comparable events.

The comparison of administrative phenomena can and should proceed immediately, but as the field develops, the comparison of alternative theories will be of utmost importance.

COMPARISONS OF PHENOMENA

The study of comparable phenomena—similar yet somehow different—is indispensable in the search for variables, their range of variation, and the consequences of those variations.

The dominant schools of administration have established curricula and research programs on the assumption that each field of administration rests on unique elements, on constants and variables which are not merely different in degree from one field to another but are different in kind. The challenge to this position has come from those who assert that administration, in whatever context, is basically the same phenomenon. They have advanced a series of abstract models or theories of administration, management, organization, decision-making and communication. The comparative approach seems to be the most promising way of settling this issue. If in fact there are important similarities in the several types of administration, comparisons should reveal them. Yet to the extent that the more abstract formulations may conceal important variations, comparison should act as a correcting factor.

This raises the important question of what is to be compared. For reasons which are more accidental than logical, "comparative public administration" has been synonymous with cross-cultural or cross-national studies of administration, and "comparative business administration" has referred to business outside of the United States, or to the foreign operations of American firms. While the cultural dimension undoubtedly is essential to our understanding of administration, as our earlier discussion of environments makes clear, the comparative study of administration cannot be limited to cultural comparison alone.

The three functions of administration indicated earlier—having to do with organizational structure, organizational purposes, and organizational exchanges with the environment—are appropriate subjects for comparison. Each of these is subject to variation or difference and thus is amenable to comparative research and conceptualization. If organizations differ in structure, we must seek to understand why this occurs and how it affects the contexts of administration. If organizations differ in purposes, we must examine the effects of purposes on other aspects of administration. If organizations operate in different kinds of environments, we must learn how environments impinge on and shape organizations, administrative functions, and administrative processes.

Another urgent task at this stage in the development of administrative science lies at the conceptual level. Present conceptions of the relevant variables allow only crude bases for differentiation. If organizational exchange with the environment is an important aspect of administration, we can compare this in differing contexts only to the extent that we can conceive of differences among environments and differences of exchange relationships. But as yet there is no adequate "typology of environments," no authoritative catalog of exchange relationships which would permit us to classify with complete confidence two instances as similar or different. If organizational structure is an important aspect of administration, we need concepts which will allow

9

the sorting out and classifying of specific cases. Here we have several varieties of concepts, but none which we can embrace with assurance. And finally, we lack a conceptual framework for dealing with organizational goals or purposes.

These problems will require a great deal of effort before they are solved. It is significant, however, that the mere statement of administration in comparative terms focuses attention on these weaknesses of our present conceptual equipment.

COMPARISON OF THEORIES

The comparison of phenomena provides only a partial solution to our problems. The comparison of *alternative theories* or models in reflection against the same phenomena or pattern can mark the turning points in the development of administrative science.

Opportunities to make the crucial observations which differentiate weaker from more powerful theories do not occur frequently, but we must be alert to them when they do. Such opportunities will become more frequent as our theories become more general, hence more abstract. The less abstract theories seldom overlap each other, so they do not offer competing predictions about what will occur in the same kind of situations.

The two aspects of comparison go hand-in-hand. Studies of comparable phenomena can lead to greater generalization by way of abstraction, and this in turn makes possible the comparison of competing theories.

The Importance of Process

Administration was defined by what it *does,* by the functions it appears to perform or the requirements it seems to satisfy. Such a definition points to the importance of *identifying patterns* of administrative action and of *discovering their association* with the functions of administration.

The comparative approach is indispensable for uncovering the states or outcomes which are associated with particular patterns of administrative action. Administrative science cannot, however, rest with the discovery of association or correlation. Ultimately, we believe, the study of administrative processes—of *how* particular patterns bring about particular functional consequences—will be essential, and vice versa.

Administration is a dynamic phenomenon, and it is imperative that the strategy employed for investigating it gives assurance of focusing on dynamics rather than statics. Reliance on correlation or association—useful in providing clues—does not provide that assurance, as experience has demonstrated repeatedly in the social sciences.

There is, for example, the trap of spurious correlation, whereby two events appear to be associated but in fact have no connection or are connected only by being associated with still a third event. There is the danger of projecting into correlation an element of inevitability, and thereby assuming a linear, evolutionary development rather than a dynamic development. There is the ever-present possibility of over-looking two-way interaction of variables, or "feed-back loops," and thus obtaining a most distorted set of half-truths about administration. There is the danger, which has plagued many of the social sciences in their recent history, of "single-factor" analysis, which assumes that a particular consequence results from one variable when in fact a complex pattern of variables is responsible for that consequence.

A focus on administrative processes seems to offer the best assurance against the temptation to be content with association, and reduces our reliance on the particular genius of the investigator. In the definitional context already advanced, those *patterned sequences of behavior* which bring about, maintain, or curtail organizational structure would constitute an administrative process. Likewise, those *sets of behavior* related to establishing, maintaining, or dropping organizational purposes constitute an administrative process. The *patterned sequences of behavior* which provide or deny modes of interaction with relevant environments would also constitute an administrative process. In each case, the crucial question is *how* one pattern of behavior leads to another pattern of behavior, and so on through a chain until a functional requirement is satisfied.

If the history of other sciences has a lesson for us, it warns that sequences of activity should neither be conceived as random nor as inevitably determined. Organizations and those who administer them are not free agents, nor are they automatons who respond automatically to forces in a field. Within the limits established by reality, alternatives, choice points, or "branching" points are presented to organizations.

We have only vague notions about the frequency and the nature of these choice points, but until they are understood together with the behavior which results in the selection of one course rather than another, a serious gap in our understanding of administration will remain. What sequences of activity lead to the establishment or modification of organizational structure in one form rather than another? What patterns of behavior bring about the adoption or rejection of organizational purposes? What activity patterns bring about the identification of relevant parts of the environment and lead to the selection of alternative systems of interaction with that environment?

The growing diversity of conceptual schemes for investigating such processes reveals that *process* can be treated on several levels of abstraction, which can be viewed as the now classic rungs on the abstraction ladder. We have implied *three* administrative processes, one for each of the postulated functions of administration. It makes sense, we believe, to speak in more general terms of *the* administrative process, and to conceive of it as a general model which takes on more specific characteristics depending on the administrative function involved.

Whatever the number and nature of such conceptions which ultimately prove useful, the development of process models can lead to hypotheses about administration that go beyond taxonomy and allow for the development of prediction.

Relations with Other Fields

No dynamic discipline has rigid, unchanging boundaries or definitions of its field. The approach to administration taken above is no more than an approximation which, through further research, will be modified and expanded repeatedly through the thoughtful activities of a great many people. Clearly, however, administrative science overlaps several established disciplines, and its gradual development will grow not only out of the efforts of those who consider themselves students of administration but also out of work by those squarely in the established disciplines. Administration has many facets, each of which has been of concern to at least one of the several disciplines.

The present content of administrative science consists largely of concepts, data, relationships, and hypotheses first developed in psychology, sociology, anthropology, economics, political science or such emerging fields as cybernetics and game theory. Progress has been slow; the development of new understandings out of combinations of older knowledge is a formidable task, and much remains to be done. The contents of neighboring fields often have relevance for administration which has never been brought into view. The perspective of administrative science needs to be trained upon such contents—either by specialists in that discipline or by administrative scientists sufficiently close to the discipline to translate it accurately—first to discover such items and translate them into administrative frameworks, and second to interpret their meanings in new contexts.

Ultimately the results of such searching of a multiplicity of disciplines, together with newly emerging data and conclusions from other research, must be integrated into larger systems of understanding which we call administrative theories. Progress toward new knowledge always is slow; it is especially difficult where the necessary synthesis is of parts whose meanings often are concealed by diverse terminologies, and have been tailored to fit a variety of discrete conceptual schemes. Just who will do the necessary translating, interpreting and integration, and what forms these will take, is problematic. But in light of the approach to administration taken in this paper, a few notes on the possible contributions of other fields may be in order.

If administered organizations are subsystems of larger systems, they must be examined in light of their interdependence with the larger systems. We must look to cultural anthropology and sociology for their understandings of the dynamics of complex societies. Economics can contribute insight into the role of the firm and similar units in the larger economic system. Political science, history, and law can illuminate important aspects of the interaction between organizations and their roles in larger governmental and judicial systems.

If administered organizations are designed to persist over significant periods of time, history should have much to reveal about the rise and decline of such organizations in relation to the larger context. If specialized delimited purposes are characteristic of administered organizations, contributions should be expected from a number of fields of study. History, for example, might illuminate the adaptive aspects of administered organizations which revise their purposes as the larger system changes. Students of business and government relations have contributions to make, as do students of civil-military relations or union-management relations.

Complex organizations are made up of smaller units or groups and consequently the study of groups both in the field and in the social psychologist's laboratory can provide valuable information about organizational dynamics. Again, because administrators in organizational contexts are part of a larger analytic category of individuals in a social context, social psychology will have much to contribute toward an understanding of the ways in which administrative processes vary with the nature of administrators.

The newer fields of study, such as game theory, cybernetics, information theory, and general systems theory, likewise have much to contribute. Not only have these tended to be multi-disciplinary, but they also appear to have broken out of traditional disciplines precisely because those who developed them attached fundamental significance to the study of processes. These new fields can be reasonably described as *process disciplines,* and as they develop and refine models of process phenomena, administrative science will have additional, essential resources upon which to draw.

It appears inevitable that for some time to come, we will have much more to learn from other fields than to contribute to them. Hopefully, however, administrative science will have creative roles in the array of disciplines. As a multi-disciplinary field, it must seek syntheses, and synthesize results in new understanding. As an hypothesis-testing field, administrative science must seek new knowledge about social behavior in a particular large context, and this knowledge should have significance for the established disciplines.

Summary

The objective has been set as a valid theory which will encompass all types of administration and be adaptive to all cultural or historical contexts. A strategy for moving toward that objective has been outlined. The strategy involves focusing on complex organization as the unit of analysis, but to see the organization both in a larger context, in interaction with its environment, and in terms of its parts. The strategy also requires identification of organizational requirements and, thus, of administrative functions. It calls for comparative studies which will point up the effects of variations in important variable dimensions, and calls for an ultimate analysis of administrative processes as explaining how observed relationships among phenomena are brought about. Finally, we have asserted that progress toward the objective requires the contributions of many disciplines and the synthesis of these into new understandings of administration.

Footnotes

1. Helpful comments on an earlier version of this paper were made by Robert W. Avery, Warren Bennis, William Dill, James T. Liu, Manning Nash, Loretta Stankard Nelson, and Charles Redfield. The shortcomings, of course, are ours.

2. For a more detailed statement of this point, see E. H. Litchfield, "Notes on a General Theory of Administration," *Administrative Science Quarterly*, 1:3-29, June, 1956.

3. Governmental administration may be very much involved, however, in police activities directed toward *controlling* mobs or crowds, or *serving* publics.

4. Further study may reveal empirical contradictions to these distinctions. Royal families, for example, may reveal closer similarity to the administered organization than to the typical family of the society; and in certain cultures the kinship group may also reveal a large element of administration. Absolute monarchies or totalitarian governments may be interpreted as attempts to make government and society coterminous, and to the extent that such attempts are successful the society may be considered an administered organization. Certainly in modern warfare, this situation is approached.

5. This generalization rests on inadequate empirical evidence. In emergency situations, such as a community disaster, the crowd or public may become organized and administered only for the duration of the emergency. There is some justification, however, for thinking that usually this organization is created by an amalgamation or coordination of previously-existing administered organizations. There is also the often-noted tendency for specific-purpose organizations to identify new goals, rather than to dispand, when original goals have been attained.

6. The overlapping of organizational roles in a dynamic society results in much confusion among the several part theories of administration. Does industrial administration include hospital administration when a union builds and operates hospitals? Does educational administration become public administration when the school is a governmental unit, ecclesiastical administration when the church operates the school, and business administration when the corporation activates an educational program for its members? These kinds of confusion underscore the need for a more general science of administration.

7. This is not to deny that the organizational context often influences the way in which such activities are carried out, or that a particular type of activity may have one meaning when placed in the organizational *Gestalt*. These are, however, matters which need not concern us for purposes of distinguishing administrative from non-administrative activity.

8. Some will challenge this view on grounds that we have overlooked the administration of "substantive programs," and they will point to instances in which it is common to insist that the administrator's credentials include a "license to practice" the ultimate organizational task. Examples would include the psychiatric hospital, where the administrator must also be a reputable psychiatrist, or the research organization, where reputation as a scientist often is a requirement for the administrator.

Again we are lacking in the necessary evidence, but there is some reason to believe that the requirement of "substantive qualification" is limited to those types of organizations doing tasks which traditionally have been done outside of organizations. Indeed, the requirement of "substantive qualification" may appear less essential a generation later, once cultural patterns for the articulation of the task and the organization have been developed. In any event, we believe the administrator's role is primarily concerned with administration for substantive programs rather than of them.

part II

ORGANIZATIONAL COMPARISONS

*"If organizations differ in structure, we must seek to understand
why this occurs, and how it affects the contexts of administration."*
(p. 9).

In each of the following three chapters structural variations are
found between organizations which in many important respects are
similar.

Thompson reports on two military units with parallel purposes, resources, and formal structures. That study sought to explain variations
in terms of informal organization, but found technology an important
determinant of organizational structure, a point further explored in
Chapter 10. Richardson compares cargo ships having identical purposes and technology and comparable task environments. Here the conclusion is that crew organization varied because crews were recruited
from social systems having different attitudes toward authority. Thomas
compares organizational units of a social welfare agency where objectives and formal prescriptions are "held constant" but size and location
vary. Seeking to understand the effects of size, he concludes that size
per se has less effect on performance than does the environmental setting.

Of these three studies, the only one in which social or economic
aspects of the environments do not appear to be significant is the case
of the military units. These were components of a larger organization
which had as an important function the neutralization of social and
economic factors in the environments in order to permit maximum concentration on the military aspects. This insight was not contained in the
original study; it becomes more apparent when that chapter is juxta-
posed against those by Richardson and Thomas.

Reprinted by permission of the author and of the publisher from AMERI-
CAN JOURNAL OF SOCIOLOGY, *November, 1956. Copyright 1956 by The
University of Chicago.*

chapter 2

Authority & Power in "Identical" Organizations

James D. Thompson

Power structures have been observed in small groups and in large communities, but these usually have been informal arrangements either in
informal groups or in the interstices between formal organizations, form-
ing a superstructure above formal government. Yet the usual definitions of power are properly applicable to the internal structures of formal organizations. One reason why research workers have seldom regarded actual power in such organizations may be that the classics
on bureaucracy have stressed the rational aspects of organization, with
emphasis on authority to the neglect of unauthorized or illegitimate
power. And it was not long ago that informal organization was "discovered" in bureaucracies.

Studies of informal organization in industrial and other large systems have been directed primarily toward relations between production
workers or between them and their supervisors; executive behavior has
seldom been considered.

This paper reports some results of a study of authorized and real
power structures in two Air Force wings with the same regulations, directives, and charts, reporting to the same headquarters, and comparable in equipment, personnel, length of time in existence, and mission.
They operated under like weather conditions. Attention is focused on
"top" executives and on differences in communication channels which
were associated with differences in power structures.

It was hypothesized (1) that the real power structures in both wings
would deviate from the more limited authority structures and (2) that
the two power structures would differ from each other.

Power was defined as the ability to determine the behavior of others, regardless of the bases of that ability. Authority, in contrast, was defined as that type of power which goes with a position and is legitimated by the official norms. Power consists of some combination of authority and influence, but for purposes of this study influence was treated as a residual category.

A power structure was defined as a relatively fixed, regular, and continuous power relationship between two or more individuals or groups, and an authority structure as a relatively fixed, regular, and continuous power relationship between offices as they are formally prescribed.

Communication was defined as a kind of interaction in which sentiments, ideas, or facts become shared, and a communication channel as a relatively fixed, regular, and continuous communication relationship between two or more individuals.

Collection and Analysis of Data

Data were collected by the author and other members of the research team[2] during six weeks spent in each of two wings. The principal techniques were direct observation, semistructured interviews, work-contact questionnaires, self-recorded schedules of contacts made by executives, and power ratings made by judges in the wings. Regulations, directives, and charts in effect at the time of field work also were analyzed.

Attention during field work was focused on two major aspects of co-ordination: *allocation* and *communication*. The allocation category was divided into five areas: tasks (or responsibilities); manpower; facilities; authority; and sanctions (rewards and punishments).[3] Data on allocation were obtained primarily through interviewing and observation.

A series of interviews was conducted with each of a dozen executives in each wing and organized around three general questions: (1) What allocation decisions were made? (2) Who made them? (3) What were the consequences for the groups and activities under the respondent's jurisdiction? Weekly "staff meetings" and other sessions of executives were observed and recorded in detail, and the data were classified according to the same general questions. Critical incidents which related to these questions were also observed and recorded.

Channels of communication were determined from work-contact questionnaires completed by all available members of each wing and from records of actual contacts kept by major executives during a critical week in each wing.

Questionnaires asked the respondent to list the individuals with whom he had contact as frequently as several times a week. Contacts within his own work group were separated from other contacts. The plan was to administer the questionnaires to all executives and all their assistants, who together made up the "executive subsystem" of the wings. Similar questionnaires were administered throughout the "maintenance subsystem" and in one of the three squadrons which comprised the "operations subsystem."

Completed questionnaires were obtained from 71 per cent of members of the executive subsystem in Wing A and from 68 per cent in Wing B. Percentages obtained in the other subsystems ranged from 67 to 81. The distribution of those from whom questionnaires were not obtained resembled randomness, and it is believed that the data obtained approximate the channels of communication within the wings.

All questionnaire entries were coded and entered into a matrix. The completed matrix was then "folded over," so that data regarding interaction between any two individuals appeared in one cell, regardless of whether the facts were supplied by one or both of the individuals.[4] (Results reported here refer to interaction as reported by either party; if reported by both parties, it is tabulated as one interaction.)

The Authority Structures

Each wing was composed of six working squadrons and a headquarters. Flying activities were carried out by crews belonging to the three tactical or combat squadrons, which "owned" the aircraft and performed minor maintenance on them. Specialized and heavy maintenance activities were the responsibilities of three maintenance squadrons.

The chief executive of a wing was the wing commander, whose principal assistants were his deputy, his six squadron commanders, and the three members of his "wing coordinating staff," namely, a director of operations, a director of matériel, and a director of personnel. These eleven, plus an assistant to the director of matériel known as the "maintenance control officer," were the key executives on whom this study focused.

Each squadron commander was officially responsible *directly* to the wing commander for the control over and the quality of the activities of his squadron. Each had one or more squadron staff officers responsible for certain matters and answerable *directly* to him. To assist him in coordinating the activities of the six squadrons, the wing commander could turn to his coordinating staff. Regulations did not limit these offices to advisory positions, however. The director of operations was officially responsible to the wing commander for the development of the wing's combat capability; the director of matériel for the direction and coordination of all phases of maintenance, supply, and logistics within the wing; and the director of personnel for personnel actions in all squadrons.

Although relationships between squadron commanders and wing staff officers were not prescribed, regulations did specify that appropriate squadron staff officers would be "supervised and directed" by wing staff officers. At the same time, however, the squadron staff officers were officially responsible to their squadron commander.

A status differential existed among the executive offices, since the authorized ranks of the coordinating staff were one notch higher than those of squadron commanders. Movement "upward" in the hierarchy was movement from squadron command to wing staff positions.

In summary, the authority structure appeared to be a blend of the "line" and "functional" concepts of administration which left some authority in both types of channels without fully integrating the channels.

Overview of the Power Structures

In both wings members of the coordinating staffs were found to exert power *over* squadron commanders, despite the absence of authority to do so. This was particularly true of the directors of operations and matériel and less so of the director of personnel. Repeatedly and systematically, directors made decisions about allocation which limited the freedom of squadron commanders to act. Directors enjoyed priority in manipulating variables and could freeze these into conditions for squadron commanders.

Allocation of operation tasks was dominated in both wings by the directors of operations, who drew up monthly training plans which were then divided among the tactical squadrons, fixed dates and deadlines for many requirements, and decided which of the squadrons would perform special activities assigned to the wing. Within the limits of restrictions by higher headquarters, the directors of operations decided who, what, and when, thereby forcing squadron commanders to take as fixed conditions which, to the directors of operations, were variables.

Similarly, the directors of matériel controlled the allocation of tasks among maintenance squadrons—and within maintenance sections of combat squadrons. They, too, set deadlines and priorities.

Despite the presence of a director of personnel in the authority structure, the allocation of manpower in both wings tended to be dominated by the directors of operations and matériel, depending upon the experience and training of the men subject to allocation. Routine matters were handled by squadron commanders and the directors of personnel, but, when key men or positions were involved, initiative was retained by the director of operations or matériel. This was true because of the crucial relationship between allocation of tasks and of men capable of carrying them out.

The allocation of facilities was handled through regular command or "line" channels—squadron commander to wing commander—for routine items, but, when the facilities were directly linked to operations or maintenance performance, the appropriate director took control, deciding which squadrons or sections within them would receive scarce tools or supplies.

Detailed policies and procedural guides by higher headquarters succeeded in minimizing "politics" with respect to sanctions—such as promotions in rank and discipline. Other less tangible rewards—more or less covered by the term "job satisfactions"—were controlled, perhaps inadvertently, by those wielding power over task and manpower allocation. This meant that many things regarded as rewarding or punishing were decided by the directors of operations and matériel and were beyond the power of squadron commanders.

Qualitative data, then, indicated that *in both wings* directors of operations and matériel exercised unauthorized power over squadron commanders and over the directors of personnel. Less clear was the position in the power structure of the deputy wing commanders and the maintenance control officers: their roles appeared to differ in the two wings.

Major Differences Between Wings

In Wing A the director of operations dominated maintenance executives, on the theory that maintenance existed to serve operations. On several occasions he planned major operations on the basis of his own inaccurate estimates of maintenance capabilities and later, to the general confusion, was forced to change his plans. The director of matériel was handicapped, in staff meetings, by the fact that he had to transact business with operations executives without the help of his chief assistant, the maintenance control officer, whose position gave him detailed information about maintenance schedules and capacities. Furthermore, when maintenance executives complained about lack of cooperation on the part of operations, it was the director of operations (not the combat squadron commanders) who promised and took action.

In Wing B the directors of operations and matériel worked more closely together, checking on each other's needs and capacities at several stages of their planning. Furthermore, they united sometimes against what they felt were arbitrary dictates of the wing commander. The director of matériel was strengthened, in executive discussions, by the presence of the maintenance control officer, who, being recognized in Wing B as a staff officer, attended all staff meetings.[5] (Because of the absence during part of the field work of the deputy wing commander of Wing A, qualitative data on his role were inconclusive.)

Finally, there were sharp differences between the two wings in the relationships of other executives to the wing commanders. In both, of course, the wing commanders were at the top of the hierarchy. But the commander of Wing A preferred to let his subordinates—in particular the director of operations—take the initiative; he reviewed and approved acts of his subordinates and held veto power. In Wing B, however, the wing commander more often exercised initiative, with the result that the hierarchical distance between him and his subordinates appeared to be greater.

Power Hierarchies Obtained from Judges' Ratings

As an independent check upon the qualitative analysis, the directors and squadron commanders were asked to give power rankings, that is, to "name the top five or six officers in the wing, in addition to the Wing Commander, who have the most to say about how the wing gets its work done and meets requirements." *After* the executive had named those he considered most powerful, he was asked to rank them. When judges felt unable to rank more than three or four, they were not pressed, with the result that there were several "ties" in the lower ranks.

The rankings were weighted using the simple device of five points for first place, four for second, and so on. In cases of tie votes, the average value was given to each. The weighted ratings obtained by each officer named were then totaled, to give each a score (Tables 1 and 2).

The order of the deputy wing commanders and directors of matériel is found to be reversed between wings, and the maintenance control officer is much higher in Wing B than in Wing A. The director of personnel is also higher in one case than in the other.

Perhaps of more significance, however, is the distribution of percentages. In Wing A the deputy received 21.8 per cent of the total score, while the director of matériel received 16.2 per cent; but in Wing B the deputy received 15.8 per cent and the director of matériel 26.8. Cumulative percentages show the two directors of matériel in very different situations. In Wing A more than half of the total score went to men above the director of matériel, while in Wing B it was less than one-third of the total score.

TABLE 1

Power Hierarchy in Wing A, Excluding Wing Commander, as Determined From Aggregate Scores Received From Nine Judges

Executive	Ranking in Hierarchy	Score	Per Cent of Total Score	Cumulative Percentage
Total	...	133.0	100.0	....
Director of operations..............	1	39.0	29.3	29.3
Deputy wing commander...........	2	29.0	21.8	51.1
Director of matériel...............	3	21.5	16.2	67.3
Director of personnel..............	4	17.0	12.8	80.1
Commander, Bomb Squadron A.....	5	7.5	5.6	85.7
Commander, Bomb Squadron B	6 and 7	6.5	4.9	90.6
Commander, Bomb Squadron C		6.5	4.9	95.5
Executive officer	8	4.0	3.0	98.5
Maintenance control officer.........	9	1.0	0.7	99.2
Wing intelligence officer...........	10	1.0	0.7	100.0

TABLE 2

Power Hierarchy in Wing B, Excluding Wing Commander, as Determined From Aggregate Scores Received From Eight Judges*

Executive	Ranking in Hierarchy	Score	Per cent of Total Score	Cumulative Percentage
Total	...	113.9	100.0	....
Director of operations..............	1	35.5	31.2	31.2
Director of matériel...............	2	30.5	26.8	58.0
Deputy wing commander...........	3	18.0	15.8	73.8
Maintenance control officer.........	4	12.0	10.5	84.3
Director of personnel..............	5	11.0	9.7	94.0
Commander, Bomb Squadron A	6, 7 and 8	2.3	2.0	96.0
Commander, Bomb Squadron B		2.3	2.0	98.0
Commander, Bomb Squadron C		2.3	2.0	100.0

*One prospective judge was unavailable

Another important question about the power hierarchies is the extent to which judges agreed on the locus of power. Tables 3 and 4, showing the number of times each executive was named in the various ranks, reveal general agreement on the higher rankings. (Tables here show maximum value, not average.) In both wings the rankings for the top men cluster. The directors of operations were rated either first or second by all judges. But, with descending rank, clusterings of frequencies gradually disappear. Moreover, there is a major incongruity in the case of the deputy wing commanders. When they were named, they were ranked high—but they were not always named.

It appeared that power is perceived differently by various executives, depending upon their positions. If this were so, it should be pos-

TABLE 3

Distribution of Rankings of Wing A Executives, Excluding Wing
Commander, As Reported by Nine Judges

Executive	Number of Times Named in Each Rank*				
	1	2	3	4	5
All executives	9	10	8	5	4
Director of operations..............	4	5	..	..	..
Deputy wing commander...........	5	1	..	..	..
Director of matériel...............	..	1	3	3	1
Director of personnel..............	..	2	2	2	..
Commander, Bomb Squadron A......	..	1	..	..	..
Commander, Bomb Squadron B......	..	..	1	..	..
Commander, Bomb Squadron C......	..	..	1	..	..
Executive officer	..	..	1	..	..
Maintenance control officer........	..	..	..	..	1
Wing intelligence officer...........	..	..	..	..	1

*Tie votes given maximum value in each case rather than average value.

TABLE 4

Distribution of Rankings of Wing B Executives, Excluding Wing
Commander, As Reported by Eight Judges*

Executive	Number of Times Named in Each Rank†				
	1	2	3	4	5
All executives	9	7	10	6	5
Director of operations..............	4	4	..	..	..
Director of matériel...............	2	3	3	..	..
Deputy wing commander...........	3	..	1	..	..
Maintenance control officer........	..	..	2	3	..
Director of personnel..............	..	..	1	3	2
Commander, Bomb Squadron A......	..	..	1	..	1
Commander, Bomb Squadron B......	..	..	1	..	1
Commander, Bomb Squadron C......	..	..	1	..	1

*One prospective judge was unavailable.
†Tie votes given maximum value in each case rather than average value.

sible to group judges according to similarity of position and find a
higher degree of consensus than in aggregate scores. To examine this
possibility, an "index of consensus" was developed. In order to demonstrate the logic and mechanics involved in the index, procedures used
in computing one for the aggregate scores will be described, using data
in Table 1. Since in essence the purpose is to find the "goodness of fit"
of a given hierarchy—the extent to which it agrees with estimates of the
judges—it is assumed for the aggregate index that the five executives
with the largest total scores actually were the five most powerful executives and that their relative rankings as determined by the scores are
correct.

Since each judge named only five and score points were based on five possible rankings, only the first five in the hierarchy are considered. If the nine judges in Wing A had been in perfect agreement, the director of operations would have received 45 points, the deputy 36, and so on as indicated in Table 5, under "Expected Score." In the adjoining column are entered "reported scores," from Table 1. The differences between expected and reported scores are then computed and entered in the third column of Table 5. In this case the differences total 40. This means that 40 points were "misplaced" by the judges or that there were 40 points of disagreement, leaving 95 points of agreement. This was converted into an index by determining the percentage of agreement (95 divided by 135) between reported and expected scores, and multiplying by 100.

The general formula for computing the index of consensus is:

$$C = 100 \times \frac{\text{Sum of expected scores minus difference between sum of expected scores and sum of reported scores}}{\text{Sum of expected scores}}$$

The index can vary between 0 and 100, with 0 indicating equal amounts of agreement and disagreement or absence of a pattern, and 100 indicating that all judges named the same executives in the same order.[6]

The aggregate index of consensus for judges in Wing A, on the hierarchy shown in Table 1, is 70.4, while there was more consensus

TABLE 5

Computation of Index of Consensus on Power Hierarchy of Wing A, as Determined From Aggregate Scores of Nine Judges

Executive	Rank in Hierarchy	Expected Score (1)	Reported Score (2)	Differences (1 – 2) (3)
Total		135	133.0	40.0
Director of operations	1	45	39.0	6.0
Deputy wing commander	2	36	29.0	7.0
Director of matériel	3	27	21.5	5.5
Director of personnel	4	18	17.0	1.0
Commander, Bomb Squadron A	5	9	7.5	1.5
Commander, Bomb Squadron B ⎰	⎰ 6	0	6.5	6.5
Commander, Bomb Squadron C ⎱	⎱ 7	0	6.5	6.5
Executive officer	8	0	4.0	4.0
Maintenance control officer	9	0	1.0	1.0
Wing intelligence officer	10	0	1.0	1.0

$$C = 100 \left[\frac{\text{Total Col. 1—Total Col. 3}}{\text{Total Col. 1}} \right] = 70.4$$

27

among judges in Wing B, where the index was 78.4 on the hierarchy shown in Table 2.

Power Perception and Position

Observation suggested two meaningful ways of grouping the judges: (a) by command and staff categories and (b) by operations and maintenance categories.

The power hierarchy in Wing A appeared clear to members of the operations system within the wing, who had a consensus index of 91.7 in relation to the following ranking:

1. Deputy wing commander
2. Director of operations
3. Director of personnel
4. Director of matériel
5. { Executive officer
Intelligence officer
Maintenance control officer

Members of the maintenance system in Wing A, however, were in less agreement; they had an index of only 65, for the following hierarchy:

1. Director of operations
2. Director of matériel
3. Commander, Bomb Squadron A.
4 and 5. Commanders, Bomb Squadron B and C

Using the alternative method of subgrouping—by command and staff—yields even less consensus in Wing A. Staff members agreed only 57.8, and command judges 75.6, on the following hierarchy:

1. Director of operations
2. Deputy wing commander
3. Director of matériel
4. Director of personnel
5. Commander, Bomb Squadron A

Do the power hierarchies upon which the subindexes are based actually fit the power structure as perceived by judges better than the aggregate index, which was 70.4? To determine this, it is necessary to develop a method for determining *total* consensus to compare with aggregate consensus. By total consensus is meant a measure of agreement resulting when judges are arranged into subgrouping, each subgrouping having its own estimate of the power hierarchy. If all judges in the staff agreed on a particular hierarchy, the index would be 100 for that subgrouping, and if all judges in the command subgrouping agreed on another hierarchy, the index would be 100. In that case the total index would also be 100, and it could be concluded that there was one hierarchy in effect for staff members and another for commanders.[7]

An index of total consensus is obtained by adding the points of difference for the two subgroupings, adding the expected scores for the two, and computing an index as before. In Wing A, in the staff and command subgroupings, the result is a total index of consensus of 69.7, slightly lower than the aggregate index. According to these calculations, the staff and command subgroupings do not result in "better-fitting" power hierarchies in Wing A. For the operations and maintenance subgroupings, however, the total index in Wing A is 78.3, much better than the aggregate.

The reverse is found in Wing B, where staff and command subgroupings do result in greater total consensus. Staff judges agreed 86.9 on the following hierarchy:

1. Director of operations
2. Director of matériel
3. Director of personnel
4 and 5. Deputy wing commander and maintenance control officer

And command judges agreed 78.7 on the following:

1. Director of operations
2. Director of matériel
3. Deputy wing commander
4. Maintenance control officer
5. Director of personnel

The total index based on staff and command subgroupings in Wing B is 81.8, whereas it is only 76.3 for the operations and maintenance subgroupings in Wing B. This is even less than the 78.4 index of aggregate consensus for that wing.

These data indicate that the judges in Wing A perceived power in relation to areas of activity (operations and maintenance), while judges in Wing B perceived it more in accordance with the traditional distinctions between staff and command channels.

Test of Hypotheses

It was hypothesized that the real power structures in both wings would deviate from the more limited authority structures. This can be accepted without reservation. At both bases the directors of operations and matériel held more power than did squadron commanders. This was supported by observation and in the reports of staff judges as well as those of squadron commanders. While the panel judgments do not show that the power of directors was power *over* squadron commanders, they support observations that the directors of operations and matériel were at or near the top of their power structures.

It is also clear that in both wings executives concerned primarily with operations activities had greater power than those concerned primarily with maintenance activities. This appeared in observations and in the judgments of panel members. In both wings, moreover, combat squadron commanders appeared on the fringe of the executive power structure, but maintenance squadron commanders were excluded.

Both directors of operations exercised power *over* the directors of matériel, which again was outside authorized relationships. This conclusion is supported by observation and also by interview data.

It was also hypothesized that the real power structures of the two wings would differ from each other. This can also be accepted without reservation. Domination of maintenance by operations executives was more pronounced in Wing A than in Wing B, where the director of matériel was in second place on the judge's lists. The maintenance control officer in Wing A was all but overlooked; his counterpart in Wing B was placed in the hierarchy by judges, a distinction confirmed by observation and interview data.

From analysis of the estimates of judges, a power hierarchy appeared sharply defined for operations executives in Wing A but poorly delineated for maintenance executives. In Wing B, by contrast, a power hierarchy was well defined for maintenance executives but poorly defined for operations executives. This leads to the conclusion that the operations system was more tightly structured than the maintenance system in Wing A, while the maintenance system was more tightly structured in Wing B. In the former the power of the deputy wing commander was felt primarily in operations, while in Wing B the power of the deputy was felt primarily in maintenance.

Finally, command and staff channels were more important in Wing B than in Wing A, where the "functional" concept of organization was favored.

Distribution of Work Contacts

There were fewer regular contacts (i.e., contacts occurring as often as several times a week) involving executives in Wing A than in Wing B.[8] According to questionnaire data, which were obtained from more than two-thirds of all members of the two wings, and which are summarized in Table 6, executives in Wing A were involved in 331 regular contacts with individuals and in regular contact with one or more members of 202 groups in the wing. Wing B executives were involved in 424 regular

TABLE 6

Number of Individuals and Groups in Regular Contact With Executives in Wings A and B

Executive	Wing A Number of		Wing B Number of	
	Individuals	Groups	Individuals	Groups
Total	331	202	424	257
Average	33	20	42	26
Wing commander	23	18	26	20
Deputy wing commander...........	14	13	34	28
Director of operations..............	54	23	47	24
Director of matériel................	22	17	36	25
Maintenance control officer..........	28	22	51	35
Director of personnel..............	46	24	35	20
Commander, Bomb Squadron.......	51	29	54	23
Commander, Maintenance Squadron A	36	23	44	30
Commander, Maintenance Squadron B	31	17	53	29
Commander, Maintenance Squadron C	26	16	44	29

contacts with individuals in 257 groups. On the average, the Wing A executive had regular contact with 33 individuals in 20 groups; the Wing B executive, with 42 individuals in 25 groups.[9]

Reasons for the greater volume of executive contacts in Wing B are not certain. Possibly executives in Wing B had more regular contacts because in that wing both "functional" and "line" channels were used frequently; the channels may have been competing. It is equally conceivable, however, that the differences are due to the larger number of written regulations and directives existing in Wing A.

Since interaction is a means of coordinating the activities of two or more subsystems, the direction of executive contacts is an important topic. Differences in the distribution of contacts appeared when contacts were tabulated according to the subsystem of the individual or group in contact with each executive.

Of the 202 groups in contact with executives in Wing A, 29 per cent were executive groups, 34 per cent were maintenance groups, and 37 per cent were operations groups.[10] Executives in Wing B contacted 257 groups, only 22 per cent of which were executive groups, while 44 per cent were in maintenance and 34 per cent in operations. Percentages for operations were not significantly different, statistically, but the others are significantly different at better than the .05 level.

31

Similar patterns appear in executive contacts with individuals. Of 331 contacts for executives in Wing A, 26 per cent fell within the executive subsystem, 38 per cent in operations, and 36 per cent in maintenance. Executives in Wing B had 424 contacts, of which 20 per cent were with members of the executive subsystem, 33 per cent in operations, and 47 per cent in maintenance. These differences between wings are significant, statistically, at more than the .05 level.

These differences between wings appear to reflect, at least in part, a greater recognition by Wing B executives of the interdependence of maintenance and operations, since in Wing B executives had not only more but a larger share of their contacts with individuals and groups in maintenance. This corroborates with the power structure data, indicating that the director of operations in Wing A was more prone to dictate to maintenance than was the director of operations in Wing B. The fact that executives in Wing A had a larger share of their contacts with members of the executive subsystem reflects the greater concentration of power at the top.

Interaction is also a major means of linking hierarchical levels. For purposes of this analysis individuals having regular contacts with executives will be identified with one of two broad levels—management or production. Management includes executives and their immediate assistants, such as secretaries, clerks, and office managers, junior executives responsible for the more detailed implementation of policies set by senior executives, and the immediate assistants of junior executives. Production includes those who, within a subsystem, decide allocation and assess the performance of production groups, those who specialized in direct supervision of work groups, and the workers themselves.

Table 7 shows that executives in Wing B contacted almost twice as many individuals at production levels as did executives in Wing A. This difference can be accounted for in part by the greater number of individuals contacted by executives in Wing B, but this does not, however, account for all the difference. Of a total of 331 contacts, 18 per cent were with individuals at production levels in Wing A, while 27 per cent of 424 individual contacts were at production levels in Wing B. This is statistically significant at the .05 level.

In both wings the bulk of the contacts of executives at the production level were between squadron commanders and the maintenance control officers; they provided the primary direct links between the executive and the production levels. The major differences between wings seem to be between maintenance squadron commanders: in Wing A they had 93 contacts, of which 26 per cent were at production levels;

TABLE 7

Contacts of Executives of Wings A and B, By Level in Organization

Number of Individuals Contacted Regularly

Executive	WING A			WING B		
	Total	Management Level	Production Level	Total	Management Level	Production Level
All executives	331	271	60	424	309	115
Wing commander	23	23	0	26	23	3
Deputy wing commander	14	14	0	34	30	4
Director of operations	54	48	6	47	42	5
Director of matériel	22	22	0	36	34	2
Maintenance control officer	28	18	10	51	35	16
Director of personnel	46	46	0	35	35	0
Commander, Bomb Squadron	51	31	20	54	33	21
Commander, Maintenance Squadron A	36	23	13	44	26	18
Commander, Maintenance Squadron B	31	25	6	53	33	20
Commander, Maintenance Squadron C	26	21	5	44	18	26

in Wing B, 141 contacts, of which 45 per cent were at production levels. These percentage differences are statistically significant at better than the .05 level.

There were also indirect links between some executives and production levels. These linkages were provided by junior executives and their assistants. An important question is the extent to which junior executives of the powerful executives communicated with production levels and whether they bypassed squadron commanders.

Tabulation revealed 66 regular contacts between management and production levels in the operations subsystem of Wing A, compared with 37 in Wing B.

(The power of operations in Wing A is also reflected in tabulations of contacts between individuals at management levels in operations and at management levels in maintenance. In Wing A there were 24 regular contacts between maintenance and operations at the management level, but only 8 in Wing B. This may reflect the greater dependence of maintenance upon operations in Wing A, although no conclusion can be drawn in the absence of information about initiation and content of communication.)

Within maintenance there were more contacts between management and production levels in Wing B than in Wing A. Since there were only 2 contacts between the matériel directorate and production levels in one wing and none in the other, the differences are accounted for by the maintenance control sections. In Wing A the maintenance control sections had 45 regular contacts with individuals at production levels, while for Wing B the figure was 134.

The association between number of indirect links with production levels and the power of the executive is the same in maintenance control as it was in operations. The more powerful director of operations (Wing A) had more indirect links with production levels. The more powerful maintenance control officer (Wing B) had more indirect links with production levels. This generalization also holds for directors of matériel, since maintenance control officers were subordinate to them, and links between maintenance control officers and production would also be accessible to directors of matériel.

In the wing where the maintenance control officer was powerful and had many indirect links with production, the maintenance squadron commanders also had relatively numerous contacts with production. Table 7 shows that the three squadron commanders in Wing B made 64 contacts with individuals in production while their counterparts in Wing A made only 24. These data again suggest that dual channels bring about competition between channels and hence a greater volume of communication in Wing B, where both channels were used.

Conclusions

Despite its many characteristics of "bureaucracy," in the technical sense of that term, the roles in an Air Force wing are not completely standardized.[11] A specified office does not necessarily bring forth the same behavior in two wings. Presumably, too, the role might change in time in a given wing.

What accounts for the deviations? Major deviations of power structures from authority structures apparently came about because of the technical requirements of operations rather than because of personal relations. The perceived necessity for inter-squadron coordination, for instance, led wing commanders to approve the exercise of power over squadron commanders by staff directors. The payoff importance of operations activities insured dominant positions for the executives concerned. The importance of manpower in wing performance meant that those responsible for performance had to assume power over manpower allocation.

Personal skills and personal relations undoubtedly had influence *within* the general power structures brought about by technical requirements. This is most clear in the case of wing commanders with quite dissimilar personalities. The commander of Wing A was a self-assured, secure individual who delegated authority or initiative and did not hesitate to reverse or modify his decisions when his subordinates turned up new information. The commander of Wing B, however, appeared less secure, reserving authority and initiative, and fearing loss of "face" if he altered a decision.

In Wing A the director of operations was dictatorial, and the wing commander was available to executives as an appellant judge; whereas in Wing B the commander was dictatorial, executives had no avenue for appeal, and instead the directors of operations and matériel formed something of a coalition.

This research supports the belief that in complex organizations power and communication are associated. At present, however, the nature of the relationship can only be inferred.

In the wing (A) which had greater concentration of power in fewer hands and a smaller power nucleus, executives had fewer links directly with people at production levels. This appears due primarily to the meager communication between squadron commanders and production levels, a conclusion which would agree with the idea that competing channels lead to increased communication.

Yet, when the wings are broken down by subsystem, there appears to be a positive association between the power of the subsystem executive and the number of links between management and production. The director of operations was relatively more powerful in Wing A than in Wing B, and in Wing A there were more contacts in operations between management and production levels. Maintenance executives were relatively more powerful in Wing B than in Wing A, and there also were more contacts between management and production levels in maintenance in Wing B. In Wing A executives as a group had fewer direct contacts with production levels, but their assistants had more. Evidently Wing A was more centralized, with longer lines of communication.

But the concept of "centralization" seems to call for refinement. In Wing A power seems concentrated in the director of operations and, of course, the wing commander. In Wing B, while power appeared to be more evenly distributed, the wing commander exercised it more. From the viewpoint of hierarchical levels, both wings were centralized. But, from the standpoint of relationships between subsystems (vertical specialization), power in Wing A appears to be lopsided, like a wheel with an axis which is off-center.

Footnotes

1. This research was supported in part by the United States Air Force under contract number 505-037-0001 monitored by the Human Resources Research Institute, Air University, and executed by the Institute for Research in Social Science, University of North Carolina. Project directors: Gordon W. Blackwell and Nicholas J. Demerath. Permission is granted for reproduction, translations, publication, and disposal in whole or in part by or for the United States government.

2. Frederick L. Bates, Jack L. Dyer, Raymond W. Mack, Richard Stephens, and George S. Tracy.

3. The frame of reference was taken with modifications from Talcott Parsons, particularly from *Toward a General Theory of Action*, ed. Parsons and Edward A. Shils (Cambridge, Mass.: Harvard University Press, 1951).

4. Slightly more than 30 per cent of contacts reported by one person were also reported by the other. This was true in both wings. There is evidence that men tended to list their more important contacts (at least outside their own work groups) and to omit the less important. This would explain the absence of mutuality: contact between A and B might be quite important to A but insignificant to B.

5. One example of the complexity of power phenomena involves a comparison of the maintenance control officers. In Wing A this position was weak when viewed at the executive level. Other members of the research team, concentrating on maintenance activities, found that this officer was quite powerful in the day-to-

day activities *within* the maintenance system. In Wing B the locus of his power was reversed.

6. Zero is theoretically possible but not practically so, since we determine expected scores from the hierarchy established from the estimates of judges. There must be some consensus before we can determine expected scores.

7. Total index of consensus cannot be obtained by averaging the two indexes except where the two are identical.

8. Because field plans did not call for a census in two of the bomb squadrons, figures for their commanders are not comparable with those for other executives and are omitted from tables and discussion.

9. Respondents in the executive subsystem of Wing A named an average of 19 other individuals, while those in Wing B named an average of only 16. The larger volume of reported contact in Wing B thus does not appear to be due to greater co-operation in completing questionnaires.

10. In interaction and activity most of the executives were members of both the executive subsystem and another. They and their assistants are here considered in the "other" subsystem, although for purposes of comparison both deputy wing commanders are considered in the executive subsystem, along with wing commanders, directors of personnel, adjutants, comptrollers, and their assistants.

11. In a study of departmental executives in a British factory, Burns noted that "there were wide differences in the distribution of activities for individuals occupying the same work role, pointing to hidden forces in apparently similar situations" (Tom Burns, "The Directions of Activity and Communication in a Departmental Executive Group," *Human Relations*, Vol. VII [1954]). For another study of executive communication see Sune Carlson, *Executive Behavior* (Stockholm: Strombergs, 1951).

chapter 3

Organizational Contrasts on British and American Ships[1]

Stephen A. Richardson

To be effective, an organization must have a structure appropriate for the particular purpose and the resulting necessary tasks. At the same time, the form of organization and the values and needs of its members must be adapted to one another. Variations in organization, then, can be expected to follow from variations of the cultures from which members of an organization are drawn. The effects of cultural factors can be seen in comparing organizations which function in a wide variety of countries and have identical purposes and similar environments.

The social organization on British and United States merchant ships was selected for study because cargo ships have identical purposes, closely comparable environments, and a set of conditions as near to the research ideal as is likely to be found in a natural setting without experimental manipulation. Cargo ships or freighters of approximately seven thousand tons, carrying crews of forty men, were selected for study.

We will first describe the purpose and environment which are common to foreign-going cargo ships of all nationalities. Then we will describe how British and United States seamen arrange their shipboard lives to meet these common conditions. For the purposes of this paper the description will be limited to some differences found between the two nationalities in training, social control, and stratification.[2]

Methods Used in Collecting Data

In evaluating a study it is helpful for the reader to know something about the methods used in carrying out the study. The author had first-hand experience for nine years on British and United States merchant ships, from 1937 to 1946. He sailed in all deck department ranks from able-bodied seaman's apprentice to chief officer and holds a British master mariner's certificate. The author kept a daily diary during this nine-year period. In 1947 the author returned to sea in connection with this study. Two passages were made, one as chief officer of a British ship and one as an able-bodied seaman on an American ship. Detailed daily observations were made and recorded.

In 1948 seventy-two interviews were conducted in port with men of all ranks in the deck department of British and American ships and with American union officials. Because of the conditions under which interviewing took place, a flexible procedure was used. A set of topics for the interviews was developed from the personal experiences of the author and from documentary sources. The set of topics was memorized and used as a guide, but none of the actual questions asked were pre-formulated.

Various drafts of the larger study were read by seamen and union officials of both nationalities, and the subsequent evaluations and discussions were taken into account in revising the final report.

Common Purpose and Environment

A merchant ship's purpose is to transport cargo and passengers. This demands three main focuses of work for the crew: (1) aiding and facilitating the loading and discharging of cargo and passengers; (2) bringing the ship and her contents safely to her appointed destination, and (3), throughout the life of the ship, maintaining and repairing her so that she will give efficient service.

A ship and her contents are a large capital investment. She is exposed frequently to such hazards as storms, collision, fire, and shipwreck. The safety of the ship depends in large measure upon the quick judgments and actions of experienced and skillful seamen. The social organization of the crew must therefore have a clearly designated hierarchy of responsibility and must make provision for rapid communication and execution of orders. Because potential hazards to the ship exist at all times, the organization must function continuously.

A ship's movements impose limitations as to when a member of the crew may form and sever connection with the ship. A seaman joins a ship when it is in his country and reasonably close to his home. With few exceptions, he must remain with the ship until it returns to his home country. This period may be from a month to two years. During the voyage, the crew therefore has a smaller turnover than any comparable organization ashore.

Members of the crew spend their working hours and leisure time at sea, isolated from other people. In foreign ports the friendships they can form ashore are limited by the brief duration of the ship's stay and by the limited channels that may be used to establish social contacts. Life at sea has in most cases been found unsuitable for families. Members of the crew must therefore be separated from their families for the voyage.

The Social System of Merchant Ship Crews

To fulfill the purpose of a ship and to adapt the seaman to the environment which has been described, a clearly defined social system has been evolved through centuries of experience. This system must be sufficiently clear so that a new crew made up of men who have never before met can immediately coordinate the complex running of a ship.

Before describing and analyzing some of the differences found in the social system on British and American merchant ships, we will outline the organization of the crews of both nationalities and the way in

FIGURE 1

Typical manning and formal organization of crew of a 7,000-ton-gross United States and British merchant ship. Crew totals forty.

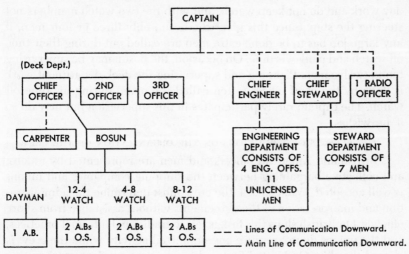

which the crews function. The crew is divided into four departments which work in close cooperation: deck, engineering, stewards, and radio. In this article, attention will be focused on the deck department, with other departments discussed only in relation to this department. Figure 1 shows the manning and basic working organization which with little variation is typical of British and United States cargo ships of about seven thousand tons (e.g., World War II Liberty ships).

There are two main categories of work for the crew while the ship is at sea. These are:

Navigating and propelling the ship: While at sea, a ship is continuously under way, and most members of the crew are divided into three shifts, or watches. Each watch alternates four hours on duty with eight hours off duty. A watch on deck is made up of one officer, two able-bodied seamen, and an ordinary seaman.[3] Although the deck watch-keeping officers are in full charge, the captain is at all times responsible for the safety of the ship and is on call if an unusual situation is suspected or special vigilance is required. The chief engineer is at all times responsible to the captain for the ship's machinery. Radio officers receive and transmit messages at internationally agreed-upon times. Competence of all officers is tested by a governmental examination system. The watch-keeping routine at sea is broken only in extraordinary circumstances. The entire crew is trained in the procedures to be adopted in case of emergency.

Ship's maintenance: During the day, the carpenter works on his own, and the bosun[4] works with any able-bodied seamen who are on day work and do not keep watch, and with the two watch members not steering the ship. Since this gives the bosun only three or four men, if any large job has to be done extra men are called out during their time off watch and paid overtime. On occasion, the bosun may be supervising ten to twelve men. Planning and supervising the deck-department work is done by the chief officer (often called the mate) during his time off watch. The captain rarely participates in this supervision but may do so if he wishes.

THE EFFECTS OF THE UNIONS ON THE ORGANIZATION OF THE CREW

British and American officers and men are represented by unions, and collective bargaining between the shipping companies and unions is well accepted. While at sea, the crew must determine the administration and interpretation of the agreements without assistance from shore officials. On British ships this task is left to traditional informal practices, and the unions do not require any organized activity while the crew is aboard the ship. On United States ships, however, unions representing the unlicensed personnel require a number of types of activity while at sea. Because of the widespread effects that union activity has had on American ships these will be described first.

At the beginning of the voyage, a meeting is called which is obligatory for all members not on duty. At the meeting, the deck, engine-room, and stewards departments each elect a delegate. The types of qualifications looked for are sea experience, education, thorough knowledge of the contract, fluency of speech, and the ability to stay sober at the pay-off at the end of the voyage. The department delegates act as official union spokesmen to the head of their department. A ship's delegate or chairman is also elected to coordinate the departments and act as delegate to the captain for all unlicensed personnel when matters

FIGURE 2.

Union organization of unlicensed personnel on United States ships.

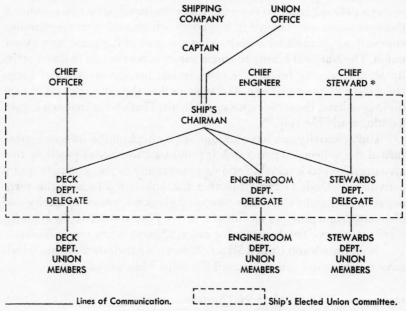

_____ Lines of Communication.   ⌐ - - - - - - - - ⌐ Ship's Elected Union Committee.

*Member of unlicensed personnel's union

arise involving more than one department. The chairman and departmental delegates constitute the ship's committee. Delegates check up on members' subscriptions, hold meetings which must be attended, educate the membership about union policies and rules, watch over members' interests, and maintain union solidarity and discipline (see Figure 2). The unions believe that any hierarchy within their ranks aboard ship might decrease their unity and strength in action; therefore union educational policies stress that all members are equals and brothers. This also tends to prevent delegates from exploiting their position for personal or political ends.

Union activity at sea is instigated mainly by the ship's committee. The union headquarters offers a wide range of suggestions and facilities, which are reflected in the agenda for union meetings of the crew. The agenda includes union business, reports from the ship's committee on the handling of complaints, education, political action, and "good and welfare." Any matter can be brought to the floor by crewmen in the form of a motion. Under the heading of "good and welfare," it is said that "everyone gets a chance to blow his top."[5] While political and educational activities take place only on some ships, the ship's committee always handles complaints, watches over living conditions, and serves a policing function in seeing that members live up to the terms of the agreement and behave in a manner which will give the shipping company no grounds for withdrawing any part of the gains won by the union. The National Maritime Union summarizes the aim of union activity aboard ship as follows: "Everyone has his special job and keeps checking with everyone else. The same policy, the same method of handling problems, the same rights apply to all. That's what makes a happy, livable, workable ship."[6]

Union activity can have an important effect on the informal structure of the unlicensed personnel. It provides a number of positions that give prestige and leadership and an opportunity to participate in group activities. It tends to bring together the unlicensed men in the three departments, maintains union interests, gives a sense of solidarity and distinction, and provides meaningful activity in a restricted environment where men have few facilities for entertainment when not at work.

Both British and United States officers have their own unions, which have no organized activity aboard the ships while at sea.

Differences Between the Social System on British and United States Ships

For the effective maintenance and survival of the social system on a ship there are two important requirements: (1) a continuous supply of trained men and (2) ways to control deviance from normative or ideal patterns of behavior if the degree of deviance becomes a threat to the functioning of the system. We will now focus attention on some of the national differences that appear in the way these requirements are met.

TRAINING OF DECK DEPARTMENT OFFICERS

On British ships, the four-year apprenticeship for youths intending to become officers is generally spent with one company. This training begins at age sixteen or seventeen, and the company takes the responsibility of teaching the apprentice the business of a seaman and the duties of a navigating officer. The apprentice "binds and obliges himself . . . to faithfully serve [the company] and any shipmaster . . . and obey their and his lawful commands [perform various duties] . . . nor absent himself from their service without leave nor frequent taverns or alehouses, nor play at unlawful games."[7] About three-fourths of British Merchant Service officers receive their training as apprentices or cadets, and the remainder put in the required sea time as ordinary seamen and able-bodied seamen.

In the American Merchant Marine, a man is required to have three years of training before he can become an officer. Youths who train as cadets spend two of their three years at a shore-based maritime academy and two six-month periods at sea, either in maritime-academy training ships or in regular merchant ships. Training begins at eighteen or nineteen years of age.

Only about 10 per cent of the officers in the American Merchant Marine are trained as cadets. The remaining 90 per cent sail as ordinary seamen and able-bodied seamen for three years and then take the examination for their license.

Among British officers, primary loyalty is found to be to the shipping companies, and to be a "company man" is considered advantageous. Among American officers, primary loyalty is found to be to the unions. For them the expression "company man" has disparaging connotations, the most important of which is its use as an opposite to "union man."

A number of factors in the training of officers suggest an explanation for this difference in loyalty. A youth sixteen to seventeen years old is in the process of gaining emotional emancipation from his parents, and is doing so through increased membership in peer groups outside his family. When the British boy goes to sea as an apprentice, he is separated from his family and his friends and placed in a social structure composed almost entirely of adult men. Here the peer group is limited to one or two somewhat older apprentices, since he is not allowed to associate with able-bodied seamen or ordinary seamen. However, the captain as shipping-company representative has certain responsibilities to the youth and plays a role closely analogous to that of a father. Because the youth is in need of stability, a sense of belonging, and friendship to replace what he has lost, he is highly motivated to use the captain, who represents the company, as a substitute for his father. The company is interested in training its apprentices in its ways and follows the youth's training and development with interest because it is likely that if he shows promise he will remain with the company throughout his career.

Although the apprentice is given a great deal of work that is normally done by the unlicensed personnel, he is trained to identify himself with the officers even though he does not hold officer's status.

The few American officers who are trained as cadets have little or no connection with any shipping company. Two-thirds of their training takes place ashore in schools which they enter when they are older than British apprentices, and where they associate mainly with a peer group. This type of training precludes the possibility of a relationship with a shipping company such as exists between British companies and officers. The majority of American officers spend their first three years at sea as ordinary seamen and able-bodied seamen. Although they go to sea at a somewhat older age than British seamen, they still have to make the difficult transition from shore to ship life. They have, however, a wider range of men with whom they may make friends and more chance of finding persons of their own age with whom they may associate.

The union and its elected representatives in the crew provide guidance and training for youths coming to sea as ordinary seamen. In return the youths develop a strong loyalty to the union. For American deck officers who first go to sea as ordinary seamen, the union plays a role comparable to that played by the company for British apprentices. When American able-bodied seamen become officers, it is natural for their allegiance to be transferred to the officer's union rather than to the companies, which they have been trained to consider as more unfriendly than friendly to the seaman.

Among the unlicensed personnel, the difference in loyalty may be explained in part by the greater militancy and youth of the American unions. The American union-controlled hiring halls, the union-organized activity at sea, and the union discipline, as compared to the British jointly controlled company-union hiring halls and the lack of union activity and discipline at sea result in different attitudes toward the companies and the unions.

MECHANISMS OF CONTROL USED BY UNLICENSED SEAMEN

An intricate set of checks and counterchecks are continuously in play between the mate, bosun, and deck crowd.[8] The captain and officers' interest and responsibility is to initiate the work and see that it gets done. The deck crowd's interest is to control authority which is not customarily acceptable or is illegitimate. Only the differences in the kinds of controls used by the deck crowd will be examined here.

 British ships: When the able-bodied seamen or ordinary seamen think the mate has infringed on an official regulation (e.g., not kept an accurate check of the number of hours overtime) the offended person will generally enlist the sympathy of the deck crowd, since there is close identity of interest and a tendency to stand together for mutual protection. The first formal move generally is to take the complaint to the bosun, although this is often little more than a gesture to prevent any comeback from him that would occur if he were ignored. The deck crowd often feels that the bosun is on the chief officer's side. A direct approach to the department head would probably meet with refusal and an order to see the bosun. This was well described in two interviews:

The bosun is rather suspect, because he works so close with the mate. The men are afraid he can be too easily called [talked around by the mate]. He is more used to acting for the mate than the men, so he may not be a good spokesman. [British able-bodied seaman]

Often the men try the bosun to get him to clear up the trouble and he has failed. [British second officer]

If the complaint is not settled by the bosun himself or by his referring the matter to the mate, the second step is for the aggrieved individual, a spokesman, or a delegation to go to the mate. There is no formal way of selecting a spokesman, but one appears in almost every deck crowd. The ability to talk well and think fast seems to be the prerequisite. In interviews, an able-bodied seaman said a delegation was sent to accompany the spokesman "for moral support," and the second officer explained that the delegation was sent "to give him moral courage and to see he says his piece."

If the complaint cannot be settled with the chief officer, the delegation may then go to the captain. The use of delegations for giving moral courage is evidenced by the more common usage of a delegation for the captain than for the chief officer. Omitting some of these steps may be done intentionally as a sign of hostility to or disparagement of a disliked bosun or mate.

United States ships: The unions have laid down rules for handling complaints against infringement of rules. The elected union delegate handles all grievances. This arrangement reinforces the union structure aboard the ship since it allows the ship's committee to have control and to interpret communications, and it prevents individual members from taking complaints directly to the captain and heads of departments. The discussion of any grievance centers around the interpretation of the union contract, which describes in great detail the rules and conditions of work. Having all complaints handled by the union delegate has the advantages of saving time and having an experienced man handle the disputes. It also ensures consistency in the treatment of comparable disputes. There is the disadvantage, however, that the chief officer receives complaints at second hand and has no opportunity to gauge the feelings underlying the complaint, to learn how widely those feelings are shared, and in some cases to know who instigated the complaint. The delegate system also makes it difficult for the chief officer to give a man more overtime than he has earned, a procedure sometimes used by British chief officers to reward better workers.

An American bosun has described how the procedure affects the bosun, if it is functioning well:

The bosun likes the system of having the delegate handle all the beefs with the mate. The delegate gets the dirt and leaves the bosun clear of being involved in friction with the mate. As the bosun is clear of beefs he [is] in a more favorable position in handling the men. He keeps in touch with all beefs as these are aired at the union meetings. If the deck crowd are dissatisfied with anything the bosun does, he is talked to by the delegate and they try to straighten it out. If this is not possible the delegate takes the beef to the mate. The delegate would not go over the bosun's head.

The success of this procedure depends on its acceptance by the chief officer and on the willingness of the bosun to work in cooperation with the union. The bosun is in a difficult position, however, if the chief officer resists the union form of communication. If the chief officer is antiunion, he can weaken the union structure on board by discouraging the delegate and by encouraging communication through the bosun. In one way this strengthens the bosun's position, especially if his actions are fully backed by the chief officer, since then he is working on the side of the officers. He is, however, a union member, and by working with the officers, who tend to be identified with the company, he may antagonize the men, thus losing their support and incurring the strong controls that the union can apply to deviant members. If the bosun resists the chief officer's attempt to undermine the union communication procedure, the bosun will antagonize the chief officer. This places him in a difficult position since close cooperation between chief officer and bosun is essential in the smooth running of the crew. The difficulty of the bosun has been increased as the result of the loss of some of his traditional status symbols. Whereas he used to eat separately from the deck crowd, he now eats in the same mess-room; and whereas he used to have a single cabin, he now tends to share a cabin with the deck maintenance crew. This, together with his membership in the same union as the men he supervises, has made his status less well defined and increased the difficulties of his position as "football" in the communication struggle.

It is probable that, as a result of increased experience with the union system of communication, its operation will become smoother.

48

The American unions have also developed a set of formal rules governing the role the deck-crowd union members should play in exercising self-regulatory controls. An able-bodied seaman outlined the delegate's job in this way:

The delegate's job is to keep the guys in line. Charges may be brought against fellow union men for inefficiency, not cooperating, refusing work, drunkenness, being antiunion, stealing from a shipmate, pulling knives. . . . The crew tries to take care of what happens. I think the Old Man likes the men to straighten out their own troubles. All the delegates may go to the Old Man and straighten things out with him. Then the delegates will call a meeting for the membership to endorse action or decide what should be done.

Some practical difficulties which lie in the way of the delegate's carrying out his job were raised by a second officer:

Discipline hardly lies with the union delegate. Union education is good on this matter, but one or two troublemakers are enough to wreck this. The delegate has got to live with the men, and if the trouble starts in Singapore, it is a long time for him to swim against the tide [until the end of the voyage].

The formal system of handling complaints has focused interest on the problem of formal and informal control. The subject was more often brought up by Americans than British and was spoken of at greater length. Controlling deviant behavior is a problem of great importance because it is conceived of not as a personal but as a union-owner issue. From the union's point of view, this approach has value in maintaining members' interest in the union. From the point of view of the chief officer, bosun, and deck crowd, a lack of agreement in interpreting the formal grievance rules leads to caution in adopting a flexible give-and-take system, and sometimes a struggle ensues between the chief officer and the deck crowd for the bosun's allegiance.

INFORMAL CONTROLS ON BRITISH AND UNITED STATES SHIPS

It is possible for behavior to deviate widely from expected or ideal forms of behavior without technically infringing upon any written agreement. To counteract such deviations by officers, a number of informal controls are commonly used by crews on British and United States ships.

Work slowdowns: Close supervision of most of the work on deck is difficult, especially if the bosun is party to the slowdowns. Slowdowns have to be very marked before the captain or chief officer can find grounds for action—great ingenuity can be exercised in doing nothing, and doing it industriously. A slowdown is most commonly used to counteract too close supervision by the mate or too rigid application of working rules without allowing for any flexibility or give-and-take. It is also used to prevent the chief officer from deviating far from the role expected of him in his relations with the men.

Quality of work: Reduction in the quality of the work on deck serves the same purpose as work slowdowns, and these two forms of control are generally used together. Within certain limits, it is difficult for the chief officer to obtain sufficient evidence of poor workmanship, especially where the work is of such a nature or in such a position as to be difficult to check with periodic inspection.

Misuse of ship's equipment: This may take the form of misusing equipment or dumping overboard small articles not easily checked. The degree to which this is done will depend largely on how well equipment is watched by the chief officer. Misuse of equipment is a more destructive reaction than work slowdowns and is likely to lead to further deterioration of relations, whereas slowdowns and poor work can vary in seriousness, and any sign of improved relations instigated by the chief officer can be encouraged by increased output and quality of work.

Leaving the ship: If the work relationship has been poor between the deck officers and the men, and if the men's complaints have met with little or no satisfaction from the captain, a great deal of hostility accumulates. This is often harmlessly dissipated at the end of the voyage, but the men may all leave the ship or make a formal complaint to the union if there are grounds for action against the captain or chief officer. A complete turnover of the crew at the end of a voyage, especially if this happens on several consecutive voyages, may indicate to the shipping company's officials that the cause may be a captain or officer. The men leaving the ship spread the information of the cause for leaving, and it may in extreme cases reach the stage where the shipping company has trouble in getting a new crew so long as the officer causing the difficulty remains on the ship. A formal complaint achieves the same purpose directly.

Effects of Social Stratification on Patterns of Behavior

If the social structure of the crew is conceived as occupying a vertical scale with the captain at the top and a first-voyage ordinary seaman at the bottom, it should be possible to place all crew members on this scale and to determine the range within which groups form. This grouping may be called social stratification, and the distance along the scale may be called social distance. There are a number of indicators of social stratification and distance which are recognized implicitly or explicitly by members of British and American crews. These include wages, qualifications formally required for holding an office (such as examinations and length of sea service), number of persons supervised, food and living conditions, and such behavior as the use of titles in addressing people. Together these indicators influence the behavior of every member of the crew with respect to every other member, providing pressures toward maintaining approved patterns of behavior.

Comparison of British and American crews on indicators of social stratification and distance showed that American seamen consistently play down behavioral and physical symbols that strengthen status and social distance. Some examples of the differences will now be given.

FOOD AND THE DIVISION OF THE CREW AT MEALS

The value of the eating arrangements aboard ship as a measure of social stratification was recognized by Herman Melville in *White Jacket* when he observed that "the dinner table is the criterion of rank in our man-of-war world."[9]

The British crews have more divisions than the American. The British bosun and carpenter eat with the engine-room supervisory men; this group is often called the petty officers. The American bosun and carpenter and other petty officers eat with the able-bodied seamen and ordinary seamen, but generally at a separate table. Interviews showed a close positive relationship between status and the quality of food on British ships. The same was true of American ships in an earlier period, until unions won the right of equal food for all. This right is carefully guarded by unlicensed personnel, whose delegates compare the quality of food being served officers and men. The British able-bodied seamen and ordinary seamen collect their meals from the cook, carry food to their messroom, and after eating do their own cleaning up. American able-bodied seamen and ordinary seamen are provided with a steward, who takes orders from the men, acts as waiter, and afterward cleans up the utensils and messroom. Both British and American officers are served at meals. Whereas on British ships only officers have tablecloths at meals, on American ships tablecloths are provided for all hands.

Although union membership has had little effect on status on British ships, the American union organization among unlicensed personnel at sea has tended to decrease social distance between fellow union members of different status, because the union teachings of brotherhood and equality are in contradiction to the official social hierarchy. Social pressures are applied to the bosun, chief steward, and carpenter to make them work in close cooperation with, and give their loyalty to, the able-bodied and ordinary seamen rather than form a separate petty-officer group. Through union efforts, the pay differential and differences in living conditions have been reduced between bosun, carpenter, chief steward, and the able-bodied and ordinary seamen.

On American ships the consistent playing down of symbols that strengthen status and social distance as compared with British practice appears to be closely related to the sentiments the men have toward social distance and authority. While interviewing, I found a consistent difference between British and American seamen in the degree of awareness and acceptance of social distance between statuses. On American ships, early in the interviews, I met such expressions as:

The bosun, he's one of the boys. He's just another fellow.

[Able-bodied seaman]

The mates, they just act big because they don't do no lousy jobs, and walk up and down the bridge doing nothing. I'm as good a man as any of them.

[Able-bodied seaman]

As the interviews developed, seamen did give various reasons why there was a need for social distance, and these explanations would often be accompanied by surprise, as if these were ideas they had never before explicitly recognized.

On British ships, in contrast, social distance was accepted as a matter of course, and it was stressed among the men that one of the reasons that officers and men for the most part kept separate was that the men had no wish to mix with the officers and preferred companions from their own or a similar status.

Conclusion

The description of the purpose and environment of a ship showed that it was necessary to have a clearly designated hierarchy of authority to meet the hazards and emergencies which the ship may encounter at any time. During nonemergency activities which account for most of the routine aboard ships, the full measure of vested authority remains latent, and a form of authority more suited to nonemergency routine work and living is manifest. There is always the possibility, however, that the powers necessary for emergency action may be misused by the captain and officers for dealing with nonemergency issues. Comparison of British and American crews suggests that the British realize and accept the authority of competent persons and are not as fearful of the misuse of authority as Americans. This acceptance of authority is closely related to acceptance of social stratification and the symbols of these differences. Status symbols function as cues for self-regulation, in conformity with the status and role requirements of the ship. British seamen are conditioned before coming to sea to accept authority, and consequently the change in attitudes required when a man becomes a seaman is slight. Acceptance of authority, by trainees, facilitates training and a willingness to rely largely on informal and traditional practices for dealing with behavior of the captains and officers which they consider deviant.

Among American crews a far greater fear and suspicion of authority appears to exist. Social stratification is not widely accepted and is often denied. Many symbols of social stratification and authority have been removed, and, because they are suspect, the remaining symbols do little to enhance self-regulation of the men in conformity with the status and role demands of the ship's social organization. If the symbols of social stratification are ineffective, alternative procedures are necessary for training Americans for the requirements of life at sea and for maintaining the necessary social system. The alternative procedure has been a far greater formalization of the social system than the British. Greater formalization is evident in training men for the system, in maintaining the expected patterns of behavior, and especially in placing constraints upon authority.

Examples given have included the formalization of working conditions through a detailed union contract, formalizing the system of handling complaints, and the training of officers and men to a far greater degree than the British through specialized shore-based training institutions. The unions have played an important part in this process of formalization. The cultural differences between the British and Americans operating through their beliefs and attitudes have, then, important effects in the operation and maintenance of a social system developed to meet an identical purpose and similar environment.

Footnotes

1. Gratitude and thanks are expressed to an American seaman, Professor G. C. Homans of Harvard University, for his advice, criticism, and encouragement during the fieldwork and writing of this study, and to the many Maritime Union officials and seamen who generously gave their time and provided the material and many of the ideas that appear in this study.

2. This study was completed in 1949, as an honors thesis for the Bachelor of Arts degree, in the Department of Social Relations at Harvard University. A full report can be found in S. A. Richardson, *The Social Organization of British and United States Merchant Ships*. Mimeographed copies are available through the New York State School of Industrial and Labor Relations, Cornell University.

3. Able-bodied seaman is a rank obtained after a man has spent three years in the deck department and has passed the required examination. The rank of ordinary seaman is given men in the deck department when they first go to sea.

4. The position of bosun is analogous to that of foreman. It requires an able-bodied seaman's rating and sufficient sea experience and supervisory ability (as judged

by competent seamen) to be responsible to the chief officer for the work of the able-bodied and ordinary seamen.

5. National Maritime Union, Pilot, Education and Publicity Department Publication No. 16, *Heart of the Union* (November 1947).

6. *Ibid.*

7. Indentures to Anchor Line Ltd., Glasgow.

8. On U. S. ships the term "deck gang" is used. These terms, used by the men themselves, have no derogatory connotation.

9. *The Romances of Herman Melville* (New York, 1931), p. 1126.

chapter 4

Role Conceptions and Organizational Size[1]

Edwin J. Thomas

The growth of organizations from modest-sized structures, often housed under one roof, to bureaucratic giants has brought a proliferation of administrative units and their dispersion over wide geographical areas. Although the units of these bureaucracies are generally part of the same organizational structure and are committed to achieving common objectives by means of uniformly applied operating procedures, the physical separation of bureaus and offices allows differences among them to germinate and grow. An important source of such differences is the number of persons in the local administrative units. These different sized units are a promising site for research on large-scale organizations because some of the characteristics that would normally vary freely in unrelated organizations are held equal.

Much still remains to be learned about the relations between the size of an organization and the behavior of its members.[2] A central question of practical and theoretical significance is the extent to which an organization's size facilitates or impedes efforts to attain its formally stated objectives. To answer this question research must be focused upon two related problems: delineation of the differences in behavior of members in organizations varying in size; and consideration of how these behavioral correlates of size affect the organization's capacity to achieve its goals. Such research should add to the further understanding of those non-formal characteristics of large organizations that affect organizational behavior.

This study compares the role conceptions, the degree of role consensus, and the quality of work of welfare workers in different sized organizational units of a state welfare department. The objectives of the welfare program and the formal requirements for the performance of roles were the same throughout the organization. In comparing small and large units in the department many formal characteristics of the welfare bureaus were thus held constant. Of course, not all of the possibly influential variables were controlled because of differences in history and location of the bureaus.

Attention in the presentation of findings is given to the relationship of the variables to organizational size and, in the discussion of results, to interpretation of why the variables were associated with size and to the relationship of the size of the welfare bureau and their effectiveness in the attainment of one of the organizational goals.

The Organization

The Michigan State Department of Social Welfare administers a program of public assistance through bureaus located in 83 counties. Bureaus range in size from those of one person, who makes investigations and serves as bureau supervisor, to one with hundreds of employees. If sufficiently large, a bureau includes public assistance workers who investigate applications for financial assistance, case and bureau supervisors, and clerical personnel. Within a bureau the chain of authority runs from bureau supervisor to case supervisor and from case supervisor to public assistance worker, with each case supervisor generally supervising six to seven workers.

As noted earlier, the formal requirements of the role of public assistance worker are uniform throughout the organization. All workers have met the same minimal requirements for the job, all perform the same types of functions, and all follow the same rules and procedures as set forth in the manual of operation for the investigation of applications for assistance. At the same time, however, the role can be conceived and performed in different ways because of certain ambiguities in how it is defined (apart from other reasons). Consider, for example, the role of workers who handle cases in the Aid to Dependent Children Program (these are the workers studied in this investigation). The federal laws define the ADC task too generally to be of much help in determining many concrete decisions.[3] In contrast, the manual of operation, while very specific with respect to conditions of eligibility for financial assistance, does not cover numerous service problems met by the worker. Thus there is latitude for individual variability in performance and for different conceptions of the role.

Procedure and Findings

The sample of 109 public assistance workers who handled ADC cases consisted largely of females, and most were married. A majority had worked in public assistance for less than four years, 22 per cent for less than a year. While three-quarters of the workers had college degrees, only 9 per cent had specialized in social work and none had obtained a Master's degree in social work.

The sample was drawn from small, medium, and large administrative units. The "small" bureaus were those in which there were at least two but no more than five workers, and no more than a two-level hierarchy. A random sample of six small bureaus was drawn containing a total of 18 workers, all of whom participated in the study. The "medium-sized" bureaus were those that had six or more workers or a three-level hierarchy, but no more than three such levels. Five medium-sized bureaus were selected on a non-random basis, contributing 59 workers who handled ADC cases. The offices ranged in size from six to 22 workers and tended to be located in the more highly industrialized, urban counties. There was only one large bureau, Wayne County; it had a five-level hierarchy, with the positions of ADC division head and director above the level of case supervisor and below the level of bureau director. Thirty-two workers were selected from a pool of 96 ADC workers assigned to two different divisions by choosing four supervisory units at random. The mean number of workers in the small offices was 3.8; comparable figures for medium and large size were 17.4 and 45.5, respectively.

There was a direct relationship between the size of the bureaus and the number of hierarchically ordered strata, since bureaus in the sample were selected by criteria of size and number of strata. For the 83 bureaus in the state there was also a marked positive relationship between the number of employees and the number of strata.[4]

The amount of specialization of function for the worker increased with size. Specialization for three of the four categories of cases was found in the largest bureau in the sample. In the two next largest ones, only a few of the workers had caseloads made up exclusively of ADC recipients, and for the remaining bureaus specialization by type of case was not found.

Characteristics of the workers in the units also differed by size. In the smaller administrative units there were found more older workers, more workers without college degrees, more who had married, more having children, and more workers with long experience in public assistance. The workers in the smaller units, as compared with the larger ones, moreover, lived in a more rural environment.

The personal characteristics of the workers were the only correlates that could be controlled statistically in the analysis of results reported below. There was no satisfactory way to separate the effects of specialization, degree of stratification, and population setting from those of the numbers of workers. Hence, even when the effects of personal characteristics were controlled, there was no way to determine whether it was the number of workers or some other factor that produced the effects. The results presented below were analyzed first without controls for variables operating concomitantly with size and, subsequently, with controls for the personal attributes of the workers. The different sized bureaus are labeled "small" or "large" as a matter of convenience; it should be understood that not merely the number of workers differentiates the offices.

Questionnaires were administered to the participating workers and to their case supervisors in the 12 administrative units. The questions referred to a wide range of variables. One of these, termed *role consensus,* is indicated by the degree of agreement between the public assistance worker and his supervisor about the importance of functions performed by workers. The amount of agreement was assumed to reflect the degree to which workers and supervisors shared a frame of reference regarding the importance of workers' functions. Eleven areas of knowledge and skill (for example, determining financial eligibility, job mechanics, and casework methods) relevant to performance of the role of the public assistance worker were rated for importance on a seven-point scale by workers and supervisors and discrepancy scores were computed.

Another variable, termed *breadth of role conception,* refers to the number of activities or functions conceived as part of the role. In the questionnaire the workers were presented with nine activities (for example, budgeting and referral for vocational counselling) and were asked to indicate for each function whether they "always," "sometimes," or "never" performed it in cases for which that activity, as a type of service, *was needed.* Numerical values were assigned to responses and total scores were computed. The higher the score, the more broadly the role is conceived.

Another aspect of role, often implicit rather than formally defined, is the ethical commitment that it requires of individuals. In public welfare, as well as in other service fields, those responsible for giving the services are guided by ethical precepts. A test of *ethical commit-*

ment was devised to measure some of these, more exactly termed a test of commitment to the ethics of professional social work, since it consists of items relating to seven ethical areas highly endorsed by a sample of 75 professionally trained social workers.[5] The content of the items, given in Table 1, may be clustered into two categories: (a) how the worker should behave with a client, and (b) who should receive the benefits of social work services and under what conditions. To complete the validation, the responses of the professionally trained social workers

TABLE 1

Percentages of Workers, Supervisors, and Members of Professional Association Selecting "Correct" Alternatives for Items of the Test of Commitment to the Ethics of Professional Social Work

Content of Item*	Inferred Underlying Value**	Group		
		Workers (N=109)	Super-visors (N=26)	Members of Professional Group (N=75)
1. In interviewing, sacrifice directness *versus* ask direct questions	humanitarian *versus* utilitarian	49	54	63
2. Motivate by offering information *versus* urge directly	non-coercive *versus* coercive	72	88	97
3. When client is upset, discuss feelings *versus* ignore them	concern *versus* non-concern for client's feelings	83	88	92
4. When client makes you angry, analyze your anger *versus* ignore it	awareness *versus* non-awareness of self as an instrument of change	72	92	97
5. Financial aid given to all *versus* to those who use it wisely	help universally *versus* help selectively	38	68	69
6. Illegitimacy demands focus on helping individual adjust *versus* changing individual	acceptance *versus* non-acceptance of deviance	28	38	74
7. Client making curtains in messy house, compliment *versus* mention house-cleaning	positive *versus* negative methods to motivate	60	75	96

*The first of the alternatives for each item is the "correct" one.

**The first of the polarities of underlying values is the one matched to the "correct" alternative for its corresponding item.

were compared with those of the sample of public assistance supervisors and workers drawn in this study. In contrast to the professionally trained group, the majority of whom had obtained Master's degrees in social work, the public assistance workers generally had little such specialized training. Table 1 shows that the "correct" alternatives are most highly endorsed by the professional group and least highly endorsed by the workers, with the supervisors' responses falling between these extremes.

A final set of measures is related to the quality of the worker's performance on the job. It was possible to learn about the cognitive aspect of performance through indications of the analytic skill of workers as indicated by their ability, first, to identify the problems of families and, second, to propose appropriate treatment plans. To measure the first item, the workers were asked to describe the problems they noted for the members of a family depicted in a case vignette; responses were transformed into a numerical score of diagnostic acuity.[6] To measure the second aspect of analytic skill, the workers were asked to describe what they would do for the individuals described in the case if they had the required time; responses were coded and scores were obtained for *appropriateness of treatment plans.*[7] A motivational aspect of performance was inferred from responses to a question about how much the worker would like to work on the case described in the vignette.[8]

Results

Workers' conceptions of their roles differed according to the size of the welfare office. In the smaller bureaus there was found to be greater *role consensus* between the worker and his supervisor about the importance of functions that workers perform (Table 2), greater *breadth of role conception* (Table 3), and higher *ethical commitment* (Table 4).

TABLE 2

Number of Workers Having Large and Small Discrepancy Scores in Role Consensus, *by Size of Administrative Unit*

Size of Administrative Unit	Discrepancy Score	
	Small (0-1)	Large (2-3)
Small	14	0
Medium	54	4
Large	21	11

$$X^2 = 15.00, \; p < .01$$

TABLE 3

Number of Workers Conceiving Their Roles Narrowly
And Broadly, by Size of Administrative Unit

Size of Administrative Unit	Breadth of Role Conception	
	Narrow (0-4)	Broad (5-8)
Small	4	14
Medium	20	37
Large	18	14

$$X^2=6.48, \ p <.05$$

TABLE 4

Number of Workers Scoring High and Low on Ethical Commitment,
By Size of Administrative Unit

Size of Administrative Unit	Scores on Ethical Commitment	
	Low (1-4)	High (5-7)
Small	3	15
Medium	35	23
Large	26	6

$$X^2=20.04, \ p <.001$$

Quality of Performance. The size of the administrative unit was found to be associated with all indicators of the quality of the worker's performance. Those workers scoring high on the three measures are much more likely to be in the small bureaus than in the larger ones (Table 5).

TABLE 5

Number of Workers Scoring High and Low on Measures of the Quality
Of Performance, by Size of Administrative Unit

Size of Administrative Unit	Scores on Diagnostic Acuity		Scores on Appropriateness of Treatment Plan		Motivation to Help Recipients	
	High (4-8)	Low (0-3)	High (5-7)	Low (0-4)	High (3-7)	Low (1, 2)
Small	13	5	14	4	15	3
Medium	23	36	21	38	21	38
Large	6	25	10	20	12	19

$$X^2=13.46, \ p <.01 \quad X^2=11.26, \ p <.01 \quad X^2=13.30, \ p <.01$$

The Effects of Personal Background Factors. Analyses were made with controls for age, education, experience on the job, marital status, and number of children. This procedure involved the relationship between organizational size and a dependent variable, holding constant the control factor whenever it was found that the control characteristic was associated with the dependent variable. The .05 level of significance was used as a choice point.

Using this technique, age is the only control factor related both to the size of bureaus and the magnitude of discrepancy of *role consensus.* Although the smaller bureaus had more older workers and more workers with small discrepancy scores, the effects of size remained with age held constant.[9]

Two of the control factors are closely associated with the *breadth of role conception.* Broadly conceived roles were found more often for older workers and for those with lengthy experience in public assistance; the first relationship yields a X^2 of 17.73, the second a X^2 of 16.21, both giving p values of less than .001. When age and experience are controlled, size is no longer related to the *breadth of role conception.* Since there were more older workers and workers with longer experience in the smaller units, age and experience, and not other factors associated with size, account for the breadth of conception of roles.

Both the education and experience of workers are related to scores of *ethical commitment.* The less well educated and those with longer experience on the job most frequently show high as opposed to low scores on ethical commitment; the X^2 is 8.51 for the former ($p < .01$) and 4.05 for the latter ($p < .05$). The effects of size remain, however, when education and experience are each held constant.[10]

The only control variable found to be related to any of the three indicators of the quality of the worker's performance was the number of children the workers had; those workers having children had higher scores on motivation to help recipients than did those having no children ($X^2 = 5.40, p < .05$). The effects of size remained for workers with or without children.[11]

Discussion and Conclusions

Why should the variables examined here be associated with organizational size? Like many others, size is not a "pure" variable—a single unitary phenomenon. Size is more like an index because of its relationship to a complement of variables associated with the number of persons in the organization. The findings of this study provide suggestions about these variables, but offer few clues about *why* they are associated with size or about their interrelationships. We now turn to these questions.

Most of our results may be accounted for plausibly in terms of the population and the community setting of the county in which the welfare bureau was located. The size of the bureau itself depends largely upon the population size of the county, since the more populous counties are likely to contain more individuals in need of welfare assistance. Although organizational size bears no necessary relationship to the population of the area in which the organization is located, one may be an index of the other to the extent that (a) the organizational unit serves a portion of the population, as does a welfare bureau, and (b) the unit is located by such arbitrary geographical criteria as county, state, or region.

The association of the workers' personal characteristics with the size of welfare bureaus probably indicates that the pool of potential employees in the counties with large populations differs from those with small populations. Available information indicates that some of the contrasts between workers in the smaller and the larger bureaus parallel those between rural residents and residents of cities.[12] This study provides no information about whether or not there is also selective retention of workers as a consequence of bureau size.

Roles were found to be more broadly conceived by workers in the smaller bureaus. The control analysis shows that age and experience account for the breadth of conception of roles. Welfare workers in rural areas change jobs less often than their urban counterparts, partly because there are fewer occupational alternatives and fewer welfare jobs from which to choose that pay as well or better than public assistance.[13] Rural welfare workers therefore would be expected to be older and more experienced than urban ones. Furthermore, rural areas contain fewer specialized social services, making it necessary for the welfare worker in the rural area to take over informally more functions as part of her role than her urban colleague.

Another correlate of organizational size is the ethical commitment of workers. Differences in ethical commitment can not be attributed to variations of professionalization, for none of the workers had had professional training in social work. The community setting of the welfare offices and the rural background of the workers account for the workers' ethical orientation most adequately. High scores on the test indicate a generally more positive approach to recipients—an approach probably growing out of a more intimate relationship with recipients in the smaller communities. The writer has been told by experienced welfare workers of the differences between working in the smaller and the larger urban communities. In the small community they note that there is more frequent community contact with recipients; perception of recipients as individuals more often than as "clients"; less social distance between worker and recipient, due in part to similarity of ethnic background; and greater need to attend to more of the recipients' problems. Consequently, the worker in the small bureau is more likely to be willing to assume greater personal responsibility for the recipient and to have more compassion for the recipient as a person than the worker in an urban bureau.

The attitude of helpfulness toward others and the "positive" approach to recipients engendered by the small community probably explain why workers in the small bureaus evidenced performance of higher quality than those in the larger ones. The measures of quality of performance were skill in analyzing problems of recipients, appropriateness of treatment plans, and motivation to help recipients—all of which reflect the extent of the worker's willingness to do a complete and adequate job of helping recipients. That the rural workers are more willing than those in urban settings to help recipients and to put forth the extra effort needed to analyze thoroughly the recipients' problems and to propose suitable treatment is consistent with the earlier observations about the small community.

The community setting of the bureaus does not readily explain why size is related to role consensus. Past theoretical and empirical work indicates that consensus is likely to be greater in small than in large groups.[14] In this study, the size alone is probably not the only organizational characteristic which contributes to role consensus.

Another correlate of organizational size is the extent to which there was vertical and horizontal differentiation. Size enables differentiation to occur by providing a larger number of persons over whom functions may be distributed and by increasing the range of individual skill and ability needed to give feasibly different assignments to persons. In the organizational units studied here, differentiation in the larger bureaus was further facilitated by administrative policy stipulating the proportion of supervisory personnel required for a given number of workers and by the belief that specialized handling of cases is efficient only in the largest bureaus.

This discussion of the correlates of organizational size suggests that the number of workers may be a less potent variable in affecting the behavior of members than the community setting of the organizational unit. Studies of organizational units of an extended bureaucracy differing in size should be undertaken where it is possible to differentiate them in terms of the population size and type of community in which the units are located.

From another viewpoint, some of the variables used in this study can be said to reflect organizational effectiveness in providing services to families. These variables include the measures of the quality of work, ethical commitment, and breadth of role conception signified by the number of different services workers would perform for families were they needed. These three indications of service are negatively associated with the size of the organizational unit: the smaller bureaus show greater commitment to the ethics of professional social work, greater breadth of role conception, and better quality of work. To the extent that these variables reflect differences in performance of workers, the results indicate that the organizational goal of providing services to recipients was more effectively attained in the smaller welfare bureaus.

The findings of the study do not help to answer the question of how effectively the bureaus attained the organizational goal of determining eligibility for financial assistance.

Why were the small bureaus better able than the larger ones to provide services to families? If the interpretations of the findings presented above are correct, it is largely because the influences of the small community encourage a service orientation toward recipients. The impact of community setting thus may be viewed as reaffirming the significance of the secondary organizational goal, that of providing services, through orienting workers more toward the service aspects of their roles. The part played by the actual size of the welfare bureau is probably minimal, except in so far as it serves to mediate, through primary relationships, the service goal. The fact that role consensus was greater in the smaller bureaus may indicate greater cohesion of the primary groups and readier acceptance of the goal to provide service.

Footnotes

1. The findings reported here are based upon data collected in one phase of a research project financed by funds from the State of Michigan for research and service in the utilization of human resources. The project was located in the University of Michigan School of Social Work. The author is indebted to W. J. Maxey, Lynn Kellogg, and Willis Oosterhof of the Department for the consultation and cooperation given in the study; to Mrs. Donna McLeod of the research

staff for assistance in collecting data and in statistical analyses; and to Morris Janowitz, Leo Meltzer, Henry J. Meyer, and Robert Vinter for critically reading an early draft of this paper.

2. One of the few empirical studies of the size of organizations is Frederic W. Terrien and Donald L. Mills, "The Effect of Changing Size Upon the Internal Structure of Organizations," *American Sociological Review*, 20 (February, 1955), pp. 11-14. Discussions of organizational size are found in Theodore Caplow, "Organizational Size," *Administrative Science Quarterly*, 1 (March, 1957), pp. 485-491; and Kenneth E. Boulding, *The Organizational Revolution*, New York: Harper, 1953.

The importance of size as a variable was noted long ago by Spencer, Durkheim, and Simmel, whose observations are well-known on this subject. Examples of recent laboratory work include: Robert F. Bales, "Some Uniformities of Behavior in Small Social Systems," in G. Swanson, T. M. Newcomb, and E. Hartley, editors, *Readings in Social Psychology*, New York: Holt, 1952, pp. 146-159; Robert F. Bales and Edgar F. Borgatta, "Size of Group as a Factor in the Interaction Profile," in A. Paul Hare, Edgar F. Borgatta, and R. F. Bales, editors, *Small Groups: Studies in Social Interaction*, New York: Knopf, 1955, pp. 396-413; A. Paul Hare, "Interaction and Consensus in Different Sized Groups," in D. Cartwright and A. Zander, editors, *Group Dynamics: Research and Theory*, Evanston, Ill.: Row, Peterson, 1953, pp. 483-492.

3. The ADC program was set up to enable needy children who are deprived of a parent to receive financial assistance so that a homemaker can remain in the home to care for them. More recent legislation expands the purpose, adding that it should "help maintain and strengthen family life," and help families "attain the maximum self-support and personal independence consistent with the maintenance of continuing parental care and protection. . . ." From "Social Security Amendment of 1956," Section 312.

4. Relationships between the number of vertical strata and the mean number of workers and clerical personnel were as follows: for one stratum, 2.0 employees; for two strata, 5.6 employees; for three strata, 18.5 employees; and for five strata, 213.0 employees.

5. This group consisted largely of members of the local chapter of the National Association of Social Workers. Almost every respondent had received the degree of Master of Social Work. The questions of the test took the same form for each ethical area. First a problem was presented followed by two opposing alternatives for action a worker might take in such a situation. The assumption underlying the instrument was that each course of action implied a different ethical justification. It is not assumed that all ethical guidelines directing the efforts of workers were sampled in the test, although the ones specified are assumed to be important.

6. Responses were coded into the following categories: non-existent problems (scored —2), superficially conceived problems (—1), problems manifest in the case (+1), and appropriately inferred underlying problems (+2). Scores were the algebraic sum. Kendall's *tau* is +.74 for the scores of two coders (N=20).

7. Responses were coded into plans inappropriate to the case (scored —2), plans to aid with manifest problems (+1), and plans to help with appropriately inferred underlying problems (+2). Scores were the algebraic sum. Kendall's *tau* is +.80 for the scores of two coders (N=20).

8. For the most part, the interrelationships among these variables are positive. Scores on diagnostic acumen are directly related to scores on appropriateness of treatment plans ($X^2 = 18.25$, $p < .001$) and on ethical commitment ($X^2 = 9.31$, $p < .01$); they bear no relationship, however, to motivation to help recipients. Scores on appropriateness of treatment plan are not related to those on ethical commitment, but are related to those of motivation to help recipients ($X^2 = 6.85$, $p < .01$). Scores on ethical commitment are positively associated with those on motivation to help recipients ($X^2 = 4.11$, $p < .05$).

9. The percentages of workers under 39 years of age with low discrepancy scores for the small, medium, and large bureaus are 100, 84, and 69, respectively; for workers 40 years or older the comparable percentages are 100, 100, and 40. The Ns are too small to compute statistical tests.

10. The percentages of workers with bachelor's or higher degrees having high scores for the small, medium, and large bureaus were respectively 60, 32, and 13 ($X^2 = 5.31$, $p < .06$); for workers having attained less than a bachelor's degree, the percentages for small, medium, and large bureaus were 91, 47, and 37 ($X^2 = 8.24$, $p < .02$). The percentages of workers with less than four years' experience having high scores for the small, medium, and large bureaus were respectively 50, 31, and 17 ($X^2 = 10.56$, $p < .01$); for workers with more than four years of experience, the percentages for the small, medium, and large bureaus were 78, 48, and 16 ($X^2 = 9.92$, $p < .01$).

11. The percentages of childless workers having high scores in the small, medium, and large bureaus are, respectively, 71, 22, and 33 ($X^2 = 5.80$, $p < .06$); for those workers with one or more children, the percentages in the small, medium, and large bureaus are 91, 44, and 57 ($X^2 = 7.39$, $p < .05$).

12. Persons residing in rural areas are less well educated, more often married, generally more fertile, and less mobile occupationally than urbanites. See Noel P. Gist and L. A. Halbert, *Urban Society* (Fourth Edition), New York: Crowell, 1956.

13. This conclusion is supported by information provided by the Michigan State Department of Social Welfare.

14. See Emile Durkheim, *The Division of Labor in Society*, Glencoe, Illinois: Free Press, 1949, pp. 80-131; and A. Paul Hare, *op.cit.* pp. 507-518. It may be noted the small group provides conditions well-suited to the development of consensus: there is likely to be a relatively rapid rate of interaction and a relatively smaller divergence of opinion and behavior, due to a smaller range of opinion and behavior than in large groups.

part III

ENVIRONMENTAL COMPARISONS

"If organizations operate in different kinds of environments, we must learn how environments impinge on and shape organizations, administrative functions, and administrative processes." (p. 9).

The preceding chapters pointed up the importance of environment for organizational structure *even when purposes and technologies were held constant.* In the following three chapters, this restriction is relaxed and the impact of environment is more squarely the focus of attention.

Comparing university research units in the same university, Bennis finds that they can have quite different environments, and that these can have important consequences for the ways in which the units define and articulate purposes. Harbison and his colleagues compare organizations with similar objectives but with quite different technical resources and procedures. This study underscores the interaction of organization and environment, for the kinds of skills produced in a society's members are important for the kinds of structural arrangements its organizations can adopt. The variations in this study cannot be explained without reference to the differing class structures and mobility patterns of the larger social systems in which industries are set.

Miller emphasizes the cultural differences inherent in manifestations of power and authority, contending that coordination and fulfillment of tasks in Euro-American contexts rests upon vertical chains of authority and permanent roles, but that this is not necessarily the case in other cultural settings. The implications of this for cross-cultural activities are basic and clear, but Miller's study contains another important, though subtle, lesson. Effective authority is culturally defined by the ways in which people relate to one another; hence, it is subject to change and redefinition even in Euro-American settings.

part III

ENVIRONMENTAL COMPARISONS

chapter 5

The Effect on Academic Goods of their Market

Warren G. Bennis

Research in the physical sciences is perhaps more certain to be directed toward useful ends than research in humanistic fields, because the former is most commonly carried on in organized laboratories, where consultation is almost inevitable and a consensus of opinion as to what is worthwhile is easily formed, and has its effect on the investigator, whereas in most humanistic and social subjects the researcher can work in comparative isolation.—J. Franklin Jameson[1] (1927).

As the design engineers in an industry feel harried by the demands and expectations of product engineers who want to produce, and the sales engineers who want to sell, so the design engineers of social science are under the pressures just indicated from the production and sales staff who insist on putting on the social science assembly line what is still necessarily in the handicraft and mock-up stage. In many quarters, the promoters of social science have aroused such unfillable expectations as to risk a disillusioning bust of the whole enterprise.—David Riesman.[2]

In less than two decades we have seen the emergence in the United States of a new industry: the organized production of new social knowledge. While Slichter and other economists cite the rise of industrial, mostly physical, research as one of the main developments in the national economy, the use of teams of social scientists working on practical problems has turned social research into a million-dollar business.[3] Although comprehensive and comparable statistical data on the growth of social science research are nonexistent, certain clues indicate the magnitude of this development: (1) The combined expenditures for social research of the twenty largest universities in 1928 would probably support only one present-day university research organization.[4] (2) While the government disbursed practically no funds for social research twenty-five years ago, in 1952 eleven million dollars was spent on psychological research alone. (3) The National Science Foundation estimates that a hundred million dollars was spent on research in the social sciences in 1953.

Perhaps the most important circumstances in stimulating large-scale programs of research are the increased specialization of the social disciplines which has created a need for interdisciplinary and team research,[5] the magnitude of world problems, the proved usefulness of social science findings for policy-makers, the availability of large sums of money from foundations and the United States government, and the quantifiability of social data. These developments have created sweeping changes in the structure of social research. A new type of intellectual organization is emerging, replete with big budgets and the growing pains of managerial responsibility. The purpose of this paper is to examine an organization which has been under study by the author for over fifteen months and describe its chief organizational syndrome: exposure to market forces.

The organization, the "hub," is located in a large university, is under the jurisdiction of its College of Social Studies, and is equivalent to an academic department. Its growth was spurred both to strengthen the social sciences at the university and to offer social scientists the opportunity to influence the nature of American foreign policy by tackling problems of major interest to the government. Hence, its main activity centers around international affairs and economic development.

The total personnel numbers about eighty-five: twelve equivalent to full or associate professors, twenty-six research associates, twenty research assistants (chiefly graduate students), twenty-two secretaries, and four administrative assistants. These persons are connected with one or the other of two main research projects: a Development Program to examine three countries with contrasting geographical and economic environments and a Communications program to study the interaction of words, impressions, and ideas which affect the attitudes and behavior of different peoples toward one another. Each program has its own director who attempts to co-ordinate the activities of the staff prescribed by the research goals.

The Hub is almost completely dependent upon outside financing by a large private foundation.[6] An indication of the anxiety concerning the granting of funds was shown in the Hub's 1953-54 Annual Report, the first sentence of which reads: "The most important event in the life of the Hub last year was the receipt at the year-end of a substantial grant from the foundation for the conduct of research. This grant removed a major uncertainty which had hovered over a major portion of the Hub's forward planning. . . ."

The program on Communications has been established with a four-year grant, while that on Development has been awarded a grant on a year-to-year basis. While even four years is short, considering the gestation period of research, the Development project was threatened by the yearly scrutiny of the foundation and by its annual uncertainties. For the preceding two years the foundation had not announced the grant until the end of May.

Market Versus Task Orientation

One chief conception of work in a research organization varies with the degree of control the organization maintains over exogenous forces—in this particular case, market forces. Where financial security provides protection from the market, the organization and the scientists within it are safe from the vagaries of the market. This situation we call "task orientation." Where there is little protection from the market place, the organization becomes intimately concerned with financial matters. Attention, for sheer sake of survival, is diverted from the task to the sponsors of research. This we call "market-orientation."

Unless there is some degree of insulation from competitive and market pressures on the science organization, professional standards are likely to be lowered, if not entirely rejected. In industrial laboratories, firms with large research budgets and some modicum of protection from the market have an opportunity to offer their scientists more freedom and hence more opportunities for "pure" research.[7] If the market structure of a particular project is insecure and tenuous the individual researcher faces a peculiar type of role conflict: duty as a scientist qua scientist and the demands of the market. Putting it differently, he is torn between organizational demands and his own professional demands. Hans Zinnser once described how the competitive milieu affects scientific performance in medical work:

It puts a premium upon quantitative productiveness, spectacular achievement and practical success, which will bring administrative applause, often because of its advertising value in institutional competition. These tendencies to be fair, are in every university known to be

73

resisted by men who have the determining influence; but the psychology of the situation is too logical to be offset by individual idealism, the natural pressure too strong.[8]

The thesis presented here is that the Development program, because of its tenuous financing, is market-oriented while the Communications program is task oriented. How was this difference in forces (market structure) reflected in the data?

The Problems

One of the questions asked of all Hub researchers in the course of an interview was "What do you consider the three main problems of research at the Hub?" The 186 responses were then categorized in five classes: organizational, external, substantive, bureaucratic, and interpersonal. We are concerned here with the "external problems" category, which deals specifically with those issues concerned exclusively with "instability and uncertainty due to precarious relations with the sponsor of research." Almost 30 per cent of the total responses fell into this category. The Communications staff made the fewest responses in this category (four times) and when they did, barely mentioned the foundation. The following representative responses were made by the Development staff:

I would take a job at X college in preference to the Hub based not on criteria of teaching over research but just that the Hub's future is not as certain as X college.

One of the major problems here has been and continues to be the uncertainty of the budget. You have to know the scale of funds before you can plan. We got only a fraction of what we had planned for. Now we're looking for other funds, etc. We cannot recruit too well because we cannot make a firm offer. If we had a budget—a firm one—we would have no personnel problems.

The main problem here is doing research and justifying ourself to the foundation. The thing that's annoyed me the most is that we spend so much time looking at our navel without doing anything—except justifying our existence.

The main problem is the uncertain environment. This is an uneasy life . . . tougher than a real university life . . . this time-uncertainty and shoe-string operation. If I were given dough when I first came here—say so many thousand per annum, I may have hired not *better* but people more akin to project needs.

I have to spend up to 25 per cent of my time working on the foundation submission.

The tightest pressure I've felt is the annual soul-searching with the foundation. I've been through it two years now and it wears me out.

74

Ever since January, tension has been awful. Everyone has been watching, waiting, and, in general, usurping valuable time because of the terrible fear of not getting the contract renewed because of budget cuts. This takes a large part of group conversation.

"I've Just Received Word From The Foundation That . . ."

Few members of the Hub, according to responses to a cartoon,[9] were free of anxiety concerning relations with the foundation. In point of fact, of the eighteen cartoons used, the one dealing with foundation relations attracted the second highest responses, twenty-five completions. This particular cartoon depicted five men seated around a table, one of whom is shown saying, "I've just received word from the foundation that. . . ." Those interviewed were asked to complete the statement of the speaker by filling in the space above the speaker's head. In addition to the straight-line box extending over the speaker, there was a cloudlike "bubble" over another member's head. Subjects were also asked to supply a response in this space to the speaker's statement but to consider it an unspoken, private thought. Thus, with a device borrowed from the cartoonist, it was possible to derive public or "overt" responses as well as private or "covert" reactions. Of nineteen overt statements, seventeen dealt specifically with the question of grants. Moreover, Table 1 shows that in their covert remarks thirteen subjects revealed anxiety about financing.

TABLE 1

Attitudes Toward Foundation

(N=25)

Grant was awarded........	8	Insecurity from uncertainty.	13
Grant was cut.............	9	Hostile to foundation.......	3
Other	2	Personal insecurity stemming	
Total	19	from fragile situation.......	7
		Total	23

Again there was a clear distinction between responses from the Communications project and those from Development. Of the seven responses showing "severe" insecurity in the covert box, six were made by Development personnel. By "severe" we mean that the individual voiced serious personal problems as a result of foundation vagaries, such as: "My job will be lost" or "Whew! Another year accounted for. . . At last." This is not to say that the Communications staff was unconcerned about the foundation. But, judging from their responses, they tended to react more *aggressively* to the foundation. At the same

75

time they were less worried about *personal* insecurities and more concerned with having "to revise my work" or deleting research problems of great interest. In short, while the Development staff was anxious about the possible loss of a job the Communications group was concerned with the research goals. Examples of cartoon responses are shown in Table 2.

TABLE 2

Overt and Covert Responses to Cartoon

Overt	Covert

Communications Program
Responses

"... they'll give us half the money we asked for."	"Oh God! Some jerks have no sense of the realities of life. We'll either have to get more money or revise our objectives completely."
"... have cut our grant in half."	"There goes our non-economic research!"
	"Here we go! Another 'revision'."

Development Program
Responses

"The Development grant will probably come up for action at the May meeting of the Board of Directors."	"How can you run a research outfit with all this uncertainty and delay? That foundation is all 'snafu'd' and unless they get straightened out they're not going to measure up to X or Y foundations—no matter how much money they have."
"We will not be given a final answer to our submission until mid-summer. By that it seems as if our request will be cut in part even if finally accepted."	"Planning research under foundation sponsorship is uncertain!"
"They are greatly pleased with our plans and will cut our request only by 75%."	"We still got away with murder. (Will I keep *my* job?)"
"They will continue the present subsidies through the coming year."	"I'm delighted. That means my own subsidization will continue unimpaired."

In addition to the data presented here the effects of the situation upon project functioning were reflected in the Communications program in the following ways: (1) more perceived freedom and scope for the staff member; (2) less time spent in writing up research proposals and progress reports; (3) greater satisfaction with the work in progress.[10] Perhaps equally important was the impression gained that more frequent offhand, somewhat parenthetical allusions to the foundation were made by the Development program. Many of these remarks were humorous. It can be argued that they were a mechanism for dealing with tension. This argument is strengthened by the fact that there seemed to be an increase in these remarks as the time drew near for the foundation decision. The following are examples:

STAFF MEMBER (*pointing to foundation proposal which is nearing completion*): There it is—about seven thousand dollars a page. . . . We have talked of matters serious—but of that—it is a matter of life and death.

(*Backing up intellectual point*): All I'm saying is what our submission to the foundation says.

CHAIRMAN OF SEMINAR: Well, that settles it!

We sent off the submission to the foundation and, after we totaled up what all the problems of development would cost, found that it would break the foundation, so we cut it down a little.

Why are we studying X country? Well, the last time this came up we had to hunt around for a slip of paper. Unfortunately today I couldn't find that, so I have to give you my own ideas for it. Where is the submission?

Usually one does not think of knowledge and research findings in terms of the pricing mechanism, but it does offer insight in understanding the difficulties of organized research. Because of methods of financing, the Development group was in a more "competitive" position than was the Communications group, which was protected from the market forces for at least four years. While the latter was aware of the foundation's importance, the Development personnel saw the foundation as a towering, overshadowing Jehovah. (One of the Development directors once substituted the name of the foundation in the phrase "God willing!") Each year during the past two years, with growing intensity from January to May, the question asked by the Development personnel has been, "Will the funds come through?" More indirectly, "What does the foundation want from us?" Or "How can we make our research proposals so attractive that we can get funds other institutions won't get?"

Without stretching the analogy, there was a good deal of concern with a form of market activity, "product differentiation." This was evidenced when a project group from the Hub visited a neighboring research group financed by the same foundation and working on the same country. The latent function of this trip, it can be argued, was to look over the "competitor," to insure the marketing of a unique and more appealing product. The effects of the anxiety over uncertain economic returns were reflected in various ways. At times it took the form of advanced gamesmanship, that is, how to impress the foundation and still keep the research plans fluid. As one member put it: "They (the foundation) want a research proposal now, but, after all, our hypotheses will come only after six months or so." Indeed, one of the most important functions of the Hub director was to keep a balance between the pressures of exogenous influences (demands of the country under study, foundation, users of research) and the pressures made upon him by individual researchers to keep insulated from market demands.

Another effect of the uncertain environment was the attitude toward the foundation. In reality the foundation exerted no pressure on the substantive efforts of the Hub. However, social and objective realities in this case were not consonant. Thus various individuals felt that the foundation placed unbearable constraints on research proposals; that the main problem at the Hub, as one member quoted before said, "was doing research and having to justify ourself to the foundation."

We see here a tendency, not uncommon in an organized milieu, to project blame upward and away.[11] This tendency may be exacerbated in social research, where uncertainty and the unknown are daily companions, where physical and social comparisons are ambiguous, and where authority is not definite. Hence, the foundation, much as in the other cases the civil service or "bureaucracy," may be made the scapegoat.

Footnotes

1. Cited in F. A. Ogg *Research in the Humanistic and Social Sciences* (New York and London: Century Co., 1928), p. 17.

2. "Observations on Social Science Research," from *Individualism Reconsidered*, (Glencoe, Illinois: Free Press, 1954), p. 475.

3. Sumner Slichter, address at the Business Executive Conference at the University of Omaha, Omaha, Nebraska, May 15, 1953.

4. Ogg, *op. cit.* reported that the following universities spent under $350,000 on social research in 1926-27: California, Chicago, Illinois, Indiana, Kansas, Michigan, Minnesota, Missouri, Nebraska, Harvard, Yale, Columbia, Johns Hopkins, and Cornell. The total budget of the research organization which will

be described here is larger; indeed, it maintains the largest budget in the College of Social Studies.

For accounts of the growth of expenditures in social science see H. Alpert, "National Science Foundation," *American Sociological Review,* XIX, and Number 2, (1954), 208; R. G. Axt, *Federal Government and Financing Higher Education* (New York: Columbia University Press, 1952); B. Barber, *Science and the Social Order* (Glencoe, Illinois: The Free Press, 1952), p. 132; W. G. Bennis, "The Structure of Social Science: An Organizational Study" (paper read at the American Sociological Society Annual Meetings, Urbana, Illinois, September, 1954) pp. 2-3; L. P. Lessing, "National Science Foundation Takes Stock," *Scientific American,* March, 1954; *Federal Funds for Science: National Science Foundation,* 1950-52 (Washington: U. S. Government Printing Office).

5. The Russell Sage Foundation, Brookings Institution and the Social Science Research Council stress this development as one of the most significant in the social sciences in the past two decades. See M. Graham, *Federal Utilization of Social Science* (Washington, D. C.: Brookings Institution, 1954), pp. 18-21; *Effective use of Social Science Research in the Federal Services* (New York: Russell Sage Foundation, 1950), p. 21; *The Social Sciences in Historical Study* (Social Science Research Council Bulletin 64, 1954) pp. 31-33.

6. Since the field work for this paper was completed, i. e., during the very first days of the organization's life, important changes have been made toward a more permanent footing of research projects. The Hub director and other officers, fully aware of the problems of tenuous short-term financing, submitted a proposal urging a long-term commitment, and a five-year grant was issued by the foundation just as this study was closing.

7. W. Bennis, "Role Conflict and Market Structure" (Massachusetts Institute of Technology, 1953) (mimeographed).

8. Cited in L. Wilson, *Academic Man* (Oxford University Press, 1942) pp. 206-7.

9. These cartoons evolved out of the problem areas mentioned by Hub members in the initial interviews. The most prominent problems were reduced to simple sketches which allowed for "projections" by the subjects. The original impetus for the use of cartoons was made by H. A. Shepard, and June Moyer is responsible for the drawing.

10. These data were taken from the author's unpublished doctoral dissertation "The Social Science Research Organization: A Study of the Institutional Practices and Values in Interdisciplinary Research" (Massachusetts Institute of Technology, Department of Economics and Social Science, 1955).

11. Paula Brown's study of a government laboratory indicates that people tend to attack and blame the far-off civil service and that there is a "reluctance to accept responsibility for making decisions easily rationalized." Thus the projection of blame upward ("Bureaucracy in a Government Laboratory," *Social Forces,* XXXII, No. 3 [March, 1954], 266). For a laboratory experiment showing somewhat similar social processes see L. Festinger, "A Theory of Social Comparison Processes," *Human Relations,* VII, No. 2 (May, 1954), 119.

chapter 6

Steel Management On Two Continents

Frederick H. Harbison, Ernst Köchling,
Frank H. Cassell[1] and Heinrich C. Ruebmann

Introduction

The success of any industrial enterprise is obviously dependent upon
the effectiveness of its managerial organization and its supervisory
personnel. There are differences in management in different industries
and even within the same industry in a single country. And these
managerial differences may be the single most important competitive
difference. But, the differences may be even greater and more significant when comparisons are made on a cross-national basis. In Europe,
for example, the concept of the function of management is quite different
from that in the United States, as are the variances in the avenues of
access to managerial positions.

In order to highlight some of the similarities and contrasts in
management in two different industrial societies, the Industrial Relations Center of the University of Chicago undertook this preliminary
pilot analysis of managerial and supervisory personnel in two well-
known steel companies—the Dortmund-Hörde Huttenunion of Dortmund, Germany and the Indiana Harbor Works of the Inland Steel
Company, East Chicago, Indiana.[2]

In terms of total employment, these two companies are nearly the
same in size. Inland's Indiana Harbor Works employs slightly over
18,000 persons and Dortmund-Hörde Huttenunion has a total employment of about 17,000 persons. However, the steel-making capacity of
Inland is 5. million tons per year as compared with 2.5 million tons at
DHHU. This difference in tonnage capacity is attributable to a number

of factors including differences in processes, machinery, ores, product-mix, and even of the products themselves. Both companies, however, have fully integrated steel-making operations including blast furnaces, coke plants, steel-making furnaces, blooming mills, sheet mills, and structural mills. Inland has one large works which is nearly two-and-one half miles from one end to the other. DHHU has two works, one at Dortmund and the other at Hörde about 6 miles away.[3]

The selection of these two companies for this pilot study was somewhat fortuitous. Originally, the German Iron and Steel Federation suggested two companies in Germany. However, for various reasons it was not possible at the time to get the necessary statistical data from the second German company. Inland Steel was selected for two reasons: first, its total employment was comparable to that of DHHU, and second, its management was particularly interested in cooperating in the study. It is understood, however, that it will be necessary to secure information from several additional companies in each country if fully definitive and reliable cross-national comparisons are to be made. A plan has already been developed to extend the analysis to other companies not only in Germany and the United States but also in France, England and possibly the Benelux countries as well. Accordingly the principal usefulness of this pilot study is to establish the framework for more comprehensive studies.

The Criteria of Comparison

This study was designed to compare the numbers of persons in various levels of management or supervision and the nature of the educational background of those holding managerial positions. Another purpose of the study was to identify trends in managerial organization and in access to supervisory and managerial positions, and to relate these trends to pertinent factors in the technological development of the steel industry.

Management, for purposes of this study, is subdivided into two categories: top management and middle management. In top management we include the following comparable positions: 1. The Technische Direktor at DHHU and the Vice President of Steel Manufacturing at Inland; 2. The Direktions Assistenten at DHHU and Assistants to the Vice President at Inland; and 3. The Oberengeneure at DHHU and the General Superintendent and the Assistant General Superintendents at Inland. In *middle management* the following are included: 1. The Betriebslieter at DHHU and the Superintendents at Inland; 2. The Assistenten at DHHU and the Assistant Superintendents at Inland; and 3. The Assistenten (in Industrial Engineering and Time Study, Metallurgy, Production Control and Construction) at DHHU and the Senior Technical Staff in comparable positions at Inland.

In *supervision* the following comparable positions are included: 1. The Obermeister and Meister at DHHU and General Foremen and Foremen at Inland; 2. The Vorarbeiter at DHHU and the Assistant Foremen at Inland. At Inland, however, the persons holding these positions are considered to be an integral part of management and are not eligible for membership in unions. At DHHU these persons, though engaged for the most part in supervisory functions, are considered members of the working class and eligible for union membership.

The remaining personnel fall into two comparable categories: 1. The Arbeiter at DHHU and the Hourly Paid Workers at Inland; and 2. The Angestellte at DHHU and the Clerical and Junior Technical Employees at Inland.[4]

The comparison of the educational background of managerial personnel is more difficult because of the very great differences in the systems of higher education in Germany and the United States. The diploma from the German Universities or the Technisches Hochschule is quite comparable to the Master's Degree of American universities or engineering schools. But, there is no real equivalent in Germany for the American AB or BS four-year college degree, for it represents a more vocational type of training than broad university training. Thus, the college degree in the United States, though not comparable to the University or Hochschule diploma in Germany, has a higher status in America than the Fachschule certificate has in Germany. For the purpose of the study, nevertheless, we have arbitarily decided to equate the Fachschule certificate to the College degree. Thus, we have classified the educational background of managerial and supervisory personnel into three categories: first, those with Master's Degrees in the United States or university degrees in Germany, designated on Chart 1 as "A"; second, those with the American college degree or the German Fachschule certificate, designated "B"; and third, those with no degrees or higher education, designated "C".[5]

The Results of the Comparison

An analysis of the statistical data, set forth in Chart 1, brings out some very interesting results. The most significant findings can be summarized as follows:

First, in *top management* the formal educational training of the DHHU executives is much greater than that of the Inland executives. At DHHU, 17 out of 20 executives in this category have a university degree, and the remaining 3 have the Fachschule certificate, whereas at Inland, only 2 out of 12 top executives have a Master's degree, 6 have a college degree, and 4 have less than a four year college education.

CHART 1

Comparison of Technical Management in Steel Operations, Inland Steel Company, Indiana Harbor Works, and Dortmund-Horder Huttenunion, 1954

Position Level	Dortmund-Horder				Inland Steel			
	Total	A	B	C	Total	A	B	C
Vice Pres., Steel Mfg. (Technische Direktor)	1	1	0	0	1	0	1	0
Assistant to Vice Pres. (Direktions Assistent).........	5	4	1	0	4	1	1	2
General Superintendent & Assts. (Oberengeneure)	14	12	2	0	7	1	4	2
Total (Top Management)	20	17	3	0	12	2	6	4
Superintendents (Betriebsleiter).	60	45	15	0	38	1	19	18
Asst. Superintendent (Assistenten)	80	47	32	1	69	8	33	28
Senior Technical Staff (Assistenten)	43	27	16	0	430	20	77	333
Total (Middle Management)..	183	119	63	1	537	39	129	379
General Foremen & Foremen (Obermeister & Meister).....	319	0	0	319	1,044	18	159	867
Leader (Vorarbeiter)	623	—	—	—	112	—	—	—
Total (Supervision)	942				1,156			
Junior Technical & Clerical (Angestellte)................	857	x	x	x	1,024	x	x	x
Workers (Arbeiter)	15,800	x	x	x	15,431	x	x	x
Total Employment (All Personnel)	17,179				18,163			

KEY: A—in Germany, Univ. or Technischeshochschule Diploma; in U.S., an M.A.
B—in Germany, Fachschule Certificate; in U. S. College degree (AB or BS).
C—in both countries, no degrees or certificates.

The difference in the number of personnel in the top management category—20 at DHHU as compared with 12 at Inland—is explained largely by the fact that Inland has one central works whereas the DHHU operations are divided into two separate works and a central administrative office. It is quite apparent that more of the Inland executives have risen from the ranks, without benefit of formal education, than is the case at DHHU. It is also apparent that much greater stress has been given to formal higher education in top management positions at DHHU than at Inland.

Second, in *middle management,* the formal educational training of the DHHU personnel is again greater than their counterparts at Inland. Three-quarters of the Betriebsleiter at DHHU have a university degree, and the rest have the Fachschule certificate, whereas at Inland only one superintendent has a Master's degree and only slightly over half have a college degree. In the case of the superintendents the difference in numbers of personnel—60 at DHHU as compared with 38 at Inland—is probably explained by the existence of the two works at DHHU and by the greater specialization and subdivision of functions at Inland.

The contrast in the Assistant Superintendent category, however, is not so great. Of 80 Assistenten at DHHU, 47 have the university degree and the rest, with one exception, have the Fachschule certificate, whereas at Inland, of 69 assistant superintendents, 8 have a Master's degree and 33 have a college education. It is apparent, therefore, that Inland is stressing formal education for its junior managerial force and that the trend is in the direction of more education qualifications for higher management positions in the future. The slightly lower proportion of highly trained assistenten at DHHU is to be explained by the great losses of young men in World War II, the category of persons who would otherwise have been attending the universities or technisches hochschule. In other words, DHHU would prefer to have highly trained men in these positions if they were available.

Third, in *middle management,* the number of senior technicians and assistant department heads in departments such as engineering, research, metallurgy, production control and industrial engineering at Inland is much greater than persons in similar positions at DHHU. At Inland there are 430 persons in this category, of whom 20 have a Master's degree and 77 have the college degree.

(Of the remaining 333, a large percentage have technical institute training and university extension training, but no academic degree. All, however, are well-trained technicians.) At DHHU there are only 43 persons in this group, the majority, of course, having formal university degrees. It is quite apparent that the investment in the so-called technical staff at Inland is perhaps nearly ten times as great as that at DHHU. One may infer from this that the top and middle line executives at Inland have many more assistants and many more trained people to actually perform technical work than do their counterparts at DHHU.

Fourth, in *supervision,* Inland employs proportionately many more General Foremen and Foremen than does DHHU. This holds true in almost all departments. The ratios of foremen and meister to workers and arbeiter in a few comparable departments are shown in Chart 2. The Inland supervisors, moreover, commonly have much greater formal education than their counterparts, the Obermeister and Meister, at DHHU. Some foremen at Inland have Master's degrees and 15.2 per cent have college degrees, whereas practically none of the meister and obermeister at DHHU have any higher educational training. At Inland the college graduate foreman is a relatively recent development and it is to be expected that as these men move into higher management its educational level will be raised.[6]

At DHHU a greater burden of supervision is placed upon the leader

CHART 2

Ratio of Foremen and General Foremen to Workers in the Blast Furnace, Coke Plant and Open Hearth Departments, Inland Steel Indiana Harbor Works, March 1, 1954

Department	Number of Foremen and General Foremen	Number of Workers	Ratio
Blast Furnace	65	976	1-15
Coke Plant	68	702	1-10.3
Open Hearth	161	2727	1-16.9
Total	294	4405	1-15

Ratio of Obermeister and Meister to Arbeiters in the Blast Furnace, Coke Plant and Open Hearth Departments for Dortmund and Hörde

Department	Dortmund		
	Number of Obermeister and Meister	Number of Arbeiter	Ratio
Blast Furnace	12	605	1-50.4
Coke Plant	—	—	—
Open Hearth	6	296	1-49.3
Total	18	901	1-50

Department	Hörde		
	Number of Obermeister and Meister	Number of Arbeiter	Ratio
Blast Furnace	11	538	1-48.9
Coke Plant	9	238	1-26.4
Open Hearth	10	447	1-44.7
Total	30	1223	1-40.7

Overall ratio of Obermeister and Meister to Arbeiter for the above three Departments of both plants is 1-44.2.

or vorarbeiter. The trend at Inland over the past five years has been toward transferring the supervisory functions of the leader to the foreman who is a full-time salaried member of management. This accounts for the very small number of leaders in the Inland organization, practically all of whom are in mechanical and electrical operations rather than steel production units.

It is obvious that Inland places much greater stress and has a much larger investment in first line supervision than does DHHU. This is perhaps the most striking contrast between the two steel companies.

It is also important to point out that at DHHU the position of obermeister or meister is commonly regarded as the highest job to which an arbeiter, without formal education, may normally rise. Very few of the meister rise into positions in middle and top management. At Inland, on the other hand, it is quite common, indeed it is becoming almost the normal practice, for foremen to be promoted into higher managerial positions. There is thus a much greater degree of upward mobility in the supervisory and managerial hierarchy at Inland which reflects the greater mobility between classes in America than in Germany.

Fifth, there are some quantitative and qualitative differences in the ranks of employees and workers. It is generally conceded that the proportion of highly skilled workers at DHHU is much higher than that at Inland, although we did not gather statistical data to support this view. This is explained by the greater investment in labor-saving and skill-saving machinery at Inland and also perhaps by the greater extent of supervision over workers at Inland.[7] The DHHU management relies quite extensively on the all-around skill of trained craftsmen who can carry out their tasks with a minimum of supervision.

The statistics show that somewhat more clerical and junior technical employees are used at Inland than are their counterparts—the angestellte—at DHHU. Here again the explanation probably lies in the greater use of mechanized processes at Inland, which leads to a proportionately greater investment in so-called "indirect" labor services. It may also be explained by Inland's emphasis on detailed cost control and analysis to determine whether heavy investments are profitable.

Inferences and Conclusions

From this pilot study one may draw several significant tentative inferences and conclusions.

The formal educational training of top and middle management

87

executives is considerably greater at DHHU than at Inland. On the other hand, the educational training of supervision at Inland is greater than that at DHHU. The DHHU executives have far fewer trained technical staff assistants than have the executives at Inland. For this reason a main criterion of successful job performance of the Inland executive is the coordination of the work of a staff, whereas the DHHU executive must himself have broad technical training, and he must also personally supervise technical operations.[8]

At Inland, a much greater proportionate investment is made in first line supervision, whereas at DHHU greater reliance is placed on trained craftsmen and skilled workmen. What then are the explanations for these findings?

The representatives of DHHU, who worked on this study and who had visited the Inland works at East Chicago, pointed out that Inland makes much greater use of automatic machinery and processes than does DHHU. The greater the mechanization of operations the greater is the need for close supervision and the less is the dependence on the skilled craftsman. The DHHU representatives further indicated that, as they modernize their works at Dortmund and at Hörde, they will require more meister with greater technical training at the same time they will need fewer craftsmen as skills are eliminated. In other words, technological development in the steel industry requires increased investment in and attention to managerial and supervisory development. The DHHU people also stressed the point that greater mechanization and the use of more advanced technology require a much greater number of technically trained staff assistants. Here again, the greater investment in senior technical staff at Inland appears to be related to the stage of technological development and the extent of investment in machinery. One may tentatively conclude, therefore, that technological development in the steel industry requires quite extensive expansion and development of supervisory and managerial personnel and at the same time necessitates rather extensive revisions in the structure and functioning of the managerial organization at all levels.

It would be incorrect, however, to attribute all of the differences in management and in access to managerial positions to technological factors. Other factors undoubtedly are important. For example, the age of an industry or a single company may have some influence on the educational background of executives. When the DHHU works were first built, a very large proportion of the top executives came up from the ranks. One of the reasons for the present large number of Inland executives who have risen from the ranks may be that the company is comparatively young. Another factor is the availability of educational opportunity as it applies to the lower levels of supervision. In the United States more young people proportionate to the total population go to colleges and universities than is the case in Germany. Another factor, of course, is the fairly rigid class system in Germany which does not exist to any comparable extent in the United States.

We should like to emphasize that truly definitive conclusions must wait upon the completion of more comprehensive studies involving a greater diversity of steel companies in Germany, the United States and other countries. These, we hope, will be forthcoming in the very near future.

Yet, even on the basis of this admittedly sketchy pilot analysis, we can safely make some valid generalizations on the potential usefulness of comparative studies of this kind. The managements of both Inland Steel and Dortmund-Horder Huttenunion are agreed that this joint study has had these practical results:

First, each company has benefited from making an inventory of its managerial and supervisory forces. This has served to focus attention in a systematic way on the problems which each company faced in the selection and training of its managerial organization.

Second, the problems of organization and personnel have been highlighted by the contrasts which come to light in cross-national studies of this kind. For example, after analyzing the findings of this survey, Inland Steel raised the question as to whether or not its investment in supervision might be perhaps too great. For its part, Dortmund-Horder Huttenunion was led to examine more intensively the possibility of training and upgrading more workers from the ranks into managerial positions. For both companies, the pilot study served to stimulate more realistic examination of the assumptions underlying the building of their respective organizations and the processes of selecting and training their managerial personnel.

Third, this pilot study may provide a basis for a more realistic program of visits by German managers to American plants and visits by American executives to German plants. Having such a basis for comparison, the exchange of information and personnel in vital areas such as management training, human relations and labor relations can be carried on with greater practical benefit to both countries.

Thus, we feel that the extension of this kind of cross-national comparative management study program can be of great long-range and also immediate benefit to the steel companies of the free world. Such a program can be carried on by the steel companies in several countries with the assistance of the steel federations in each country.

In more exhaustive and comprehensive comparisons, questions such as these might be studied:

1. Supervisory selection and training programs.
2. Executive leadership and development programs and procedures.
3. Staff and line relationships in industrial organization.
4. Criteria and procedures of recruiting labor.
5. Labor relations, human relations and employee welfare.
6. The problems of internal communication.
7. Industry-university relations in recruitment and development of technical and managerial personnel.
8. The effect of advancing technology on the proportion of (1) indirect to direct workers, (2) skilled to semi-skilled and unskilled, (3) white collar to blue collar, (4) Engineers to technicians, (5) Engineers and technicians to balance of work force, and (6) Supervision by level to work force and in relation to process and technology.

Footnotes

1. Communications to the authors concerning this paper may be addressed to Frank H. Cassell, Manager, Industrial Relations, Inland Steel Co., 38 South Dearborn St., Chicago 3, Illinois. A version of this paper appeared in *Industrial Relations*, Quebec, vol. 10, No. 2, March, 1955.

2. This particular study is concerned with only operating management of the steel works, and does not include such functions as purchasing, sales, finance or industrial relations.

3. The main products of Inland Steel are: Steel sheets, strip, tin mill products, bar mill products, structural shapes, floor plate, sheet piling, re-enforcing bars, rails and track accessories, pig iron and coal chemicals. The main products of Dortmund-Hörde are as follows: pig iron, ingots, steel bars, plates, structural shapes, sheet pilings, semi-finished products, heavy and medium plates, rolling mill products, steel castings, forgings and miscellaneous railroad products.

4. See Chart 1.

5. However, many of Inland's managerial, supervisory and technical personnel have had college training in extension and evening schools and technical institute training. Such training is not reflected in the compilation of educational attainment.

6. The injection of the college graduate into the foreman occupation has created organization morale stresses, as the non-college man foreman sees his avenues of promotion blocked. This is an area requiring much additional research.

7. On the other hand at Inland the reclassification of jobs under the job evaluation plan is resulting in jobs being reclassified *higher* in the job structure reflecting increasing requirements of the jobs to keep pace with advancing technology.

8. This is reflected in statements of Inland's organizational philosophy by Clarence B. Randall:

"A common method for making decisions (and arriving at policy) is the group conference. . . . Once policy has been established the executive must look to others for its fulfillment, *and his effectiveness lies in the skill with which he directs the activities of others.*

"Since the object of management is to draw out of the best that is in each member of the group, the emphasis must be on the encouragement of creative impulses, rather than upon restraint.

"A good administrator not only learns to delegate authority, but he also seeks to share his thinking with as many others as possible." Clarence B. Randall, *Freedom's Faith* (Boston: Little, Brown & Co., 1953).

Reprinted by permission of the author and of the publisher from THE AMERICAN ANTHROPOLOGIST, April, 1955.

chapter 7

Two Concepts of Authority[1]

Walter B. Miller

When European fur traders, soldiers, and missionaries first began to move into the western Great Lakes region around 1650, they found in the area that is now Wisconsin, Illinois, and Indiana a group of Central Algonkian tribes. Eight of these tribes spoke slightly divergent dialects of a single language, Central Algonkian. They were approximately the same size and showed considerable similarity in religion, social organization, cultural traditions, and general way of life. These eight tribes were the Potowatami, Sac, Menomini, Fox, Mascoutin, Kickapoo, Miami, and Illinois.

The Central Algonkians were village-dwelling Indians, each tribe averaging about 3,000 people. Although some agriculture was practiced, hunting was the primary subsistence activity, and hunting and warfare the focal interests of tribal members. Politically, each tribe was an autonomous and independent sovereignty, maintaining both hostile and friendly relationships with neighboring tribes in a shifting pattern of intertribal wars and alliances. The Central Algonkians had developed effective modes of exploiting their physical environment and maintaining a satisfactory social and ecological balance. They were extremely skillful hunters and, as the incoming Europeans soon learned, equally effective fighters.

But these same Europeans were struck by what appeared to them a most remarkable phenomenon: The Central Algonkians seemed to carry out their subsistence, religious, administrative, and military activities in the virtual absence of any sort of recognizable authority! Traders, soldiers, and missionaries alike were impressed by this. One of the first Europeans to contact the central tribes was Nicolas Perrot, a French fur trader and *coureur de bois*. He recorded these impressions around 1680:

Subordination is not a maxim among these savages; the savage does not know what it is to obey. . . . It is more necessary to entreat him than to command him. . . . The father does not venture to exercise authority over his son, nor does the chief dare give commands to his soldier. . . . if anyone is stubborn in regard to some proposed movement, it is necessary to flatter him in order to dissuade him, otherwise he will go further in his opposition . . . (in Blair 1911:145).

About ten years later a French aristocrat, Baron de La Hontan, made these observations on conditions among the central tribes which he contacted as a military officer:

. . . each village hath its . . . Head of Warriors, who in consideration of his valor, capacity and experience is proclaimed such by an unanimous consent. But after all, this title invests him with no power over the warriors, for these people are strangers to military as well as civil subordination. Nay—they are so far from it, that if the . . . leader should order the silliest and most pitiful fellow in his (war party) to do so and so, why truly, this shadow of a captain would receive this answer . . . *that what he orders another to do he ought to do himself.* But it is such an uncommon thing for the leader to act so indiscretely that I question if there be one instance of it . . . the savages . . . think it unaccountable that one man should have more than another, and that the rich should have more respect than the poor; they value themselves above anything you can imagine, and this is the reason they always give for it—*that one man's as much master as another, and since all men are made of the same clay, there should be no distinction or superiority among them* (in Thwaites, 1905, II:499).

In 1708 a Sieur d'Aigremont was assigned to investigate a proposal to enroll Central tribesmen as militiamen. His report to his superior included these remarks:

. . . Lamothe Cadillac . . . has proposed . . . to organize complete companies of Indians . . . it appears to me extraordinary to undertake to discipline people who possess no subordination among themselves, and whose chiefs cannot say to the others, "Do thus and so," but merely "it would be proper to do so and so," without naming any person. Otherwise they would do nothing, being opposed to all restraint. Moreover, these people have no idea of royal grandeur nor majesty, nor of the power of superiors over inferiors, and thus would not feel among themselves any emulation or ambition to reach these . . . honors, and consequently no desire to perform their duties. Neither would they be influenced thereto by fear of punishment, for, not tolerating any among themselves, they would suffer still less that others should inflict any on them.

I am persuaded that if any (French) captain would give some command to the subaltern officers or soldiers of his (Indian) company, they would tell him curtly that they would not do it, and to let him do it himself. That would, verily, be a fine example for French troops (d'Aigremont, in Thwaites 1902:150).

Similar impressions were recorded by Jonathan Carver, one of the first Englishmen to explore the Central area. He wrote, about 1770: Although (the Indians have both military and civil chiefs), yet (they) are sensible of neither civil nor military subordination. As every one of them entertains a very high opinion of his consequence, and is extremely tenacious of his liberty, all injunctions that carry with them the appearance of a command are instantly rejected with scorn. On this account it is seldom that their leaders are so indiscrete as to give out orders in a peremptory style . . . there is no visible form of government; they allow of no such distinction as (that between) magistrate and subject, everyone appearing to enjoy an independence that cannot be controlled . . . (1797:142).

It is apparent from these reactions that the Europeans saw in the Central Algonkian situation, not a system for coordinating collective action that was different from their own, but rather the absence of any kind of regulatory system. Carver's impression that "there is no visible form of government" is echoed again and again by Europeans who contacted the Central tribesmen. Such perceptions and evaluations were evidently influenced in large part by what the Europeans were accustomed to. What was it in European culture that occasioned such shocked and astonished reactions to Algonkian culture? Some insight into the nature of the cultural standards guiding the judgment of the Europeans can be gained by examining briefly three relationships in European society[2] that entailed the exercise of authority.

Three European Authority Relationships

The Lord-Follower Relationship of Sixth-Century England. English society in the sixth century in many ways resembled Central Algonkian society of the sixteenth century. Both societies were organized on a tribal basis; the size of political units was roughly the same; the technological level was similar; social organization was based on the clan system; kin ties were important binding elements of society; there were tribal and clan chiefs, and intertribal warfare was a primary cultural preoccupation.

A fundamental "bond of society" in sixth-century England was the relationship between lord and follower. Whitelock's *The Beginnings of English Society* describes this relationship in the chapter, "The Bonds of Society" (1952:29 *et seq.*):

95

Loyalty to One's Lord

The strength of the bond between a man and his lord in the Germanic races impressed Tacitus in the first century. (He writes)—

". . . it is lifelong infamy and reproach to survive the chief and withdraw from him in battle . . . . The chiefs fight for victory, the followers for their chief."

In Anglo-Saxon (society) . . . the bond between lord and retainer went deeper than material benefits on either side. (It had) a symbolic significance, and it is not mere material loss that inspires the following lament for a dead lord in a poem generally known as *The Wanderer*:

"All joy has departed. Truly does he know this who must long forego the advice of his dear lord. When sorrow and sleep both together often bind the wretched lonely man, it seems to him in his mind that he embraces and kisses his liege lord . . . then awakens the friendless man. . . . Then are the wounds of his heart the heavier, the sore wounds after his dear one. . . ."

The relationship of lord and follower involved the duty of vengeance by the survivor if either were slain. The Christian Church . . . added its sanctity to the oath of allegiance. In Christian times the man who took service under a lord swore the following oath:

"By the Lord, I will be loyal and true to N, and love all that he loves, and hate all that he hates . . . and never, willingly and intentionally, in word or deed, do anything that is hateful to him. . . ."

The binding force of the . . . allegiance was well (established) even in heathen times . . . the lord took responsibility for the man's acts . . . when the claims of the lord clashed with those of the kindred, the idea (became) established . . . that the duty to the lord should come first. A paragraph that sums up the Christian view of loyalty . . . concludes:

"For all that we ever do, through just loyalty to our lord, we do to our own great advantage, for truly God will be gracious to him who is duly faithful to his lord."

The Superior-Priest Relationship of the Sixteenth-Century Spain. Ignatius Loyola, the Spaniard who in 1534 founded the Society of Jesus, incorporated into the charter of that order ideals about the nature of authority derived from contemporary Spanish culture, but which were readily accepted and understood in France, Italy, and other parts of Europe where the order became established. In his letters Loyola described the attitudes and behavior deemed appropriate to the relationship between the Jesuit priest and his Superior:

In the hands of my Superior, I must be a soft wax, a thing, from which he is to require whatever pleases him, be it to write or receive letters, to speak or not to speak to such a person, or the like; and I must put all my fervor in executing zealously and exactly what I am ordered. I must consider myself as a corpse which has neither intelligence nor will; be like a mass of matter which without resistance lets itself be placed wherever it may please anyone; like a stick in the hands of an old man, who uses it according to his needs and places it where it suits him. So must I be under the hands of the Order, to serve it in the way it judges most useful.

I must never ask of the Superior to be sent to a particular place, to be employed in a particular duty ... I must ... be like a statue which lets itself be stripped and never opposes resistance (quoted in James 1902:307, 308).

The King-Subject Relationship of Seventeenth-Century France. Perrot, La Hontan, and other Frenchmen who contacted the Central Algonkians in the middle 1600's were products of a society whose government was based on a concept of authority that produced the doctrine of royal absolutism. The relationship of Louis XIV to his subjects represented in many ways the culmination of a long development of European ideas on the nature of authority. Bishop Bousset, tutor to the king's son, described royal authority as divinely ordained and as a response to God-given natural instincts. His conception of the nature of monarchy and the relation of ruler to subject is summarized by C. J. Hayes (1944:291):

Under God, monarchy is, of all forms of government, the most usual and the most ancient, and therefore the most natural. It is likewise the strongest and most efficient, therefore the best. It is analogous to the rule of a family by the father, and, like that rule, should be hereditary. The hereditary monarch (has) four qualities. (1) He is sacred because he is anointed at the time of coronation by the priests of the church, and hence it is blasphemy and sacrilege to assail the person of the king or to conspire against him. (2) He is, in a very real sense, the father of his people, the paternal king. ... (3) His power is absolute and autocratic, and for its exercise he is accountable to God alone; no man on earth may rightfully resist the royal commands, and the only recourse for subjects against an evil king is to pray God that his heart be changed. (4) Greater reason is given to a king than to anyone else; the king is an earthly image of God's majesty, and it is wrong, therefore, to look upon him as a mere man. ... "As in God are united all perfection and every virtue, so all the power of all the individuals in a community is united in the person of the king."

A Contemporary European Type of Authority Relationship

To most present-day Europeans, the amount of authority exercised by the sixth-century English Lord, the sixteenth-century Jesuit Superior, and the seventeenth-century French King appears extreme. However, in present-day European societies there are numerous role-relationships that share, in less extreme form, certain characteristics of these earlier prototypes. Setting aside contemporary role-relationships such as the Führer-citizen relationship of Nazi Germany or the Commissar-comrade relationship of Soviet Russia, Europeans are familiar with numerous less spectacular role-relationships that entail the exercise of authority, and which they accept as a normal and necessary part of life. Some of these are: master-servant, officer-enlisted man, boss-employee, teacher-pupil, parent-child, foreman-worker, pastor-parishioner, orchestra leader-sideman, coach-team member, director-cast member, captain-crew member, doctor-patient, chief-staff member.

It would seldom occur to the average European to question the validity of such relationships. The amount of authority they involve is not seen as excessive but as normal and right. Europeans accept the fact that the functioning of their factories, hospitals, churches, and other organized institutions depends on the authority exercised through these role-relationships and others like them. But a member of sixteenth-century Algonkian society would regard such authority as oppressive and intolerable. Although collective action was successfully coordinated in the political, economic, military, and religious spheres, it would be difficult to point to a single role-relationship in Algonkian society that was essentially analogous to the European type of authority relationship.

The Relationship Viewed Analytically. Examined analytically, a number of important characteristics of this type of role-relationship can be isolated. From a "structural" viewpoint the relationship can be considered a kind of patterned interaction between individuals, with certain distinctive features, six of which will be cited:

(1) *The directive component.* The defining characteristic of this relationship is that by virtue of occupying a given position in a patterned role-relationship, one individual is empowered to direct the actions of another, and the other is obligated to accept that direction.

(2) *Role-based.* The relationship is between role and role, not between individual and individual. The relationship of superordination-subordination is inherent in the definition of the role-relationship, and relatively independent of the personal qualities of the individuals who happen to fill these roles. This characteristic is clearly brought out by the familiar military injunction, "Salute the uniform, not the man."

(3) *Permanence.* The role-relationship is associated with a set of continuing or recurring activities, and tenure by the incumbents of the respective role positions is extended through time. Thus, the "general-private" relationship does not provide that the general direct the private under one set of circumstances, and the private the general under another, in so far as they are acting as incumbents of these roles. If the authority prerogatives of incumbents *are* altered or reversed, it is be-

cause they are acting as incumbents of other role-positions. For example, an individual who usually fills the role of "boss" may accept direction from someone who usually fills the role of "employee," if, at an office party, the employee is acting as "square dance-caller" and the boss as "dancer."

(4) *Prestige differential.* The occupant of the superior role position is accorded greater prestige than the occupant of the subordinate position. This superior prestige is manifested in various ways, e. g.: deference patterns, symbols of superior status, reward differential. The behavior of subordinate to superior serves to affirm the inequality of status. Examples of such behavior are the salute, the bow, standing at attention, waiting to be addressed before speaking, and the use of "sir," "mister," "doctor," or "your honor." Differences in wearing apparel or ornamentation are frequently associated with this differential prestige. The ornate and resplendent "royal trappings" of a monarch are an extreme example, but military insignia and other forms of personal adornment serve also to indicate differences in status. When some compensation for role-performance is present, the occupant of the superior status position generally receives more. These externally discernible differences in behavior, dress, and reward symbolize the fact that members of this type of role-relationship are differentially ranked, and that the occupant of the superordinate role has greater access to and control over valued social resources.

(5) *Functional differential.* Although engaged in a common enterprise, occupants of the two role positions each perform a different aspect of the total task. The incumbent of the superordinate role position generally plays a more passive part in relation to the actual execution of activity, and a more active part in relation to its direction.

(6) *Differential access to system of rules.* The incumbents of the two role positions have differential access to the body of rules governing their conduct. The great majority of collective enterprises are conducted according to a body of rules, or instructions as to procedure, worked out in advance. The exercise of authority can be described as a mode of transmuting such rules into action. An order can be seen as a selection and/or arrangement of one or more of these rules, communicated from one agency to another.

The incumbent of the superordinate role position has more direct access to this body of procedural directives. He has the prerogative of communicating selected directives to his subordinate, a communication having the force of a command. This process occurs when a drill sergeant orders "Squads right," a clergyman directs "Turn to hymn 36," or when an administrator pencils "Act on this" on a communique from a higher echelon.

The Relationship Viewed Conceptually. From an analytic viewpoint the role-relationship has been treated as a type of interpersonal interaction embodying certain specific features. But if the relationship is approached from a different angle, and viewed not analytically but as it is most generally conceptualized in European culture, a picture emerges that contrasts sharply both with the analytic view and with the conceptualization prevalent in Algonkian culture.

In the European cultural tradition a rather remarkable phenomenon can be noted: authority, or "power," is conceptually equated with height or elevation. It is conceived as originating in some elevated locus, and as passing down to lower levels. This metaphorical way of thinking about authority is closely tied in with European religious conceptions, many of which utilize the notion that power originates in a supernatural being or group of beings located in the heavens, or some elevated location. Central Algonkian religion places its deities at the four corners of the universe, and on the same plane as humans.

This way of conceptualizing authority is so well integrated into European culture that it is difficult to deal with authority in any other way. The equation of authority with altitude is firmly built into European linguistic systems; the terms *super*ior, *infer*ior, and *super*ordinate, *sub*ordinate, have been key terms in this discussion. A man with considerable authority is said to be in a *top* position, *high*-ranking way *up* there, one with little authority is on the *bottom*, in a *lowly* position, *down* and out. We speak of the *haute*-monde and the *under*world, of *over*lord and *under*ling, of *upper* and *lower* classes.

In addition to the metaphorical convention whereby "amount of authority" is conceived in terms of points on a vertical scale, there exists the conception that there is a passageway between the various positions on this scale, which is frequently pictured as a ladder or a flight of stairs. Thus one can "rise" or "fall" in respect to authority or status by means of this vertical passageway. A man is "on his way up," or on his way "to the top"; "elevated" to a lofty position; a "rising" young executive; or he is "slipping badly, or "falling" by the wayside. The Hebrew story of Jacob's ladder, the French use of "echelon" to describe a position in a system of authority, the Latin phrase "ad astra per aspera," and the American phrase "the ladder of success" all utilize this figurative mode of referring to changes in the amount of authority or prestige accorded an individual.

A third aspect of this mode of conceptualizing authority is pointed up by comparison with that of the Central Algonkians. While the Central Algonkian conceives of authority as the resultant of ongoing interaction between individuals, the European tends to reify authority—to picture it as a substance, generally a liquidlike substance. We speak of the "flow" of authority, of "going through channels," of the "fountainhead" of authority. As a substance, authority can be quantified, and thus we speak of a great deal of authority, little authority, no authority.

The "table of organization" chart, used so widely to represent organizational structure, utilizes these metaphorical conventions whereby authority is reified, quantified, elevated, and pictured as flowing downward. A number of boxes, representing offices or authority agencies, are placed on different vertical levels and joined to one another by lines or arrows. The "locus," or loci, of power is placed at the top; agencies with "less" authority are put at lower levels; arrows denote the "flow" of authority from one box to another; each box can serve as an area or passage through which authority can be transmitted from one place to another.

In general, the structure of authority is pictured as pyramidal, with greatest authority at a relatively narrow apex, and more diffuse authority at increasingly lower levels. MacIver (1947:82-113) speaks of the "pyramid of power" and utilizes the pyramidal form to represent different kinds of governmental structures.

Thus, in European societies, authority is frequently conceived as a substance having its origin in an elevated locus and flowing downward through prescribed channels. An authority relationship is conceptualized as a situation where one individual, situated above another, has superior quantities of authority which can flow downward to the individual below. Any one relationship within an organizational system can be depicted as a higher box connected with a lower box by a line. These characteristics of the conceptual model make it possible to call this type of role-relationship a "vertical" authority relationship.

The vertical authority relationship is a fundamental building block of European society. Without it the phenomenon of "ranked" authority—where given individuals are permanently empowered to direct others—would be impossible, and ranked authority is an indispensable feature of European organizational systems.

A society where authority is conceptualized in a different way would have to organize collective activity according to different principles. Following sections will describe how a Central Algonkian society conceived of authority and organized collective action.

The Fox Indians

Of the eight Central Algonkian tribes that flourished in the Great Lakes region in 1650, the best documented is the Mesquakie (Red Earth) tribe, better known as the Fox. One reason for this is that the Fox have retained their tribal identity despite three hundred years of violent and disruptive pressures, and are today a cohesive community of some five hundred Indians in the state of Iowa.

Viewed broadly the organization of authority in all the Central Algonkian tribes was essentially the same, but closer examination reveals certain differences. On a gradient of intensity for the characteristic "aversion to vertical authority," the Fox fall at an extreme end of the scale. The obduracy of Fox resistance to European attempts at control was outstanding even among a group of tribes noted for its resistance to subordination. Father Claude Allouez, the first Christian missionary to proselytize the Fox, said of them "These people are self-willed beyond anything that can be imagined!" (Allouez 1673: in Thwaites V. 58).

This strongly negative attitude toward vertical authority was one characteristic of a particular kind of organization of authority. The Fox authority system represents the "purest" manifestation of this kind of system found in the Central area, and so presents its essential features most clearly for purposes of analysis.[3]

Gods and Men in Fox Society

One way to gain insight into the way that authority was conceived and organized in Fox society is to look at the Fox system of religion. The pantheon of any society can be seen as a projective system, whereby the essential features of the social organization of the projecting society are attributed to a group of supernatural beings, whose relations reflect those existing among the people themselves.

In a representative European pantheon the ultimate locus of supernatural power rests in a supreme being situated in an elevated location. Below him are a series of subordinate supernatural beings, arranged in a persisting and orderly hierarchy, each possessing considerable power but less than that of the supreme being from whom their power derives, or flows. Below these are still other supernatural subordinates, arranged powerwise in pyramidal form. At some point in this system the power-flow breaks through to an earthly system. A most elevated official (high priest, pope, etc.) is at the apex of a hierarchically graded pyramid of authority positions. He derives his power from the supernatural system and delegates lesser amounts to his subordinates. Below these two pyramids are the great mass of people ("laymen") whose access to the ultimate source of supernatural power is mediated, in situations of formal worship, via the two overlying authority systems.

The Fox Pantheon. Relations between deities and between gods and men in the Fox pantheon present a contrasting picture. The basic concept of Fox religion is *manitu* (see Jones 1905). Manitu is a kind of generalized essence of supernatural power. It has been compared with concepts such as Polynesian "mana"—an abstract, impersonal power immanent in the universe. But the Fox themselves never think of manitu in this way. Manitu power is actualized or manifested only when it is acquired by some particular being, who then *becomes* manitu, and is called "a manitu." A significant characteristic of manitu power is that it is never possessed permanently by any being or group of beings; it is always held conditionally. It is lost, gained, lost again—its possession being measured by quality of performance in a particular area of activity. To succeed means that manitu power is possessed; to fail means that it is lost.

Thus neither the composition of the Fox pantheon nor the relationships between its members can be stable, as where a designated group of supernatural beings, arranged in an orderly hierarchy, possesses permanent and assured power prerogatives. The Fox pantheon is peopled by a great and heterogeneous variety of beings. Fox religious thought makes little distinction between the material and nonmaterial, the organic and inorganic, between animal and human, natural and supernatural. All varieties of natural phenomena can gain manitu power by demonstrating qualities or abilities that bring about success in a particular activity. Rain, Wind, Mountains, Lightning, Thunder, Bears, Eagles, Skunks, Snakes, Frogs, Fish, Lizards, Corn, Fire can all become manitus, since each has its own particular kind of power.

But manitu power, once possessed, is never assured. Its possession is conditional, constantly subject to loss by encounter with some being possessing superior manitu. Fox cosmology presents a picture of scores of powerful manitus jockeying with one another in a constant and unending struggle for temporary superiority. Each is potentially able to vanquish the other—for conquest depends, not on possessing an intrinsically superior amount of power, but rather on how carefully, or shrewdly, or skillfully each antagonist utilizes the resources he possesses in any particular encounter. Fox myths tell over and again of the struggles between these powerful antagonists—antagonists who are matched, not because they belong to the same sphere of the organic or inorganic world, but because each possesses a particular kind of power.[4] Eagle fights Swamp; Thunder fights Deer; Man fights Lizard; Spider fights North Wind. Each uses his own most effective weapons. If Eagle has great speed and sharp eyes, Swamp can emit terrifying flashes and devour the unwary; if Bear has massive strength and sharp, wicked claws, Skunk has a most formidable odor; if Thunder can produce horrifying noises, Deer can run with lightning speed.

But it is important to note the *results* of these combats. The combats serve merely to establish a temporary prestige advantage for the winner. The loser is subject to feelings of shame at having been outwitted. He is never subjugated by virtue of his defeat. Conquest does not in any way grant to the victor the prerogative to direct or control the future actions of the vanquished. No permanent relationship of superordination-subordination is instituted as the result of demonstrated possession of superior power, because the vanquished always has direct access to an unlimited store of manitu power, by use of which he may, and often does, defeat his adversary in the next encounter. Thus there can be no stable, vertical hierarchy of gods who derive permanent power from superiors. The power of Fox deities is temporary, contingent on personal achievement, and grants no right to direct others.

Man and Manitu. In most European religious systems large masses of people worship a limited group of deities over which one paramount deity exercises hegemony. In situations of formal worship, groups of worshipers relate themselves to the deity or deities through the medium of a religious official or group of officials who have more direct access than they to the source of supernatural power.

In Fox society, each individual is related directly to the source of supernatural power, and each has his own individual deity. At the onset of adolescence, each Fox male goes out into the forest where he fasts for four days and four nights. During the course of this fast he has a vision of a powerful manitu—an animal, bird, manitu-human, or natural object. The boy is told by the manitu that henceforth he will be under his protection, and that he will control the particular power possessed by the manitu. In the course of the visitation the manitu instructs the boy in acceptable ethical and moral behavior. This "instruction" is given not in the form of rigid commands or interdictions, but rather as advice, in the form: ". . . and this, my grandchild; if you observe the fasting periods, you will not become sick . . ." (Michelson 1936:18).

But the grant of manitu power and supernatural guardianship is not outright; the manitu needs the services of the boy as much as the boy needs his. In exchange for supernatural power, the boy agrees to present to the manitu periodic gifts of tobacco, which the manitu craves but can get only from humans, and to adhere to his guardian's ethical precepts in order to please him. The boy-manitu relationship is couched in terms of mutual obligations, not in terms of a one-way power flow. If the boy neglects his obligations, the manitu may withdraw his support; if the boy fails in some important undertaking, this evidence that the manitu has not done his part entitles the boy to seek a new protector.

Thus the Fox accept their gods as powerful only so long as they deliver the goods; when they fail to bring about a successful undertaking, they are dropped. In 1667, Father Allouez, on a mission to the Fox, told them that Jesus Christ, as represented by the cross, was a powerful manitu. He was amazed by the alacrity with which the Fox "accepted Christ," not realizing that the Fox pantheon is extremely elastic, always ready to accommodate any deity, of whatever origin, who can demonstrate the possession of power. In 1671 warriors, undertaking a war expedition against the Sioux, painted the cross on their bodies and shields, put themselves under the protection of the cross-manitu, and gained a decisive victory over their enemies. They returned, proclaiming the white man's manitu. The following year, however, another expedition against the Sioux, under similar manitu protection, was disastrously defeated. In a rage, the warriors repudiated the white man's manitu, tore down the cross Allouez had erected, and refused to let the priest re-enter the village (Dablon 1673:228).

Although the Fox pantheon lacks any supremely placed deity, it does contain a number of "important" gods, whose doings are accorded considerable attention. One of these is *Wisakeya*, felt by the Fox to be their special protector and to have presided over the creation of the Red Earth people. Despite the special place accorded Wisakeya, neither he nor any other Fox deity is regarded with hallowed respect, adoration, or worshipful deference. On the contrary, Wisakeya is pictured by William Jones, a Harvard-educated Fox: ". . . now as a buffoon doing tricks to others and having them done to him, and now as a benefactor and altruistic character. Sometimes he is peevish and whimpering, like a spoiled child, and stoops to the most degrading acts for the accomplishment of an end; and again he rises to . . . a position of wisdom and dignity" (1907:228).

The term of address used to refer to Wisakeya is "my nephew" (for a man, viz., "sister's son"; for a woman this term of address means "my son"). The Fox uncle-nephew relationship is essentially one of equality, as will be shown later. That the Fox calls his principal deity "my nephew" is as revealing as the fact that the Europeon calls his principal deity "my father."

Like veneration, hero-worship has no place in Fox culture. The

105

intensely emotional attachment of the English follower to his lord, described by Whitelock, would be incomprehensible to a Fox. One searches in vain through the body of Fox historical legends for semi-mythified heroes of the stature of Beowulf, Roland, Moses, Galahad, Aeneas, Ulysses, George Washington—who are wise, noble, and brave, and revered as the embodiment of all the most estimable virtues. The cycle of myths centering around White Robe, an outstanding Fox warrior during the period of the French wars, depicts him, not as a noble and flawless hero, but as a man racked by an internal conflict between his sacred obligation to maintain peace for his fellow tribesmen and an irresistible urge to kill.[5]

Neither toward their deities nor their mythified heroes do the Fox evince the adulation that reaches almost obsessive extremes in the hysteria of massed tribute to Hitler, Mussolini, or Queen Elizabeth; the screaming adulation of adolescent girls to a popular singer; the frenzy of a Broadway reception to General MacArthur, or the passionate devotion of a cult group to its leader. There are no charismatic leaders in Fox society, because the special, mystic, hallowed qualities of supreme power, supernatural grace, and ultimate infallibility are accorded to neither god nor hero.

Fox religion is little concerned with the afterworld, stressing instead virtuous and long life (*metoseneniwi*) in this world. The exact nature of the afterworld is kept rather vague; it is not pictured as an exalted or glorious place. The term for the afterworld is "where the sun goes down"; it is "over yonder" not up in the sky. The "land of ghosts" is much like a Fox village, where life goes on essentially "as it is here" (Michelson 1925b:399). In the land of ghosts one resumes the Fox type of reciprocal relations with one's deceased kin, who are now manitus. Characteristically, Fox who have lived a good life are rewarded by going to that part of the land of ghosts where "they are forbidden nothing . . . they do whatever they please. And they are always happy" (p. 415)—whereas those who have been wicked go to a village where they cannot act except by permission of the afterworld manitu! In the death as in life the greatest gift the Fox can ask of his gods is the right to control his own behavior, and the greatest torture he can conceive is an eternity of being subject to orders.

The Fox Concept of Power

The relations between gods, and between gods and men, as they are depicted in Fox religious mythology, are based on Fox ideals of right and proper interpersonal relations. The myths are direct products of such ideals, and since in myths the actions of men and manitus are not restricted by the limitations of finite reality, the behavior therein exemplifies these ideals in their purest form.

Manitu power represents to the Fox a vital and absorbing aspect of interpersonal relations—the ability to control, automatically and magically, the actions of others. Its characteristics, as they emerge from a consideration of relations within the Fox pantheon, can be described in the abstract.

Power is universally available and unlimited; it does not have a unitary locus; it is everywhere and equally available to all.

The possession of power is temporary and contingent; it is not a quality permanently possessed by any being, but can be gained and lost, possession being demonstrated by successful performance in specific situations.

Demonstrated power does not grant to its possessor the subsequent right to direct the actions of any other being.

Power is not hierarchical; since its possession is temporary and contingent, fixed and varying amounts of power are not distributed among a group of beings arranged in a stable heirarchy.

The control of power is dangerous; powerful beings are to be feared, not adorned or admired.

Thus even in its purest conceptualized form, "manitu power," the ability to control others, emerges as substantially different from the European concept of vertical authority. The concept of manitu served as a fundamental precept governing concrete day-to-day behavior in Fox life. As a guide to interpersonal relations it had this implication: it is both dangerous and immoral for one individual to exercise any substantial control over others. As a personal attitude it was manifested as an intense and deep-rooted resentment of anything perceived as an attempt to control one's actions.

The next sections will show how these ideals worked out in practice: how authority was organized, how activity was co-ordinated, and how individuals related themselves to authority.

The Organization of Authority in Fox Society

A number of formalized agencies in Fox society operated to bring about the coordination of collective action. Such agencies were limited in number, and highly circumscribed in the amount and kinds of authority exercised. Three formalized positions of authority (authority-roles), and one formal group which functioned to implement collective action (authority organ) will be described.

The nominally paramount authority-role was that of village chief. The role was a permanent one, in that it was held by the same man over

107

an extended period of time. Incumbency was determined by hereditary factors, each village chief being selected from the same lineage group —the Bear totemic group. The functions of the village chief did not involve any directive authority. On the contrary, the role-definition called for mild, nonaggressive, noninitiative behavior. The Fox name for this role was "peace chief," or sometimes "kindly chief." The village chief acted to symbolize peaceful and harmonious intergroup relations, nonaggressive behavior, and the unity of the village group. The closest his role functions came to permitting direction was that he was expected to act as arbiter and peacemaker in the event of dissension in council meetings.

The role of war leader involved a modicum of directive authority. During a war expedition the war leader was authorized to size up the situation and suggest desirable action. But this authority was limited in two ways. First, no one was obligated to accept the direction of the war leader if he didn't want to. Any warrior in the tribe who was granted manitu power in a vision could lead a war party, but war party membership was entirely voluntary, and members could leave at any time during a war expedition if they were not satisfied with the way things were going. No war-party leader would be imprudent enough to issue direct commands. The incumbent of the war-chief role, by far the most "powerful" authority role in Fox society, communicated his directives in the form of suggestions as to desirable action which war-party members could act on or not, as they saw fit.

Second, incumbency of the war-chief role was strictly limited in duration. The authority prerogatives of the war leader, circumscribed as they were, were confined to the duration of the war expedition itself. At its termination, the war leader, who had been invested for a few days with this dangerous amount of authority, was not permitted to re-enter the village until he had participated in a ceremonial wherein his temporary authority was vividly and symbolically revoked (Marston, in Blair 1912:158). Comparing the roles of village chief and war chief, we see that where even a small amount of directive authority was associated with the role, tenure was strictly limited; where tenure was extended the amount of authority was strictly limited.

The role of ceremony leader similarly involved very little authority. The ceremony leader was a man who had committed to memory one or more of the many religious rituals which played so important a part in Fox life. He put people through the paces of a given religious ceremony, signaling beginnings and endings of a preset sequence of traditionally prescribed ritual episodes. His functions did not include formulation or initiation of religious activity; he did not serve to mediate the relationship between man and manitu; and, like the war chief, his authority functions were limited to the duration of the ritual itself and did not extend beyond the area of ceremonial activity.

The village council served as the tribal decision-making agency in matters involving collective welfare or concerted action. The council was composed of the headmen of each of the extended family groupings that composed the tribe, plus any other man who demonstrated ability in council affairs. The amount of influence exerted by any councilman depended on his own personal capability and not on the status of the totemic group he represented. The village chief served as the presiding officer of the council, but had no more influence by virtue of his position than any other member; in fact, he was expected to participate only minimally in council discussion.

The mechanism whereby the adherence of the people to council decisions was obtained was the unanimous decision (Jones 1939:82). No course of action was agreed on by the council unless all members were in accord with the final decision. Since each Fox was represented in the council by a member of his own family group, and since considerable and extended intratribal discussion preceded all matters involving the collectivity, a concluded council decision had taken into account, and in some way accommodated to, the wishes of everyone involved in the execution of a given enterprise. Thus the act of decision-making itself insured the tribal validation of the decision. If there was any considerable opposition to a course of action involving full tribal participation, such a course could not be adopted, since this would make impossible the necessary unanimous decision; there was no necessity to force dissidents to participate in a policy of which they did not approve. The line between the people and the council was thinly drawn; all were welcome to attend and participate in council sessions; if a matter were of sufficient import, a formal meeting of the whole tribe was called. The whole decision-making mechanism was characterized by extreme reluctance to permit decisions as to action to be concluded by any group smaller than the participating group itself.

The Coordination of Collective Action

Since authority roles were so weakly invested with the right to direct, how, in fact, was action coordinated? Even today an observer of Fox society is struck by the fact that organized activity appears to proceed in the absence of any visible authority. A Fox taking part in a fairly large and complex organized enterprise (200-300 people) conducted each year was asked how he knew so well what to do without being told. His answer was "I just do the same as I did last year."

This answer furnishes a key to understanding the Fox method of coordinating collective action. Just as each individual related himself directly to the source of supernatural power, each individual participating in organized activity related himself directly to the body of procedural rules governing that activity. He was free to select and execute appropriate modes of action; his access to procedural rules was not mediated through another person who transmitted these rules to him.

It seems obvious that this system would hardly be adequate to insure success in a modern military landing operation, the construction of a skyscraper, or the production of a moving picture. Why, then, did it work in Fox society? In the first place, the *range* of activities involving coordinated action was quite limited. Only about five of six such activities (the war party, religious ceremonial, council meeting, some group games) were frequently recurrent; the total number of recurrent collective activities did not exceed ten or twelve. Second, the *size* of the group participating in such activities was limited. The war party consisted of about five to fifteen men; the religious ceremony involved fifteen to forty participants. Only very infrequently were larger groups involved in a coordinated enterprise. Third, since the rate of social change in Fox society was slow, the procedure of such activities was familiar to all participants. They had observed or taken part in them since early childhood; each knew his own part and how it fitted in with the parts of others; the activities changed little from year to year. Fourth, the "division of labor" in Fox society was neither complex or ramified. There were few real specialists, no secret or esoteric groups of craftsmen; in important coordinated activities such as ceremonials and council meetings, the whole range of the population—all age groups and both sexes—was customarily participant.

Thus it was possible for each participant in a collective activity to "control" the plan of action that governed its conduct. He was familiar with the procedural directives specifying the part he was to play and was able to act out these directives without being told what to do. It was as if the action plan for each activity were "built into" each participant. In activities such as the ceremonial, where a person in a position of authority presided over the proceedings, he exercised only "nominal" authority functions, such as signaling the beginnings and endings of set episodes, or recalling the proper sequence of events.

Authority and the Individual

To early European observers the Fox individual appeared unusually haughty, self-contained, and quick to resent anything he perceived as limiting his right to independent action. The reaction of the English, trader, Peter Pond (1773), "[The Fox] are insolent... and inclined to cheatery . . . when you meet them . . . they will speak in their own language if they speak at all, or otherwise they will look sulky and make you no answer," echoes that of Allouez in 1673, "These people are self-willed beyond anything that can be imagined!"

But what the Europeans perceived as resentment of authority could be described more accurately as resentment of authorities. Just as the Fox related himself directly to supernatural power, and to the procedural rules governing collective action, so he deemed it his inviolable right to respond directly to the rules governing general behavior. The intensity of Fox resentment of external direction was matched by an equally intense conformity to internalized cultural directives. The Fox individual was highly moral; he felt individually responsible for knowing and acting in accordance with the regulations of his society. An order was an insult; it implied that he was inadequate in his knowledge and performance of traditional rules of correct behavior.

Fox subsistence economy was based on tracking and killing wild game, mostly by individual hunters. Success in hunting expeditions required that individuals spend long periods in complete solitude, traverse many miles of difficult wilderness, undergo extended hardship and deprivation, and exercise considerable initiative and ingenuity to contend with animal quarry which could resort to many devices to outwit a pursuer. Such a subsistence system put a premium on qualities of individual initiative, self-dependence, forebearance, and the capacity to size up a situation and act on one's estimate.

Fox child-rearing practices produced and encouraged such qualities. From the earliest years children were encouraged to go alone into the woods and fast, learning to endure in solitude the terrors of the forest; they were sent on long trips by themselves as training for future hunting and war expeditions.

The relationship of child and father, the prototypical "authority" relationship in most European societies, is especially significant in this connection. The vertical-type authority relation between Freudian father and son, with the father the chief disciplinarian and internalized symbol of moral authority ("super-ego"), does not exist in Fox. The relationship is far closer to one of equality, a "horizontal" as against a vertical relationship—especially when the age differential between father and child is sufficiently reduced. Sol Tax, describing kinship behavior patterns in Fox, says (1937:256): ". . . the father-son relationship is much like that between two brothers . . . the father is supposed to make (the son) fast 'for his own good,' the closest thing to corporal punishment that properly occurs . . ." ". . . the father-daughter relationship is much like that of brother-sister. . . ."

Tax further points out that the right to exercise vertical authority never forms an intrinsic part of the definition of kin roles. First, the attitude of junior to senior is one of "respect," not "obedience," and second, it is the relative ages of the role-holders, quite independent of the specific roles they occupy, that determine appropriate behavior. "The relationship between uncle and nephew is one of equivalence . . . except (that the uncle plays the role of bogey-man for the nephew). Normally the 'uncle' is bogeyman to the 'nephew,' but if the 'uncle' is a child and the 'nephew' a mature man, the nephew is actually the bogeymen" (p. 282).

The Fox feeling about a dependency relationship between son and father, or son and parents, is symbolized graphically in the series of myths dealing with the finding of a manitu guardian by the adolescent boy. In these myths, when the boy goes into the woods on his manitu quest, he is considered to have died, and the parents mourn their lost son. Then, under the guidance of his own manitu, he is born again—this time, *not* as the child of his parents, but of his manitu. In some myths the boy's real father also dies while the boy is finding his manitu, or has died when the boy was very young (Michelson 1936:19). In other myths the father is depicted as an evil and unworthy person, who tries to dissuade his son from following the "right" precepts of ethical behavior revealed by the manitu and rejected by the son (Michelson 1925a:85).

All of these myths depict a symbolic severance of ties of dependency between son and father, and a transfer of these ties to an *internalized* manitu guardian. This is a way of saying that the conceptualized source of psychological security is transferred from a parental-dependency situation to a self-dependency situation. The boy dies; is lost to his parents; his real father is killed; he is born again with no real father, but now with his source of protective security inside himself in the form of his ever-present and powerful manitu guardian. The real parents are replaced by an internalized source of security and exemplar of correct social behavior.

Authority in Fox Society and as an Analytic Concept

From the viewpoint of the European observer, Fox society appears to lay great stress on the concept of "power" and at the same time to order its affairs with a minimum of overt authority. This points to certain implications of interest to the student of comparative political organization.

The Fox individual can relate himself, directly and without any mediating agency, to three things: the conceptualized source of power, the broadly representative societal decision-making agency, and the body of procedural rules governing interpersonal interaction. Is coordination of collective action in Fox society accomplished by means of "authority," as this term is commonly used by students of government or political sociology? Authority defined as "mediated access to rules" is rare; authority as "institutionalized power" (Bierstedt 1950) or as "legitimatized imperative control" (Weber 1947:324) is even less in evidence. In brief, Fox society lacks "vertical" authority, and the coordination of collective action utilizing the device of role-relationship combining the right to direct, permanent incumbency, differential prestige, differential functions, and differential access to procedural rules.

In Fox society there is little or no prestige differential between occupants of given role positions; the phenomenon of "ranked" or hierarchical authority is absent; attitudes of reverence or submissive obedience are not associated with given role positions. On the other hand, some of the characteristics of the vertical authority relationship *are* found in Fox society. There are culturally defined roles whose incumbents operate to facilitate collective action; there is permanent incumbency; directives are communicated by role-holders to participants in collective action; designated role-holders in a collective enterprise act out different aspects of the total task. But these components of the relationship type are not combined in the same way as in the case of vertical authority. Where there is permanent incumbency there is no right to direct, and where right to direct is granted, incumbency is temporary. Acceptance of communicated directives by executants in collective action is considered a matter of personal choice, not a binding, role-based obligation. The constituent elements of the

113

vertical authority relationship are conceptually and operationally separate.

This raises certain questions as to the utility of the concept "authority" for purposes of cross-cultural analysis. As generally used, this term treats as organically associated elements which evidently occur independently in Fox society. If "authority" is equated with "vertical authority," it would follow that societies lacking vertical authority also lack authority. Considerable systematic study of a wide range of diverse societies is indicated if the concept "authority" is to attain utility and applicability for cross-cultural analysis.

Footnotes

1. I am much indebted to Ben Paul, David Schneider, Robert Redfield, and Leo Strauss for their useful criticism of earlier versions of this paper.

2. "European" society in this paper will refer to those societies whose dominant cultural tradition derives from Europe as well as those properly called "European."

3. Unless otherwise specified, statements about Fox society in the following sections will refer to the society as it was in 1650, prior to white-influenced change. However, much of the analysis is applicable also to the present day, since many of the features described have remained substantially unchanged for three hundred years.

4. The best collection of Fox myths is found in Jones 1907. Other myths are contained in the voluminous material collected between 1912 and 1936 by Truman Michelson. Michelson's material on the "origin myths" of Fox totemic groups, found mainly in Bureau of American Ethnology Bulletins 72, 85, 87, 89, 95, 105, 114, and in the Bureau of American Ethnology Fortieth Annual Report (1925), contains numerous myths in full, as well as scattered mythic episodes.

5. Myths about White Robe (*Wa.pisaya*: "White fox-fur," a Fox clan name) can be found, among other places, in Jones 1907:9, 17; Jones 1939:17, 18; and in Jones 1911:231.

References Cited

ALLOUEZ, CLAUDE. "On the Mission of St. Marc to the Outagamie" (1673), *The Jesuit Relations and Allied Documents*, ed. R. G. Thwaites. Vol. LVIII. Cleveland, 1896-1901.

BIERSTEDT, ROBERT. "An Analysis of Social Power," *American Sociological Review*, XV (1950), 730-38.

CARVER, JONATHON. *Travels Throughout North America.* Philadelphia: Key and Simpson, 1797.

DABLON, CLAUDE. "Father Claude Allouez's Mission to the Mascoutench, the Outagamy, and the Tribes Toward the South" (1673), *The Jesuit Relations and Allied Documents, ed.* R. G. Thwaites. Vol. LVI, Cleveland, 1896-1901.

D'AIGREMONT, SR. "Rejection of Proposal to Enroll Indians in Canadian Militia" (1708), *Collections* of the State Historical Society of Wisconsin. Vol. XVI, 1902.

HAYES, CARLTON, J. H. *A Political and Cultural History of Modern Europe*. Vol. I. Madison, Wisconsin: The Macmillan Co. (for the U. S. Armed Forces Institute).

JAMES, WILLIAM. *The Varieties of Religious Experience*. New York: The Modern Library, 1902.

JONES, WILLIAM. "The Algonkin Manitou," *Journal of American Folklore*, XVIII (1905), 183-90.

————. "Fox Texts," *American Ethnological Society*, Vol. I. Leyden, 1907.

————. "Fox Notes," *Journal of American Folklore*, XXIV (1911), 231.

————. *Ethnography of the Fox Indians*, ed. M. W. Fisher. Bureau of American Ethnology, Bulletin 125, 1939.

LA HONTAN, LOUIS-ARMAND DE. *New Voyages to North America*. Paris, 1703. Ed. R. G. Thwaites. Chicago: A. C. McClurg and Co., 1905.

MARSTON, MORRELL. "Memoirs Relating to the Sauk and Foxes," *The Indian Tribes of the Upper Mississippi Valley and Region of the Great Lakes*, ed. Emma Helen Blair, Vol. II, 1827.

MacIVER, ROBERT M. *The Web of Government*. New York: The Macmillan Co., 1947.

MICHELSON, TRUMAN. "The Mythical Origin of the White Buffalo Dance of the Fox Indians," *Fortieth Annual Report of the Bulletin of American Ethnology* (1925a), pp. 23-349.

————. "Notes on Fox Mortuary Customs and Beliefs," *Fortieth Annual Report of the Bureau of American Ethnology* (1925b), pp. 351-496.

————. "Fox Miscellany," *Bureau of American Ethnology*, Bulletin 114, 1936.

PERROT, NICOLAS. "Memoir on the Manners, Customs and Religion of the Savages of North America," *The Indian Tribes of the Upper Mississippi Valley and Region of the Great Lakes*, ed. Emma Helen Blair, Vol. I, 1911.

POND, PETER. "Journal of a Trader Among the Central Indians" (1773), *Collections of the State Historical Society of Wisconsin*, XVIII.

TAX, SOL. "The Social Organization of the Fox Indians," *Social Anthropology of North American Tribes*, ed. Fred Eggan. Chicago: University of Chicago Press, 1937.

WEBER, MAX. *The Theory of Social and Economic Organization*. Translated by A. M. Henderson and Talcott Parsons. New York: Oxford University Press, 1947.

WHITELOCK, DOROTHY. *The Beginnings of English Society*. Harmondsworth: Penguin Books, 1952.

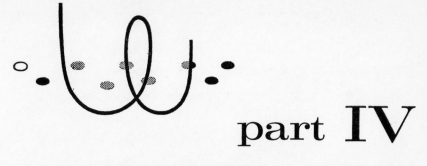

part IV

VARIATIONS IN PROCESS

". . . the crucial question is how *one pattern of behavior leads to another pattern of behavior. . ." (p. 11).*

Earlier chapters have revealed important aspects of organizational structure and of environmental relationships, and thus have been suggestive of factors to be taken into consideration in the examination of the administrative process. The following chapters turn to more explicit examination of process.

Coser's study of two wards in the same hospital indicates that the kinds of problems faced by the organization and the self-images of the administrators can be important factors in how and where decisions are made. Moreover, the locus and process of decision-making seem to be related to other aspects of organizational action, including the crucial question of whether behavior in organizational contexts is ritualistic or innovative.

Dill's comparison of business firms shows the relationship between the type of environment an organization interprets for itself and the behavior of its managers, especially with respect to their autonomy in selecting and acting on company problems. Thus we are given insights into two aspects of the administrative process: (1) the sequence of activity that relates the organization to the environment is illuminated and related to (2) those sequences of action which maintain the structure of the organization.

chapter 8

Authority and Decision-Making in a Hospital: A Comparative Analysis[1]

Rose Laub Coser

This paper presents a case analysis of the relationship between role behavior and social structure in two hospital wards. The analysis is based on daily observations made over a three-month period in the medical and surgical wards of a 360-bed research and teaching hospital on the Atlantic seaboard. Informal interviews, as well as a limited number of standardized interviews (10 each with house doctors and nurses), were used for the formulation of cues suggested by participant observation. Since only one hospital was studied, the comparisons to be made here—between the social structure of the medical team and that of the surgical team, and between the behavior of nurses on the two wards—should not be generalized beyond the case observed without further research. They are presented, however, with the aim of formulating hypotheses about the effect on role behavior of different types of authority structure in the hospital setting.

The surgical and the medical wards of this hospital were situated on two sides of the same floor, one floor each for men and women. An observer walking from one ward to the other, either on the male or on the female floor, would notice at first a superficial difference: joking as well as swearing, laughing as well as grumbling could be heard at the surgical nurses' station where some house doctors and some nurses gathered periodically. In contrast, on the medical ward the atmosphere can best be described as being more "polite." Joking and swearing were the exceptions; informal talk between doctors and nurses, if it occurred at all, was rare. Mainly medical students, who were not part of the formal ward organization, talked informally with nurses. On the surgical side, however, banter between doctors and nurses was a regular occurrence, and there one could also overhear from time to time a discussion between a nurse and some house doctor about a patient. Little if any of this occurred in the medical ward.

The behavior of the head nurse differed significantly on these two wards. While the medical nurse went through prescribed channels in her dealings with doctors, addressing herself to the interne whose orders she was expected to fill, the surgical nurse would talk to any doctor who was available, regardless of rank. She would more specifically ask that some decisions be made rather than trying to express her views through hints, which was the nurses' custom in the medical ward.

Moreover, in the surgical ward nurses participated much more fully in rounds than in the medical ward. Descriptions of rounds by medical and surgical nurses differed significantly. We heard in the medical ward, for example, from one of the nurses:

If nurses go on rounds they hold the charts, they pass them to the interne, the interne to the chief resident, and then it comes back down the line and the nurse puts the chart back. All that the nurse is there for, according to them, is to hold the charts.

Another medical nurse explained:

I get very little out of rounds. As nurses we're supposed to get something, and give something, but it never works. We're at the end of the line wheeling the charts, then I'm given orders to get something, I have to run out, when I come in again, there's something else they want me to do. . . .

In contrast, the head nurse in one of the surgical wards said this:

During rounds, the nurse gains insight into the condition of the patient, finds out changes in terms of medication and treatment. She can inform the doctor what treatment the patient is on and can suggest to the doctor that the dressing procedure can be changed; she can suggest vitamins by mouth instead of by injection; she can suggest taking them off antibiotics and point out necessary medication. . . . Occasionally the doctors would bypass the nurse, so before they forget to tell me anything I would ask; also you find out yourself when you're on rounds and that is very important.

This nurse seemed to take initiative, although she appeared to be shy and withdrawn, unlike the head nurses on the medical wards who happened to have a more outgoing personality.

In attempting to account for the different types of nurse-doctor relationship in the two wards, one could examine such factors as personality, character, and level of aspiration of the individuals. We propose, however, to discuss the phenomenon on the level of our observations, namely in terms of the network of social relations in the wards.

Social Structure of the Wards

Although the relationships in the surgical ward seemed to be easy-going, the social distance between the visiting doctor and the house doctors, and between the chief resident and those under him, was more marked among the surgeons. The contradiction between joviality and social distance was well expressed by a surgical interne: "It is not a very strict and formal atmosphere on our ward," he said, and then added: "Of course, the chief resident has everything; he's the despot, he decides who operates, so he takes the cases that he is interested in. The visiting doctor, of course, may propose to take a case over—he can overrule the chief resident."

CHART 1

Social Structure of the Medical Ward: Formal Line of Authority and Decision-Making

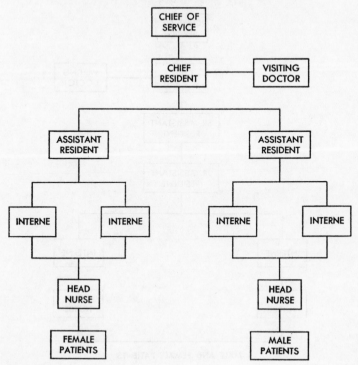

To resolve this apparent contradiction, we must compare the formal structure of authority with the *de facto* lines of decision-making. We will see that in the surgical ward the formal line of authority does not coincide with the actual line of decision-making; the process of decision-making, rather than the formal line of authority, apparently has an impact on the role of the nurse.

As Charts 1 and 2 show, the chief of service is responsible for the ward. He does not make any decisions for individual patients, however, but delegates his authority for the care of patients to the chief resident. The latter is responsible to the chief of service. In turn, the chief resident delegates the care of patients to the internes, each of whom is in charge of specific patients under the chief resident's continuous supervision. The internes pass on orders to the head nurse for the patients assigned to them. The assistant resident acts as supervisor and "consultant" to the internes.

CHART 2

Social Structure of the Surgical Ward:
Formal Line of Authority and Decision-Making

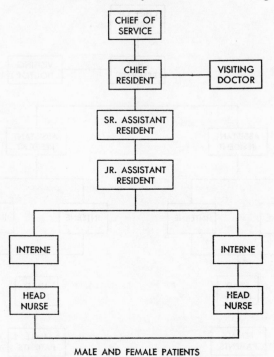

MALE AND FEMALE PATIENTS

The formal authority structure is essentially the same in both medical and surgical wards, with a simple organizational difference: there is no separation of tasks among the doctors for the male and female wards on the surgical side, as Chart 2 indicates. There, internes and residents walked up and down the steps to take care of their patients who were segregated by sex on two floors.

But the way in which the house doctors made use of the authority attached to their rank differed significantly in the two wards. In the medical ward, there was consistent delegation of authority down the line. The chief resident was heard saying on rounds to one or the other of the internes, "You make the final decision, he's your patient." Such remarks were not part of the pattern on the surgical ward, where the chief resident made the decisions. The medical house officers also based their decisions, to a large extent, on consensus, with the chief resident presiding and leading the discussion while the surgical house doctors received orders from the chief resident.[2] The following incident was typical of the authority relations in the surgical ward:

An interne and an assistant resident were conversing about an incident that had transpired that morning, when the daughter of an elderly patient had created a scene at the nurses' station about the fact that she had been notified as late as the previous evening at eleven o'clock of her father's operation the next morning. When she came to see her father before the operation, he had already been taken to the operating room and the daughter was extremely upset about not being able to see him. The interne and the assistant resident felt that in the future something should be done to forestall similar reactions from patients' relatives; they thought that the chief resident was too busy to notify relatives in due time and that therefore they would take it upon themselves to notify a patient's relatives if the chief resident would give them sufficient advance notice. They decided to take up the problem with the chief resident at the next occasion, and did so that very afternoon. The chief resident's answer was curt: "I always notify the family on time," he said with an annoyed facial expression, and walked away. He did not wish to delegate authority in the matter, trivial though it may seem.

The chief resident's "despotism," to which the previously quoted interne referred, is part of the surgical ward's culture. Although his decision-making by fiat may seem, at first glance, to be a "bad habit," or due to a lack of knowledge about the advantages of delegation of authority and of agreement by consensus, it has its roots in the specific activity system of the surgical team which differs significantly from that of the medical team.[3] We must bear in mind that responsibility for an operation, if performed by a house officer, lies with the chief resident or with the attending surgeon. They perform the important operations. As Stanton and Schwartz have pointed out, decision by consensus is time-consuming.[4] An emergency situation, in the operating room as elsewhere, is characterized precisely by the fact that a task must be performed in the minimum possible time. Whether in military operations or surgical operations, there can be no doubt about who makes decisions, that they must be made quickly and carried out unquestioningly and instantly.

The situation is quite different for the medical team. There the problems are those of diagnosis and of different possible avenues of treatment. Such problems require deliberation, and decisions are often tentative; the results of adopted therapeutic procedures are carefully observed and procedures may have to be modified in the process. All this demands careful consultation and deliberation, which are better accomplished through teamwork than through the unquestioned authority of a single person.

In his role as teacher of medical students, moreover, the person in authority teaches different lessons on the two wards: in the medical ward students and house officers are taught to think and reflect, while in the surgical ward the emphasis is on action and punctual performance. If this seems too sharp a distinction, and if it is objected that surgeons should learn to think also and medical doctors should learn to act as well, it must be borne in mind that the latter ideal situation is not always approximated, especially since the physicians themselves seem to have this image of the difference between medical and surgical men. The doctors on the medical ward, asked why they chose their field of specialization rather than surgery, said, for example: "Medicine is more of an intellectual challenge"; "I enjoy the kind of mental operation you go through"; "[Surgeons] want to act and they want results, sometimes they make a mess of it." The physicians on the surgical ward displayed a similar view of the differences between medicine and surgery and differed only concerning the value they gave the same traits. When asked why they chose to be surgeons, they said that they "like working with hands," that they "prefer something that is reasonably decisive," and that "[a medical] man probably doesn't want to work with his hands."

Thus the differences in task orientation and differences in self-images would seem to account in part for the main distinction between the two wards. This distinction can be summarized as follows: On the medical ward there is a scalar delegation of authority in a large area of decision-making,[5] and the important decisions are generally made through consensus under the guidance of the visiting doctor or the chief resident. On the surgical ward there is little delegation of authority as far as decision-making is concerned and decisions about operations and important aspects of treatment of patients are made by fiat. Charts 3 and 4 illustrate this difference.

CHART 3

Social Structure of the Medical Ward:
Informal Line of Authority and Decision-Making

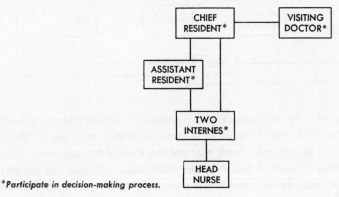

*Participate in decision-making process.

The Nurse-Doctor Relationship

Under these circumstances surgical assistant residents and internes are more or less on the same level under the authority of the chief resident or the visiting doctor; this makes for a common bond between assistant residents and internes and the strengthening of internal solidarity. The relative absence of actual prestige-grading, notwithstanding the formal rank differences, as they were observed among those who were practically excluded from the decision-making process, tended to eliminate some of the spirit of competition among the junior members. Moreover, with only little authority delegated to them, they could not be consistently superior in position to the nurse. This "negative democratization," as Karl Mannheim has called it,[6] encourages a colleague type of relationship between the nurses and doctors rather than a service relationship. Hence the banter and joking, which helped further to cancel out status differences,[7] and the relative frequency of interaction to which we referred above.

125

CHART 4

Social Structure of the Surgical Ward:
Informal Line of Authority and Decision-Making

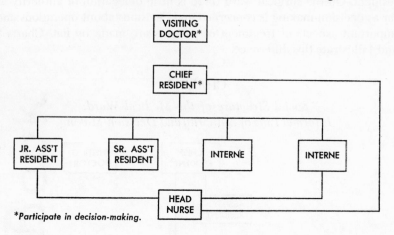

*Participate in decision-making.

Since authority was scarcely delegated, all house officers passed on orders to the nurse, who in turn communicated with all of them. Writing orders in the order book was not the task of internes only. This was confirmed by one of the internes who said: "Anyone on surgery writes in the order book," and the head nurse on one of the floors corroborated this situation when asked who gave her orders: "The internes, the residents also give orders, all give orders; we get orders all over the place and then you have to make your own compromise; you got to figure out what is most important."

Such a relation with the doctors puts the nurse in a strategic position. In using her own judgment about the importance of orders, she makes decisions about the care of patients, deciding to delay one action rather than another. This gives her a certain amount of power.

The position of the nurse in the surgical ward brings to mind Jules Henry's analysis of the social structure of a mental hospital.[8] Henry discusses two types of social organization: the "pine-tree" type, in which authority is delegated downward step by step, as in the medical ward discussed above (see Chart 3); and the "oak-tree" type, in which orders come down to the same person through several channels, as in the surgical ward described here (see Chart 4). The latter type, Henry says, is a source of stresses and strains because the head nurse must follow orders coming from different directions that may or may not be compatible. This is probably true, to some extent, in the surgical ward described here, but it is accompanied by the fact that such a position gives the nurse more power and more active part in therapy.

The head nurse on the surgical floor, often facing the necessity of compromise, must know a great deal about the conditions of patients; she is constrained to contact patients frequently and to establish a closer relationship with them. This is all the more necessary since during a large part of the day, while surgery is being performed, the surgical staff is confined to the operating room with the exception of one interne on duty in the ward. The nurse must therefore be "on her toes," checking with the duty interne only if absolutely necessary, since he has his hands full. Her knowledge of the patients is thus greater than that of the nurses on the medical floor. A medical head nurse, although she tried to impress the observer with her own importance, admitted: "The nurse knows more about patients than the doctor on surgical. On the medical floor it's about even. . . ." The doctors, in turn, knowing that the nurse on the surgical floor has more contact with patients than they themselves, rely on her information and reminders, in this way increasing her influence and decision-making role.

The doctors' expectations of the nurse differ according to ward. Asked to define a good nurse, the doctors on the surgical ward said that she should have foresight, intelligence, or that she must be a good assistant to the doctors, or that she should read. Some even noted that the same criteria apply to her as to a doctor. In contrast, the physicians on the medical ward emphasized her ability to "carry out orders" and "to do her routine work well." Only one of the medical internes declared: "Intellectual curiosity is rare but nice if you see it," thus implying that he wouldn't really expect it. Although our interviews with doctors are too few in number to draw any definite conclusions about expectations that medical doctors and surgeons have of nurses, the differences in their comments support our observations made elsewhere about some degree of autonomy and initiative among surgical nurses.

Moreover, where the rank hierarchy below the top decision-makers is not very strict and the delegation of authority not well-defined, informal relations are built across status lines. House doctors in the surgical ward sometimes abdicated their authority if they could rely on the nurse.[9] According to a surgical nurse, "The doctors want to be called in an emergency only, if they know you and they feel you know what you're doing. . . . They let us *do* things first and then call the doctor, as long as we would keep him informed." A third-year student nurse in the surgical ward had this to say: "In this hospital we're not allowed to draw blood or give I.V. I do it occasionally but nobody knows. I do it just to help [the doctors] if there are no medical students around. . . ." Needless to say, such informal arrangements enhance the nurse's prestige and enlarge her realm of power.

The surgical head nurse even made decisions about reference of patients to the social service. One of the head nurses, when asked whether she participated in the social service rounds, replied: "We should have been in on them, but I had close contact with the social worker, and I would ask her what I wanted to know. . . . Anyhow the patients would come to me for reference to the social worker." According to the formal rules, patients are referred to social service by the medical staff, but here, as in previous examples, the nurse by-passed official regulations and maintained considerable control over patients.

Ritualism or Innovation

Nurses on the surgical ward felt less tied to rules and regulations than nurses on the medical floor. This is illustrated by their reactions to the following story upon which they were asked to comment:

Interviewer: "I would like to tell you a story that happened in another hospital. An interne was called to the floor during the night to a patient who had a heart attack. He asked the nurse on the floor to get him a tank. She told him to ask an orderly. But there was no orderly around and she still refused to get it for him. Do you think she had a right to refuse, or do you think he had the right to expect her to get it for him?"

All nurses agreed that the nurse is not supposed to leave the floor if there is no other nurse around. However, while the answers of four of the five medical nurses were unqualified (e.g., "I would never have gotten the tank, the doctor definitely should have gotten it," or "I wouldn't think of leaving the floor for a minute when I'm alone, this is unheard of"), all five surgical nurses made important qualifications (e.g., "she should have called the supervisor," or "she could have said, you keep your ears and eyes open while I get it," or "she could say, if you keep an eye open in the meantime, I'll run and get it"). In spite of the small number of respondents these figures lend support to our observations and other interview material according to which the surgical nurse is more accustomed than the medical nurse to "find a way out," to use her initiative, and is more ready to circumvent rules and regulations.

Nurses are often accused of being "ritualistic," of attaching more importance to routine and rules than to the ends for which they are designed to serve. While the nurses on the medical floor were accused fairly often by the internes of "merely clinging to rules" and "not willing or not able to think," the head nurses on the surgical floor were never the targets of such criticisms. Indeed, the surgical nurses seemed to be capable of innovation and were often relied upon by doctors to use their own judgment and to initiate action, as we have shown.[10]

By relating the attitudes of the surgical nurses to the social structure of the ward, we have tried to confirm Merton's formulation in "Social Structure and Anomie," i.e., that "some social structures exert a definite pressure upon certain persons in the society to engage in nonconformist rather than conformist conduct."[11] There is reason to believe that in the wards that we observed, "ritualism" or "innovation" is largely a function of the specific social structure rather than merely a "professional" or "character" trait. Nurses are often in a position in which the insistence on rules serves as a means to assert themselves and to display some degree of power. If their professional pride as well as their power and influence are enhanced by breaking through the routine, however, they seem to be ready to use informal means or to act as innovators to reach their goals.

If the relation of the nurse's position—and that of other occupational types, perhaps—to the structure of authority and decision-making is subject to the kinds of influence described in this case, problems of morale might well be considered in the light of their structural context.

Footnotes

1. Paper read at the annual meeting of the American Sociological Society held in Washington, D. C., August 27-29, 1957.

2. We have adopted from Alfred H. Stanton and Morris S. Schwartz (*The Mental Hospital,* New York: Basic Books, 1954) the distinction between decisions arrived at through consensus and decisions that are made arbitrarily. (p. 258) "When a consensus is reached or assumed, the participants always feel it is completely unforced. There is no element of submissiveness, of defeat in argument. ... if there is any specific awareness at all it is one of discovery, of clarity, or of understanding." (p. 196) On the other hand, "we define an arbitrary decision as one made by a person higher in the power hierarchy governing a person lower in it, without regard to the agreement of the latter. Most frequently, of course, it is made to override disagreement and without consulting the subordinate. ..." (pp. 270-271).

3. For a general comparison between surgical and medical floors, see Temple Burling, Edith M. Lentz and Robert N. Wilson, *The Give and Take in Hospitals,* New York: G. P. Putnam's Sons, 1956, Chapter 16. For a dramatic description of work in the operating room, see Robert N. Wilson, "Teamwork in the Operating Room," *Human Organization,* XII, (Winter, 1954), pp. 9-14.

4. *Op. cit.,* pp. 268, 271.

5. The term "scalar" is here used as defined by Chester I. Barnard in "Functions and Pathology of Status Systems in Formal Organizations" in W. F. Whyte (ed.), *Industry and Society,* New York: McGraw Hill & Co., 1946, pp. 46-83.

6. Karl Mannheim, *Man and Society in an Age of Reconstruction*, New York: Harcourt, Brace & Co., 1951, esp. pp. 85 ff.

7. On this function of banter in status systems, see Tom Burns, "Friends, Enemies and Polite Fiction," *American Sociological Review*, 18 (December 1953), pp. 654-662.

8. Jules Henry, "The Formal Social Structure of a Psychiatric Hospital," *Psychiatry*, 17 (May 1954), pp. 139-152.

9. The concept of abdication of authority is here used in the sense defined by Stanton and Schwartz: "By abdication, we mean the situation in which a person who is supposed to make a decision according to the formal organization does not make it even though circumstances require that it be made." *op. cit.*, p. 274.

10. The type of therapy in the surgical ward also makes the surgical nurse's work seem more important than that of the medical nurse. As Burling, Lentz and Wilson have pointed out, on surgical wards, "the nurse's skills are tested daily and both her feeling and her prestige rise as she becomes more adept." *op. cit.*, p. 245.

11. Robert K. Merton, *Social Theory and Social Structure*, Glencoe, Illinois: The Free Press, 1957, pp. 131-160.

chapter 9

Environment as an Influence on Managerial Autonomy[1]

William R. Dill

Administrative science needs propositions about the ways in which environmental factors constrain the structure of organizations and the behavior of organizational participants. Until we can identify relevant environmental variables and can predict their impact on behavior, we cannot know how findings about behavior in one situation must be modified if they are to serve as prescriptions for behavior in other situations where groups are subject to different environmental "demands."

This paper reports an exploratory study of environmental influences on the top-management groups in two Norwegian business firms, each with 250-300 employees. One, which I shall call Alpha manufactured a varied line of clothing and sold it to wholesalers and retailers throughout Norway. The second, Beta, was a sales, engineering, and contracting firm. It sold, installed, and serviced a wide variety of supplies and machinery for state, industrial and private users. Both Alpha and Beta were among the larger, older firms in their industries.

The two firms differed sharply in the degree to which the department heads and top staff men thought and acted autonomously, both with respect to their peers and with respect to their superior, the owner-manager. This paper reports differences between Alpha and Beta in top-management autonomy, and it contrasts the environments in which the two management groups worked. The final section proposes relationships between environmental variables and autonomy.

131

Basic Concepts and a Frame of Reference

TASK VARIABLES

Each management group planned action on the basis of information it received about environmental events. I have denoted that part of the total environment of management which was potentially relevant to goal setting and goal attainment as the task environment.[2]

The task environment of management consisted of inputs of information from external sources. These inputs did not represent "tasks" for the organization; by *task* I mean a cognitive formulation consisting of a goal and usually also of constraints on behaviors appropriate for reaching the goal. When we study the task environment, we are focusing on the stimuli to which an organization is exposed; but when we study tasks, we are studying the organization's interpretations of what environmental inputs mean for behavior. These interpretations are subject to errors of perception and to the bias of past experience.[3]

The task environment as information inputs, and tasks, as cognitive formulations to guide action, need further to be distinguished from task-fulfilling activities, the actual behavior of men in organizations. In many studies where task variables have been considered,[4] clear distinctions have not been made among things that the organization does *(activities)*, things that the organization sets itself to do *(tasks)*, or stimuli that the organization might respond to *(task environment)*. There are many relevant inputs of information which organizations do not attend to as well as many tasks which they formulate but never act upon.

AUTONOMY

The dependent variable for this study was autonomy, or freedom from influence. A department head or top staff man was judged autonomous with respect to peers or to the president to the extent that he and his subordinates were independent in formulating tasks or in carrying through courses of action.

The measures I have used are varied. They include statements by members of management about their relations with colleagues as well as reports and observations of specific samples of behavior. The measures represent primarily short-run freedom from influence. The study, which spanned four months, was too short for analyzing long-term interpersonal influence. Over the long run, moreover, much of the instruction and suggestion that a man receives tends to get internalized so that the man, in acting, feels that he is responding to internal choice rather than to external pressure.

In reporting data on autonomy, I shall make a distinction between *upward* and *horizontal* autonomy. The former is the freedom that first-rank subordinates had with respect to the owner-manager, their common superior; the latter, the freedom that they had with respect to one another or to one another's subordinates.

INFLUENCE OF TASK ENVIRONMENT ON AUTONOMY

The relationships between environment and autonomy in Alpha and Beta were not simple.

We can assume that the behavior of each management group was a function of the inputs that were, or that had been, accessible from the environment. But even in short time intervals, vast numbers of inputs became accessible. Of these, only a small proportion could be— and were—attended to.

Most inputs were simply statements about the condition of the organization or of parts of the environment. Some inputs took the form of goals suggested or specified for management. Only rarely, however, were inputs complete task formulations that included both goals to be attained and detailed specifications for courses of action. Even where environmental inputs specified courses of action, they rarely specified in any direct way the degree of autonomy that was to prevail in management relationships.[5]

Thus to understand the degree of autonomy that a leader showed in Alpha and Beta, we must look beyond the environmental inputs to which he was exposed. We must ask which inputs he was cognizant of, how he grouped inputs and elaborated their meaning for the organization, how he ascribed such properties as urgency or complexity to the tasks they suggested, and how he mapped actual courses of action. We must ask how the thoughts and actions of different men in the same firm, each exposed to the environment in a different way, mesh or conflict. Our problem, briefly, is to explore the task environment as it impinged on management and to search for characteristics of the environment that might have influenced one key aspect, the autonomy, of management behavior.

Sources of Data

The analysis which follows is based mainly on interviews with management people in Alpha and Beta and on observations of them interacting with one another and with the environment. Before the intensive study began, the manager and his immediate subordinates in each firm were interviewed as part of a more general survey of patterns of autonomy in Norwegian management. Then over a four-month period these men were interviewed again, and additional interviews were held with all higher-level supervisors, with most foremen and foreladies, and with most specialists—salesmen, engineers, designers, technicians, accountants, and other office service personnel. Only a few clerical and hourly employees were interviewed.

These interviews were intended to elicit information about each man's career with the firm, about his job activities, and about his relationships with others in the firm. The interviews were supplemented by informal conversations with employees about jobs they were then doing and by observations of management at work. Two questionnaires were used to get additional data about what members of management did, how they worked together, and what they thought of their positions.

To gain perspective I explored the history of the two firms and interviewed men in other organizations about their relationships to Alpha and Beta. I have also drawn extensively on sources of general information about Norwegian society and the Norwegian economy.[6]

The data are far from complete, and little of what was learned deals directly with information from and about the environment *as it became accessible* to the two management groups during the study. The data, however, are rich enough to delineate major differences between Alpha and Beta and to suggest hypotheses for more carefully controlled research.

Background Information About the Two Firms

GENERAL BACKGROUND

Before going further with the analysis, let us look briefly at Alpha and Beta and at the men who led them. Alpha was founded before the turn of the century; Beta, shortly after. By the time of the study Alpha was one of the largest and most diversified firms in its branch of the Norwegian clothing and textile industry. The only son of one founder was the president, and sons of another founder still served on the board of directors. These men controlled the firm.

Beta began as a very small specialty contracting firm for products and facilities that were undergoing rapid technological change. Its most rapid growth occurred after the twenties, when the founder withdrew in favor of the present owner-manager. Functions of the firm at the time of the study included importing foreign manufactures for resale, some assembly and manufacturing work, and a wide variety of engineering, installation, and maintenance services.

Men in Alpha recognized four major sequences of activity within the organization. Each sequence, to a large extent, involved unique processes, required special personnel, and led to outputs that were clearly differentiable from the outputs of other sequences. Men in Beta clearly recognized thirteen such sequences of activity.

Over the years the volume of business for both firms had increased greatly, but the nature of products and services provided changed much more radically in Beta than Alpha. From a staff of ten to twelve men in 1910, Beta had grown to a firm of nearly three hundred at the time of the study. Over the same period the number of employees at Alpha had decreased, dropping from more than five hundred to about two hundred and fifty.

MAJOR WORK GROUPS

Each of the two firms was composed of a number of distinct work groups. Tables 1 and 2 identify these groups and suggest the extent of their involvement in the major work sequences.

Certain groups were administrative; that is, they sponsored and controlled activities for the firm as a whole, and they were regarded inside and outside the firm as loci of ultimate responsibility for decisions and actions of the firm. The top administrative group in Alpha was a relatively passive board of directors composed of major stockholders. Only one director, the firm's president, concerned himself with day-to-day operating problems; the others met bi-monthly to review accounting statements. The president of Beta had established a policy committee composed of himself and five top subordinates, which had legal power to perform many of the functions of a corporate board. This committee met at least once a month to review accounts and to discuss operating problems.

The presidents at Alpha and Beta took active personal leadership of operations but both relied for assistance on mail committees, made up of key members of top management. These committees met daily to review incoming mail and to discuss other problems which committee members wanted to raise.

The operating and service groups were organized differently in the two firms. At Alpha most of the groups had been in existence for a long time, and most did work associated with two or more of the firm's major programs. No group did work associated with a program in which no other group was involved. At Beta, the histories of operating and service groups varied more widely. The groups were frequently respon-

TABLE 1

Alpha: Top-management involvement in work groups and job sequences.

Major work groups	Group Size Rank*	Directly affiliated members of top management†	Extent of management involvement in major routine job sequences‡			
			No. 1	No. 2	No. 3	No. 4
Board of Directors	*	President (M)				
Top Executive	*	President (L)	P	P	P	P
Mail Committee	*	Pres. (L); Office Mgr., Sales Mgr., Scheduling Mgr., Production leaders 1 & 2 (M).				

ADMINISTRATIVE GROUPS

OPERATING AND SERVICE GROUPS						
Sales	13	Sales Manager (D)	P	P	P	P
Services	10	Office Manager (L)	P	P	P	P
Scheduling	11	Scheduling Manager (L)	P	P	P	S
Production—H	3	Production leader 1 (L)	P	–	–	–
Production-S } Production-U	2	Production leader 2 (L)	–	P	P	–
Production-O } Production-Y	8	Production leader 3 (L)	S	S	P	S
Production—Sp	7	Production leader 4 (D)	–	–	–	P
Production D	12	Production leader 5 (L)	S	S	S	S
Fashion	15	Stylist (L)	P	P	P	P
Industrial engg.	14	Industrial engineer (D)	P	P	P	P

*Groups in *both* firms have been ranked *together*, from largest to smallest, by the number of employees in them at the time of the study. The actual group sizes ranged from 125 to 1 (the stylist in Alpha had no subordinates). Administrative groups were not included in the ranking.

†The letter to the right of each man's title in this column indicates his primary role in the work group: D, if he had led the group since its inception as a separate unit in the firm; L, if he was the group leader at the time of the study (but not the original leader); M, if he was a subordinate member.

‡For each numbered job sequence, the expected (formal) involvement of every member of top management is indicated by one of the following symbols: P, involvement as frequent participant in routine activities and decisions; S, involvement only as supervisor or evaluator; A, occasional involvement as planner or adviser on matters which required coordination among two or more job sequences; —, substantially no involvement. P represents the highest degree of involvements in a job sequence; —, the least.

TABLE 2

Beta: Top-management involvement in work groups and job sequences.

Major work groups	Group Size Rank*	Directly affiliated members of top management†	Extent of management involvement in major routine job sequences‡												
			1	2	3	4	5	6	7	8	9	10	11	12	13
Owners Policy Committee	* *	President (L); President (D); Office manager, Division managers 1, 2, 3, & 4 (M)				S	S	S	S	S	S	S	S	S	S
Top Executive Mail Committee	* *	President (L); President (D); Office manager, Division managers 1, 2, & 3 (M)	S	S	S	S	S	S	S	S	S	S	S	S	S

ADMINISTRATIVE GROUPS

OPERATING AND SERVICE GROUPS

	Group Size Rank*		1	2	3	4	5	6	7	8	9	10	11	12	13
Services	6	Office manager (D)	S	S	S	S	S	S	S	S	S	S	S	S	S
Consumer contracting	1	Division manager 1 (D)	P	S	S	A	–	S	S	–	–	A	A	–	I
Producer contracting Equipment sales	4	Division manager 2 (D)	A	–	A	S	S	S	S	S	S	A	A	A	A
Manufacturing Retail sales	5	Division manager 3 (D)	–	A	A	–	–	–	–	–	A	P	S	A	A
Specialty contracting	9	Division manager 4 (L)	–	–	–	–	–	–	–	A	A	A	A	P	P

*See notes to Table 1

sible for more than one program apiece, and in Beta some groups had sole responsibility for their programs.

TOP MANAGEMENT

In each firm one could distinguish several people who had perceptibly higher status as "management" than others in the organization. These included the two presidents and those of their immediate subordinates who had significant professional or supervisory responsibility.[7] These subordinates will be known in this study as *key men.*

Top management in Alpha differed from top management in Beta in the following ways:

1. The group at Alpha, defined by a criterion of apparent status was larger (the president and ten subordinates vs. the president and five subordinates at Beta).

2. The group at Alpha was younger (median age, Alpha, 38 years; Beta, 50 years, and had fewer years of service with the firm (median service, Alpha 7 years; Beta, 30 years).

3. All but three of the men at Alpha held jobs that had been established and developed by predecessors. All five subordinates at Beta, however, had had the task of creating and developing the positions that they held.

4. The men at Alpha had had less formal education. Two of the eleven (vs. three of the six at Beta) had had full university training.

5. The job titles and salary rates of the men at Alpha were less likely to earn high status in the business and social community outside the firm than those at Beta.

It is the two groups of key men—ten in Alpha and five in Beta— which will receive our attention in the pages which follow.

Autonomy in the Two Groups of Subordinate Leaders

By almost every measure that was tried, the five key men at Beta seemed more autonomous with respect to one another and with respect to their common superior, the president, than the ten key men at Alpha. The major evidence is summarized below.

PERCEIVED AUTONOMY

The key men from Beta perceived for themselves a greater degree of autonomy than the key men from Alpha. This was inferred from: (1) the proportions of each group who, in interviews and conversations, *spontaneously* mentioned autonomy or lack of autonomy as a prominent characteristic of their jobs; (2) the frequencies and types of working contacts men in each firm reported with their peers and with the president; and (3) the men's responses to eight questions (in a list of forty-five) which probed the degree of autonomy that they enjoyed.*[8]

OBSERVATIONS OF CONFERENCE BEHAVIOR

The perceptual evidence is supported by behavioral evidence. In Alpha the president and five of his key men met nearly every morning as the mail committee, chiefly to review incoming mail but also to discuss other problems. The president and four key men formed a similar committee at Beta. In Beta, too, all six members of top management met eight to twelve times a year as the policy committee to review company performance, to approve major departmental decisions, and to plan for the organization as a whole.

1. *Upward autonomy.* Observations of the committees in session corroborate the proposition that key men in Alpha functioned less autonomously with respect to the president than did key men in Beta. The president at Alpha determined every day when the meeting would start, and he controlled the length of the meeting and most of the agenda for it. He was the first to see the incoming mail. The mail committee did not meet in his absence; and when a meeting was called all members on the premises were expected to attend.

Subordinate committee members at Beta were the first to receive correspondence, and they generally decided whether it should be discussed with the president. The president seldom arrived less than half an hour after the meetings began, and meetings were held daily whether or not he was expected to attend. Attendance was voluntary, and two of the four key men came only two or three times a week. The office manager, who had routine information to report, was the only subordinate who regularly stayed at the meetings until the president arrived.

These over-all impressions that the president at Alpha controlled conference activities more than did the president at Beta are supported by data on interaction within meetings.[9] Table 3 shows that the president at Alpha was more active than the president at Beta as an initiator of topics for discussion, as a direct participant (speaker or addressee) in the conversation, and as a contributor of high-influence acts (for example, "stating decisions or policy" and "giving orders, requesting action"). Most of the differences become significant, by the criteria described in footnote 8, if we take into consideration the interaction which occurred at Beta while the president was not present.[10]

2. *Horizontal autonomy.* Evidence from the meetings also indicates

TABLE 3

Roles of the presidents in conferences with subordinates.

Measure of Role	President Alpha 7 Mail-committee meetings	President Beta 3 Mail-committee meetings	1 policy committee meeting
Number of topics he initiated as a percentage of:			
Number of topics taken up when he was present	83	29*	30*
Number of topics taken up during entire meetings	83	12*	30*
Number of conversation units in which he was speaker or direct addressee as a percentage of:			
Number of units spoken when he was present	92	91*	72*
Number of units spoken during entire meetings	92	40*	72*
Number of low-influence units he contributed as a percentage of all his units	45	42	58*
Number of high-influence units he contributed as a percentage of:			
All his units	18	8	8
Number of high-influence units contributed by all members of committee	98	100	47*

*The starred (*) Beta percentages are significantly different from the corresponding Alpha percentages by the criteria outlined in footnote 8.

that the subordinate committee members had less autonomy with respect to one another in Alpha than in Beta.

Attendance at mail committee meetings in Beta was sporadic. Members generally did not stay through the entire meeting; they entered and left the meeting room at will. Silence was common in the period before the president arrived. Several minutes might pass while men read mail without a word being said. The average rate of interaction (number of conversation units recorded per minute) was 2.4 for 85 minutes when the president was not present. This contrasts with rates of 3.6 for 45 minutes when the president was present and of 4.0 for 140 minutes of interaction (president in attendance) at Alpha.[11]

Social conversation in mail committee meetings amounted to 4 per cent of the recorded units at Alpha; to 15 per cent of the recorded units at Beta.* Most of the social interchanges at Beta occurred among subordinate members before the manager arrived.

As further evidence that key men in Alpha used meeting time more intensively to counsel and influence each other, let us look at variations in individuals' participation in the discussion of different topics. In both firms the topics taken up varied greatly in their relevance to different individuals. If we assume equal variability in the two firms, evidence that men in Beta keyed their participation more closely than men in Alpha to the topics under discussion can be interpreted as evidence of greater autonomy in Beta.

A simple, strong measure of topic-to-topic variability in participation rates is the frequency with which each subordinate committee member "withdrew," or remained silent, when topics were discussed. On the average, each man was silent during 16 per cent of the major topics discussed at Alpha, and for 27 per cent at Beta.[12] At Beta, though, the two men who were least often silent were also the two who spent least time at the meetings. If we define "withdrawal" to include voluntary absence, the mean frequency of withdrawal for Alpha does not change, but the mean frequency for Beta rises to 45 per cent.*

RECOLLECTIONS OF BEHAVIOR ON "MOST IMPORTANT" TASKS

To get a sample of behavior outside scheduled meetings, I used management reports of activities. For at least two weeks every member of top management was asked to describe each day the "most important matter" he had handled that day and to answer questions about his involvement in activity on the task. The number of usable responses from key men ranged from three to twelve per man, with a median of seven. Each task reported required, in the median, two hours of the respondent's time during the day.

Although the data summarized below are subordinates' recollections of involvement in task performance, the data—as recollections—should be subject to a minimum of error. In most cases the questionnaires were filled out on the day when the behavior reported occurred, and the questions asked about behavior were specific.[13]

1. *Upward autonomy.* The "most important" task data confirm our other evidence about differences in upward autonomy between Alpha and Beta.

The president was more often reported as initiator of activity by key men in Alpha than by key men in Beta. Six of nine respondents in Alpha named the president as initiator at least once. He was named as initiator of action on eleven (14 per cent) of 77 reported tasks. None of the five key men in Beta named the president as initiator of action on *any* task that he reported.*

The president at Alpha was also more frequently involved as a participant in task performance. He was named as a co-worker on eighteen (23 per cent) of 77 reported tasks. Each key man named him as a co-worker at least once. At Beta, in contrast, the president was named as a co-worker on only six (15 per cent) of 39 tasks.* All six namings were made by three of the five respondents. It is worth noting that in all cases the president at Beta participated at the invitation of a subordinate, but that the president at Alpha initiated half the tasks on which he was named as a co-worker.

Data from a very small sample of cases suggest that, when working with the president, key men at Alpha made decisions less often than the subordinates at Beta and that the actions of subordinates in Alpha were often restricted to the low-influence roles of "collecting information" and "preparing proposals."

2. *Horizontal autonomy.* The data about handling of "most important" tasks also support the judgment that key men in Alpha had less freedom with respect to one another than had key men in Beta. The more independent they were, for example, the less one would expect them to agree with one another in their choice of one task as "most important" for a particular day. In Alpha two men agreed in their choices in eight of a possible 165 instances. The fraction is small; but in Beta no coincident choices occurred in thirty possible pairings.*[14]

In addition, key men reported more cross-departmental initiation of tasks by peers at Alpha (26 per cent of 77 tasks) than at Beta (8 per cent of 39 tasks).* In naming co-workers on tasks, key men in Alpha reported interaction with peers and with subordinates of peers from more departments, and reported such interaction more frequently, than key men in Beta.*

A variety of measures then, give consistent support to the generalization that the key men at Alpha had less autonomy than the key men at Beta, both with respect to their direct superiors and with respect to one another.[15]

The Task Environments of Top Management

Can the differences in autonomy be attributed to differences in the task environments with which the top-management groups of Alpha and Beta dealt? To answer this question, we first require a description of environmental characteristics.

COMPOSITION OF THE TASK ENVIRONMENT

For both firms the "elements" of task environment that had greatest impact on goal attainment included *customers* (both distributors and users), *suppliers* (of materials, labor, equipment, capital, and work space), *competitors* (for both markets and resources), and *regulatory groups* (government agencies, unions, and interfirm associations). The people and institutions who had active or potential interest in the outputs of Alpha and Beta were mostly Norwegian. Neither firm exported goods or services extensively. Organization-customer relations were important to both firms because in the short run they had to adapt to customers' demands and patterns of behavior. Only in the long run could either firm significantly influence consumer preferences and market structure.

Alpha and Beta were especially alert to the markets at the time of the study. For nearly a decade they had enjoyed a sellers' market, but now because of increased domestic competition and relaxation of import restrictions some departments in both firms were running at a loss. For the first time in fourteen years the government had removed or substantially relaxed price controls; and, increasingly, Norwegian companies were reluctant to honor voluntary private agreements on pricing and marketing practices.

Increased competition for markets made relations with suppliers crucial too. Some resources—notably foreign currencies and new plant or office facilities—were extremely scarce and still formally rationed. The government controlled not only new construction but also renovation of old facilities.) Even resources that were routinely in demand were difficult or expensive to obtain. Skilled workers, particularly, were scarce because industry around Oslo had grown faster than men had been trained or than housing for migrants from other districts had been provided. Skilled personnel, particularly at management levels, were sometimes recruited from abroad.

Since most materials, production equipment, or goods bought for resale came directly or indirectly from other countries, fluctuations in international political and economic conditions complicated the arrangement of purchases.

Competitors did not have the direct influence that suppliers and customers had in specifying goals for Alpha and Beta. But competitors, working toward their own objectives, could thwart or limit the attainment of goals by Alpha or Beta, and they could introduce a large

143

measure of uncertainty into the two firms' operations. Information about competitors gave management in Alpha and Beta criteria for setting goals and for evaluating performance. Dissatisfaction with performance at Alpha, for example, stemmed partly from knowledge that other mills were increasing sales while Alpha was losing customers.

The fourth significant part of the task environments of the two firms comprised regulatory agencies, organizations with powers of sanction that restricted the operation of market mechanisms.

At the same time of the study labor unions were committed to win from Norwegian employers a new general contract covering all industries, as well as specific contracts for different industries and for individual firms. Their demands included a general wage increase, guarantees of minimum earnings, pay for holidays, assurances of job security, and adjustments in incentive rates. The unions had a strong bargaining position. For many demands they had at least tacit backing from the government, and because good workers were scarce and competition was keen few firms felt they could afford a disgruntled work force.

The government, controlled by the Labor party for two decades, exercised strong controls over (1) the rate and direction of investment; (2) the use of capital in foreign trade; (3) prices and marketing practices; and (4) the pay-off on operations, through taxes and dividend restrictions. These controls had delayed the expansion of manufacturing activities in Beta for several years.

Two federations of interfirm organizations had important regulatory roles, even though their existence depended on the consent of firms like Alpha and Beta. The Employer's Association (NAF) was organized at the turn of the century to deal collectively with labor, which had previously formed a national organization. The Federation of Industries (NIF) was founded to represent firms in dealing with the government, the public, and foreign groups. Both were national federations of regional and industrial branch organizations. As institutions with wide membership and long history, NAF and NIF had acquired full-time administrative staffs, and had developed programs which member firms could not easily alter. Even on questions decided by vote of the membership, Alpha and Beta were bound by the will of the majority. The majority, in turn, was reluctant to accept any program that might induce any of the largest members, or groups of members, to withdraw.

What were the important differences between the task environments of top management in Alpha and Beta? From a host of specific differences we can abstract some major points of contrast between the two task environments. These will be analyzed in some detail.

1. *Degree of unity and homogeneity.* For each member of top management (and for his work groups), certain sectors of the firm's total task environment were of more interest than others. To what extent were the leaders concerned with the same environment? Where they dealt with sectors that did not overlap, were the sectors similar in nature and in their relation to the firm?

As individuals, the leaders at Alpha dealt with sectors of the task environment that were less differentiated than those with which the leaders at Beta dealt; where they were differentiated, the sectors dealt with by the Alpha leaders were more homogeneous.

Key men at Alpha were more often involved with the same environmental groups than key men at Beta. Most of the wholesalers and retailers who bought from Alpha ordered from all four product lines. The main purchases for all products were made twice a year at the same time. Contracts with Alpha on discounts and deliveries were seldom specific with regard to particular products or work groups. Even Norwegian families, the ultimate consumers of Alpha's output, generally purchased every year some of each major type of clothing that the firm manufactured.

At Beta the leaders were generally concerned with different, quite distinct markets. Some work groups subcontracted work for shipyards and building contractors, and most of their inquiries came from customers in the vicinity of Oslo. Others sold to specialized wholesalers all over Norway. Still another, in contrast to all other work groups, sold to individual consumers through a retail shop in Oslo. Two groups were the only ones concerned with the food-processing and storage industries and the only ones that regularly sold a major part of their output in north Norway. Even where groups shared customers, the nature of demands were quite different. Take two, for example, that served public and private industrial firms. One supplied material for maintenance and for routine inventories on a continuing basis. The other supplied major equipment and provided engineering services that a firm might need only once in twenty years.

The different leaders in Alpha worried about the same competitors, by and large, and dealt with the same union. The firm was associated with only one affiliate each of NAF and NIF. On the other hand, since Beta was not organized to fit traditional industry patterns, its leaders were concerned with different competitors. Most groups competed against other specialty contracting and engineering firms; but some groups that imported goods for resale to industrial users or to wholesalers competed with Norwegian manufacturers of similar goods. One competed against similar retail shops in Oslo, as well as against a broader class of suppliers of luxury goods to private consumers.

Not only were different groups at Beta concerned with different groups of competitors, but these competitors propounded distinct problems to each group. Some faced most difficulty in obtaining customers and in counteracting the prices of other firms. Two other groups which had customers could not supply the customers' demands; the foreign manufacturers on which the two groups depended were finding it more advantageous to sell in countries other than Norway.

Similarly, in contacts with regulatory groups, Beta had workers in each of three unions. Not all departments in the firm were affiliated with the same branches of NAF and NIF. Government regulations that applied to one work group frequently did not apply to other groups in the firm.

Other examples could be given, but the difference between the two task environments should be clear. At Alpha leaders of different work groups were more often concerned with the same customers, suppliers, competitors, and regulatory groups. Where the leaders dealt with different individuals or groups, these individuals still tended to be homogeneous in their role in the economy, in their geographical dispersion around Europe, and in the content and timing of demands that they made on Alpha. At Beta, in contrast, the leaders of various work groups were more distinctly concerned with different subportions of a highly differentiated, heterogeneous task environment.

2. *Degree of stability.* The environment of an organization, like the organization itself, is continually changing. What were the important differences between the task environments of Alpha and Beta in the manners in which they were changing?

The long-term stability of environmental systems and environmental demands was greater, and would probably continue to be greater, for Alpha than for Beta; but at the time of the study important sectors of the task environment were less stable at Alpha. Fewer abrupt, short-run changes were occurring in Beta's environment.

A few examples will illustrate the long-run difference. The market that Alpha served had changed relatively little in fifty years. Its size had increased: population had risen by 50 per cent, distant customers were easier to supply, and less clothing was made at home. Yet the Norwegian family remained the only important customer; products and means of distribution were basically the same. Demand for only one really new type of clothing had developed. Since the twenties, at least, families had not been using increments in real income to buy more clothing.[16] For Beta, however, markets that had existed when the firm was founded had grown in some cases, disappeared in others. Only two of the major work programs continued operations initiated before World War I; the other eleven had resulted from the growth (approximately tenfold) and diversification of the industries which used Beta's services, from rapid technological development of the equipment and processes Beta specialized in, and from increases in the real prosperity of the Norwegian consumer. Beta profited from increments in real income, since these were spent in large measure for durable and semidurable goods sold by shops like Beta's or produced by firms which Beta served.

At the time of the study Alpha had recently installed new, more automatic production equipment, but they had not begun to work extensively with any of the new synthetic fibers. Beta was under continual pressure to expand the scope of its operations from suppliers who wanted to market new products and from customers who wanted more complete service.

The prospects for future expansion of markets were small at Alpha, large at Beta. For the first time Alpha and its competitors had capacity to meet domestic demand, limited prospects for export sales, and no expectations of radically new products. Beta, however, was confronted with a large, unfilled domestic demand in many of its lines of activity and with the expectation of an accelerated rate of technological change within the industry. Within six years the government planned a 75 per cent increase in the country's capacity to generate electric power. Beta would benefit from this and from the new industries that would follow.

Yet at the time of the study, somewhat paradoxically, the short-run changes occurring in Alpha's task environment were greater than those occurring in Beta's. New synthetic fibers of many types were becoming available to Norwegian manufacturers. There were strong pressures to revise marketing practices to conform with American ideas. And most important, of course, was the sudden change from an in-

147

dustry with too little to one with too much production capacity. During the study, import restrictions on foreign textiles were relaxed; price controls, already superfluous, were removed; and many firms were threatening to break voluntary agreements about marketing practices. At the same time sales were falling, costs were rising. Alpha, which had to pay premium wages because of its location, was more concerned than competitors about union demands for higher pay.

3. *Disruptiveness of environmental inputs.* Inputs to an organization can vary a great deal in the directness with which they serve as checks, or feedback, on company operations. At the time of the study Alpha was more subject than was Beta to inputs that indicated the firm was not doing well. Salesmen reported resistance to pricing policies. Customers complained directly about delays in delivery of orders. Information about the progress of certain competitors contrasted unfavorably with data about Alpha's own performance. Two "outsiders," a new sales manager and a recently hired consultant, were using their knowledge of other firms to make critical observations about current policies and practices in Alpha.

Except for one or two major work programs at Beta, instances of unfavorable feedback were either less frequent or less obvious to the responsible members of management.

4. *Demands for direct personal interaction.* Top management at Alpha had fewer demands for, and were subject to fewer inducements to, direct interaction with individuals or groups in the task environment than top management at Beta. In Alpha's case more transactions with the environment were routine, and more messages could be coded for transmission in brief, standard form.

When a customer ordered clothing or when a leader in Alpha ordered raw materials, a few symbols on paper sufficed to initiate the production and delivery of the order. In most transactions with customers and suppliers there was little room for bargaining about prices or specifications; and since most commitments were of relatively short duration, there was little need for flexibility to change terms of an agreement.

Most customers of Beta, however, were not ordering standard products. They were frequently not expert enough fully to determine their own needs. They depended on leaders in Beta for technical advice, and they expected to bargain on terms of a bid or contract. For large projects, which sometimes lasted three or four years and which involved cooperation of Beta with customers, suppliers, and other contractors at the same time, details of Beta's role could not be planned completely in advance. Customers established direct contact with key men in Beta to facilitate adjustments in their demands as the project progressed.

The instability of relationships with customers and with suppliers at Beta also contributed to the greater pressures for direct personal interaction. Alpha had a steady group of potential customers, retailers and wholesalers, who restocked at least twice a year and who shopped regularly among different manufacturers to find styles that they could sell. Beta had a constant need to find new customers. Changing technology made new products and new markets available at a rapid rate, and purchasers of capital goods did not restock twice each year. Customers expected Beta in part to anticipate their needs and to suggest other transactions they might make.

In other respects, contacts with outsiders were likely to be more attractive to leaders in Beta than to those in Alpha. Such contacts were easier to make since much of Beta's work was done on customers' or on suppliers' premises. More frequently the Beta leaders who had contacts with customers or suppliers dealt with equals or superiors in education and social rank (transactions at Beta generally were more complex and involved larger commitments of resources). For leaders in Beta, too, there were fewer causes for tension and mistrust in relations with men from other firms. The industries with which Beta was affiliated were further than the clothing industry from a period of zero profits, empty prospects for new business, and intense competition. The clothing industry, in contrast, was split by threats of individual firms to abandon long-honored agreements on pricing and marketing practices. Finally, Beta had greater need for two resources, funds for foreign trade and space for expansion, that the government controlled. Personal contact with the groups that rationed these resources was essential for bargaining and persuasion.

5. *Routing of inputs.* Inputs from the task environment were routed less directly to the leaders they concerned in Alpha than they were to the leaders in Beta. Information from customers of Alpha, for example, did not come directly to the sales manager or to the production foremen. Salesmen relayed routine orders and inquiries about delivery to the sales manager or to the scheduling chief. They reported suggestions about styles to the president as often as to the fashion designer. The stylist received inputs that were more relevant to the sales personnel, and important information about consumer prefer-

ences came from the chief industrial engineer. The production supervisors, bound to tasks within the plant, had few contacts with outside groups.

At Beta, in contrast, almost all information about the market environment of any department was received or gathered either by the department head or by his subordinates. Little came through the president or through other departments. These department heads were more exposed to market inputs than the leaders in Alpha because much more of their work was done on customer's premises.

Suppliers to Alpha were conditioned by previous contacts with the firm to make first contacts with the president or with the office manager in most cases, but suppliers to Beta made more contacts with individual department leaders. Beta's multiple affiliations with competitors, unions, and branches of NAF and NIF also gave its subordinate leaders more exposure to external union and employer groups. At Alpha such contacts were usually made through the managing director.

6. *Complexity of inputs.* The order of skills required for transactions with the environment was less in Alpha than in Beta. The transactions in which Beta was involved were distinguished by their complexity in comparison with the ones in which Alpha was involved. First, the technological training and experience necessary to prepare a bid or to plan a purchase from suppliers was greater at Beta. Second, while operations in Alpha generally had a planning horizon of a few days to six months, it was not infrequent for Beta to become involved in activities with planning horizons of several years. Third, while Alpha had major problems of internal coordination of activities, the leaders there were able to deal rather independently with various external groups. The nature of Beta's relationships with external groups were such that Beta's leaders frequently could not deal with a customer, for example, without dealing at the same time with suppliers and with other groups involved in the same project. Fourth, while most of the external groups that Alpha dealt with directly were Norwegian, Beta had important direct connections with groups—particularly with suppliers—in other parts of Europe. Men in Beta had greater need for mastery of languages other than Norwegian.

Internal Constraints on Top Management

Not only did the two top-management groups confront the external task environments we have discussed above but they also were constrained by features of the organization which they led. These "internal" constraints may be regarded in one sense as part of the task environment of management, for in the short run they were outside management's control. The dimensions along which we find differences between Alpha and Beta in this area include:

1. *Stress of formal rules and procedures on autonomy in the management relationship.* An examination was made of job instructions, policy statements to employees, accounting routines, and rules for the preparation and signing of correspondence. In Alpha all these stressed the dependence of subordinate leaders on the president and on one another. In Beta they stressed autonomy as a major goal of top-management organization and specified fewer, weaker dependencies among members of top management.

2. *Departmental independence in routine work.* At Alpha nearly all members of top management (or their subordinates) were involved at some phase in each of the four major routine work programs. The programs required, for execution, close interdepartmental coordination in the parallel or sequential performance of tasks. At Beta most of the thirteen major work programs were executed by subordinates of a single top leader and usually subgroups of his subordinates handled individual programs semiautonomously. There were few instances where groups under two leaders were required to work in parallel effort or in sequence.

3. *Top-management involvement in routine activities.* More often in Alpha than in Beta top management was routinely involved as participants rather than as supervisors in major work programs. The president of Alpha, for example, made most purchasing decisions himself, and he and the sales manager set prices. At Beta the president had no direct role in routine activities, and no members of top management were involved regularly as participants in six of the thirteen major work programs. Even their supervisory roles in the six programs were quite limited.

4. *Competition for scarce resources.* Although at both firms there was frequent competition among work programs for such resources as labor, capital, and assistance from specialists in the firm, cases of simultaneous demand seldom involved as many departments or recurred as frequently in Beta as in Alpha.

5. *Barriers to management interaction.* There were fewer hindrances to interaction among members of top management at Alpha than at Beta. Communications were facilitated at Alpha since all but one member of top management and all but one small group of employees

worked in the same building. The leaders crossed paths often because the subordinates of each were scattered in many locations. Only three leaders had closed offices, and only the president had a secretary to screen visitors. A spacious lunchroom provided facilities for informal, private conferences. A loudspeaker system could be used to summon men who could not be reached by telephone.

Work groups at Beta were dispersed among four major and several minor locations. While all but one member of top management had offices in one building, major groups of subordinates to three of the five key men worked at locations five minutes to a half hour (of walking) away. All but one leader had a closed office, and there were no facilities for the men to meet regularly for lunch. The network of telephones was more extensive but less useful than the network at Alpha. Telephone contacts were difficult to make because the leaders spent a lot of time outside their offices and off the firm's premises.

6. *Number of employees under leaders.* Only two key men in Alpha had more men working under them than the median key man in Beta; and six of the ten in Alpha had fewer than thirteen, the lowest total for any key man in Beta.

7. *Barriers to identification with subordinates.* Differences in sex, education, and status in Alpha formed stronger barriers to close identification by key men with their subordinates. While all but one of the key "men" in Alpha were male, most subordinates were women. Beta employed few women, even in clerical jobs. Fewer subordinates in Alpha (36 per cent *vs.* 89 per cent) in the next lower echelons had more than an elementary or trade-school education. Of the next lower subordinates, too, the majority in Alpha were "workers" or "functionaries." The majority in Beta were themselves supervisors or specialists. None of the subordinates in Alpha were likely to be promoted into top management, but at Beta many were. All but one member of top management at Beta had among their subordinates (a) older men who functioned as close assistants and understudies or (b) younger men who were being trained as candidates for future openings in top management.

Interpretations of the Data

We have now summarized some differences between Alpha and Beta in the task environments of top management and in the degree of autonomy that members of top management displayed. What hypotheses do these findings suggest?

CONSIDERATIONS IN FORMULATING HYPOTHESES

Before hypotheses are offered, some of my major assumptions deserve review:

1. *Long-run* vs. *short-run phenomena.* The kind of theory we build depends greatly on the time span we deal with. In the short run, for example, behavior can be regarded as the outcome of the two "constants," personality and environment. Over a longer period personality and environment vary as functions of each other. Personality changes as men internalize attitudes and patterns of behavior that are consistent with their circumstances. In the case of organizations environment influences the "personality" of leaders by determining what kind of men stay with certain kinds of jobs. Shortly after my study one man in Alpha left its management because he lacked autonomy; in Beta, earlier, a middle-level manager was fired because of his failure to maintain effective relations with others in and outside the firm.

2. *Differential roles in organizations.* Hypotheses about the impact of environment on individual autonomy need to be framed with respect to role differences among individuals in their organizations. For example, in considering access to information as a factor in autonomy, we need to know not only how many members of management had access but also how those that had access could use the information.

3. *Indirectness of environmental impact.* There was little evidence from either firm that task environment *prescribed* the measure of autonomy observed in management behavior. Formal rules that governed management action appeared to prescribe; but in fact these were only effective where they reflected stable, informally derived patterns of behavior. In making demands on the firms the environment usually prescribed outcomes rather than the means by which outcomes were to be achieved.

It is more reasonable to assume that environmental factors constrained behavior by cueing management's attention to associations between current events and situations with which they had programs to deal, as well as by making some courses of action appear more attractive than others. It was probably true that management had more ways to achieve desired outcomes than they generally realized.

4. *Automaticity of response.* In both Alpha and Beta leaders seldom talked explicitly about how they would act, and their implicit choices of courses of action were made quickly. The uniformity of response to similar inputs suggests that management acted to a large extent on the basis of "programs" it had developed and adopted for dealing with different classes of inputs.[17]

A NEGATIVE FINDING: TASK IMPORTANCE,
TASK ROUTINENESS, AND AUTONOMY

A frequent hypothesis in the folklore of organization asserts that low autonomy is more likely the greater the importance of a task to the organization and the less its routineness—that unfamiliar tasks or tasks where "the stakes are high" are least likely to be handled by a single individual.[18]

Data from the "most important" task questionnaire[19] provide a crude test, since for each task they described respondents were asked to rate: (1) implications of the task for conservation of resources (as "pay-off," "cost," or "risk"); (2) the quantity of money associated with the task; (3) the number of groups in the firm perceived as having a stake in action on the task; (4) the length of time for which action on the task was likely to commit the firm; and (5) the similarity of the task to previous tasks.

Table 4 shows first, that members of management were frequently unable to estimate significant aspects of task "importance," and, second, that the reported behavior of individual leaders showed no significant links between importance or routineness and autonomy. Interview data confirm the finding that leaders had difficulty evaluating the consequences of tasks for their firms.

TABLE 4.
*Reported task characteristics vs. autonomy.**

Task characteristic	Percentage of tasks where respondent did not estimate the value of the task characteristic	Percentage of leaders whose behavior confirmed hypothesis (14 leaders)
Implication for resources of firm...............	38	14
Quantity of money involved...................	44	21
Number of people concerned with consequences..	0	36
Duration of commitments involved.............	20	36
Similarity to previous tasks....................	9	50

*Data from Alpha and Beta have been combined. Results in the two firms did not differ significantly.

For a particular characteristic certain values could be defined as indicating high or low importance (or routineness). With respect to any characteristic an individual leader's behavior was judged to confirm the hypothesis on this page if for tasks where he reported a value, the frequency with which he named others as initiators of action or as co-workers varied directly with estimates of task importance (or inversely with estimates of task routineness).

154

Examination of observation and interview data on a number of action sequences in the two firms crudely supports a hypothesis that the amount of autonomy in leaders' behavior was a function of four factors: (1) the ease of formulating independent task assignments for different work groups in the firm; (2) leaders' estimates of the probability that action on tasks would lead to unpleasant personal consequences by producing unwanted results for the organization or by producing conflict with other activities in the firm, especially in other work groups; (3) the exclusiveness of each leader's control over information about tasks or activities he was formally responsible for; and (4) leaders' estimates of the costs and gains associated with attempts to seek or to give advice.

These factors seem to account for behavior differences on similar tasks between the firms and on different tasks within the firms. Let us consider each factor briefly in relation to our observations about the task environments of management in Alpha and Beta.

1. *Ease of formulating independent tasks.* The descriptions of tasks that key men gave were more likely in Alpha than in Beta to imply the involvement of not just one work group but of many. Several characteristics of Alpha's task environment may have contributed to this difference. Because the environment of management at Alpha was less differentiated, more inputs were addressed to the firm as a whole. If they did not demand uniform action from different work groups, they frequently made it difficult to avoid coordinated action. A single customer's order might request simultaneous delivery of several products; a union complaint about incentive rates would require adjustments in all departments. Receiving inputs from common sources thus accented interdepartmental dependence and probably in the long run contributed to the development of programs of perceiving inputs that reinforced the interdependence.

At Beta a highly differentiated and heterogeneous task environment, whose elements seldom addressed themselves to the firm as a whole, reinforced tendencies of work groups to see their tasks as distinct from the tasks of other groups in the firm. The differences in language and other skills required by various groups for transactions with customers and suppliers also tended to obscure interrelationships among tasks.

At Beta, too, most environmental inputs were routed directly to the relevant key man or to one of his subordinates. There was less chance than at Alpha that the content of inputs would be distorted in transmission. At Alpha, for example, the production leaders had direct access to few parts of the environment. Most information they received came from the president, the sales manager, or the scheduling chief. The content of inputs was frequently distorted by the interpretations of the relayers.

2. *Estimates of undesirable consequences.* Within action sequences, autonomy seemed to decrease whenever environmental inputs were perceived as evidence of impending conflict or of impending personal failure if individuals acted alone. One can assume, for example, that the two presidents would be most likely to intervene where they saw a need to protect their investment or their reputation with outside groups, or that key men would seek advice from peers or superiors where they feared failure or interference from others in the firm.

We noted in our analysis of task environment that abrupt changes had occurred in Alpha's relation to customers and competitors and that most environmental feedback on Alpha's performance was negative. These changes meant that programs Alpha had used for many years no longer sufficed. A great deal of the management interaction I observed at Alpha was directed toward rebuilding sales and competitive position.

Similar conditions prevailed in two major work programs at Beta. These were the two on which the president was spending time; the others he left almost completely to subordinates. Although the environment of management at Beta was unstable, the key men had grown accustomed to the instability and could anticipate many of the changes that would occur. They had more evidence than men at Alpha of program success, less of program failure.

A second undesired consequence of action was conflict within the organization. The leaders at Alpha were confronted more frequently with situations that would lead them to expect their actions to interfere with the freedom of others to plan and act. Execution of customer orders or adjustments in labor practices, for example, raised more demands for parallel or sequential coordination of activities. Simultaneous claims on scarce resources were more frequent and more widespread. Attempts to develop new patterns of action and to meet changes in the task environment also gave rise to expectations of conflict. More than at Beta new policies or relationships with the environment suggested by one group interfered with the plans or commitments of others.

3. *Control over access to information.* Even where a key man expected conflict or feared failure, he was in a stronger position to act autonomously if he and his subordinates alone had access to inputs that indicated the results of his action. In general, the key man who had most exclusive access to environmental inputs that pertained to his work

groups and their activities was in the strongest position to avoid unsolicited advice.

Key men at Alpha had less exclusive access to information than key men at Beta. The indirect routing of inputs—and particularly the routing of all correspondence through the president—kept most leaders in Alpha well posted on matters of concern to departments other than their own. At Beta each key man and his subordinates had direct and exclusive access to large segments of their environments, and thus they could limit the flow of information to their peers or to the president. (I have already noted a higher incidence in Beta than in Alpha of subordinate initiation of action involving several leaders.)

Because the task environment of management at Alpha was relatively undifferentiated and homogeneous, we might expect the key men there to have less exclusive control of information. Since the men knew that others in management had, in the past, been exposed to similar sets of inputs, they would be more disposed to seek or to offer advice. In contrast, the heterogeneity and the instability of Beta's environment had probably prevented key men from developing ability to anticipate information that others had received.

Finally, there were environmental influences that led to more informal interaction among key men, and thus greater "leakage" of information, in Alpha than in Beta. By the nature of the firm's operations most key men in Alpha were under strong constraints to spend their working days on company premises. Their paths crossed often as each supervised his scattered work groups. Lunchtable groups usually included men who had only marginal responsibility for many of the topics the group discussed. Unplanned interaction, then, was quite frequent at Alpha. It was less frequent at Beta, where environmental pressures led members of management to spend large amounts of time away from company premises, where the on-premise work locations of key men were isolated from one another, and where adequate facilities did not exist for staging *ad hoc* conferences.

Over the long run, as we shall see in the next section, the high level of informal interaction in Alpha and the low level in Beta were probably self-perpetuating.

4. *Estimates of interaction cost.* Interaction among leaders was not all accidental; some was planned specifically for the handling of certain tasks. But in both firms, because task loads were high, the cost of meetings (in time consumed and in other jobs not done) was regarded as high. Leaders' estimates of the worth of interaction were higher at

Alpha than at Beta. This is the result of both short- and long-run environmental influences.

Interaction was probably more attractive at Alpha because of the perceived interdependence of tasks, because of the inevitable sharing of information, and because of the risks inherent in independent action. But it was also more attractive at Alpha because it was easier to arrange and because it yielded more satisfying results. Most leaders (excepting the sales manager and the president, who left the premises frequently) could be found for a conversation at nearly any time of day. Familiarity with a common environment enabled the men to talk a common language, and common access to recent inputs enabled them to begin deliberations without extensive briefing sessions. The relative simplicity and stability of the environments the men dealt with made it possible for them, even where their environments differed to become experts over time, in one another's work.

At Beta, leaders frequently could not contact one another at will. Where telephone conversations would not suffice, face-to-face meetings required at least one member of the group of leaders to come from a distant work location. Because the leaders did not have common access to one another's information flows, the discussion of many problems had to be preceded by periods of briefing. Incomplete knowledge of one another's work and the barriers to attainment of such knowledge combined to make fruitless many attempts at collaboration.

Over the years short-run decisions for or against interaction combined to strengthen interdependence in Alpha and autonomy in Beta. For by interacting frequently in Alpha, the leaders were doing a great deal to establish the common frame of reference and the type of organizational adjustments that would make continued interaction attractive. The leaders in Beta, in contrast, were not disregarding constraints against interaction often enough to develop the familiarity with one another's work that would make meetings seem worth while. At the time of the study an attempt was made at Beta to initiate two series of meetings among subgroups in middle management. Both groups served many customers in common, but they were accustomed to working independently. Neither attempt appeared likely to succeed, and there were complaints in both cases that the interaction was simply a waste of time.

Conclusion

An understanding of the factors which limit or facilitate autonomy in organizations has both scientific and practical significance. Upward autonomy is a key variable in the centralization-decentralization controversy.[20] More generally, autonomy has been linked to the success of executive training, to the efficiency of managerial control, to employees' feelings of frustration and conflict, to the costs of making decisions, to the flexibility of company response to new tasks, and to other important aspects of organizational performance.[21]

Such relationships have usually been stated as if they were applicable in many different organizational settings, and where they have not been so stated they have too frequently been so interpreted by organizational planners.[22] The investigation of environmental influences that are relevant to organizational planning is very important.

The essential argument of this paper has been threefold. First, the investigation of the impact of environmental factors on behavior in organizations is one of the most important tasks for organization theorists. Second, by conceptualizing the environment as a flow of information to participants in an organization (and as a body of accessible information), it is possible to make systematic and meaningful comparisons of the environments of different organizations. Finally, intensive field and laboratory observation of organizations in action are a necessary step to the fuller understanding of organizational processes. These observation studies (as well as interview studies and attempt at historical reconstruction of organizational action) should put explicit emphasis on the cognitive activities of organizational participants as a link between environmental "stimuli" and the participants' overt "responses."

Footnotes

1. This research was begun in Norway. Thanks are due to the Norwegian Fulbright Committee for financial aid and for permission to depart from the usual academic program and to the owners and employees of Alpha and Beta for cooperating on all phases of the study. Rolf Waaler, Harriet Gullvag, and Sverre Lysgaard generously took time from their own work to criticize plans for gathering data. Analysis of the data was carried out, in part, under a Ford Foundation grant to the Graduate School of Industrial Administration for research on decision making in organizations. During the analysis Melvin Anshen, Harold Guetzkow, Allen Newell, H. A. Simon and Donald Trow offered valuable criticisms and suggestions. A more detailed report of the study and of the findings is available in my thesis, "An Analysis of Task Environment and Personal Autonomy in Two Management Organizations" (Unpublished doctor's dissertation, Carnegie Institute of Technology, 1956).

2. Clear delineation of the boundaries of task environment requires more information than I gathered on the goals of management. C. J. Haberstroh proposes a scheme for the systematic mapping of organizational goal structures in "Processes of Internal Control in Firms" (Ph.D. thesis, University of Minnesota, 1958). He starts with the statements that executives make in research interviews, in conversations with co-workers, and in written documents. He codes separately each sentence or part of a sentence that identifies a goal or that identifies means-ends relationships. This analysis yields matrices of means-ends relationships

among goals, subgoals, and tasks. From these matrices a number of important dimensions of organizational goal structures can be identified.

3. *Task environment* may not seem to be a useful concept, since we can gain access to the environment only through our perceptions of it. In complex situations, however, it seems important to distinguish the environmental "demands" presented to a person from the person's interpretation of the demands and formulation of them into "tasks." The power of the distinction in laboratory experiments is shown in papers such as R. F. Bales, "The Equilibrium Problem in Small Groups," in T. Parsons, R. F. Bales and E. A. Shils (eds.), *Working Papers in the Theory of Action* (Glencoe, Ill., 1953), pp. 111-161; H. Guetzkow and H. A. Simon, The Impact of Certain Communication Nets upon Organization and Performance in Task-oriented Groups, *Management Science,* 1 (1955) 233-250; and H. Guetzkow and W. R. Dill, Factors in the Organizational Development of Task-oriented Groups, *Sociometry,* 20 (1957) 175-204.

4. For example, T. Burns, The Direction of Activity and Communications in a Departmental Executive Group, *Human Relations,* 7 (1954), 73-97; S. Carlson, Executive Behavior (Stockholm, 1950); C. L. Shartle, *Executive Performance and Leadership* (Englewood Cliffs, N. J., 1956).

5. Even in laboratory experiments the relationship of the experimenter's instructions to the tasks which subjects set for themselves may frequently not be as direct as the experimenter assumes them to be.

6. These sources included Norwegian newspapers and periodicals, regular and special publications of the Central Bureau of Statistics, and a variety of professional and partisan commentaries on the Norwegian economy and on Norwegian society.

7. The groups of "leading subordinates" do not include all employees who reported directly to the two presidents. Personal secretaries and a few special assistants are omitted.

8. The measures which have been starred (*), as here, yielded differences between the two groups that were larger than one could reasonably attribute to change variation. I have starred only differences (1) which I had an appropriate statistical test for, (2) which, when tested by a strong statistical criterion, proved significant at the 5 per cent level or better, and (3) which were not likely, on the basis of other information, to be overvalued by the statistical test.

9. To code interaction I broke the conversation into *units.* The main boundary between units was signaled by change of speaker, or rarely, within one man's speech, by major shifts of topic or addressee. For each unit I recorded the speaker, the apparent addressee, and the function of the unit in the discussion as apparently intended by the speaker. Six functions were distinguished: (1) giving information, (2) questioning, (3) offering suggestions, proposals, opinions, (4) stating decisions or rules of policy, (5) giving orders, requesting action, and (6) talking socially. Functions 1 and 2 were classed as "low influence" and 4 and 5 as "high influence." The conversation was episoded by topic discussed, and the nature of each topic was noted briefly. I coded seven mail-committee meetings in Alpha (560 units, 140 minutes of conversation) and three in Beta (368 units, 130 minutes), as well as one policy-committee meeting in Beta.

10. The one inconsistent finding in Table 1 is that the president at Alpha (in contrast to the manager at Beta) had a greater percentage of contributions to conversation in the low-influence categories of "giving information" or "asking questions." This is probably an artifact of the former's role as the man who summarized the contents of incoming mail to the group as he distributed it. At Beta this function was performed by clerks, who sorted the mail before the

meeting and prepared a summary list of its contents for circulation to members of top management later the same day.

11. A critical variable for this comparison, the average length of time spanned by each conversation unit, was not measured, but it was roughly comparable in the two firms.

12. The calculations omitted minor topics (1) which were discussed with only two committee members present and (2) for which the total number of units contributed by subordinate members was less than twice the number of subordinates present.

13. For data confirming the importance of getting information about people's activities soon after the activities have occurred, see T. Burns, *op. cit.*, and R. M. Stogdill and C. L. Shartle, *Methods in the Study of Administrative Leadership* (Columbus, Ohio, 1955), pp. 27-30.

14. The number of possible pairings for each firm is small relative to the number of men and to the number of responses because not all men filed responses for the same dates.

15. Were autonomy the main focus of this paper, we might explore more fully the relationship of upward to horizontal autonomy. Both types were lower in Alpha than in Beta. But there is evidence that this need not be the case—that under certain conditions low upward autonomy may lead to high horizontal autonomy. See C. Argyris, *Executive Leadership* (New York, 1953) pp. 62-86.

16. This is an example of inferences based on data gathered outside Alpha and Beta. The source here is Statistiske Sentralbyra, *Husholdningsregnskaper, oktober 1951-september 1952.* (N.O.S. XI. 128: Oslo, 1953) pp. 29-34, 40-44.

17. The concept of a "program" will be familiar to readers who have worked with electronic data-processing machines or who have read recent papers by H. A. Simon and Allen Newell that apply programming concepts to theories of problem solving. See, for example, The Logic Theory Machine, *Proceedings 1956 Joint Symposium on Information Theory*, Institute of Radio Engineers, Cambridge, Mass., Sept. 10-12, 1956.

18. This hypothesis is implicit, for example, in recent work that E. Jaques has done to compare the discretion men can exercise at different organizational levels. See his *Measurement of Responsibility* (London, 1956).

19. See p. 141 above.

20. See, for example, H. Baker and R. France, *Centralization and Decentralization in Industrial Relations* (Princeton, 1954); H. A. Simon *et al., Centralization vs. Decentralization in Organizing the Controller's Department* (New York, 1954); and P. Stryker, The Subtleties of Delegation, *Fortune*, 51 (March, 1955) 94-97.

21. The role of opportunity for autonomy as a motivational factor is discussed by C. Argyris, The Individual and Organization: Some Problems of Mutual Adjustment, *Administrative Science Quarterly*, 2 (June, 1957), 1-24. A more general review of the effects of opportunity for autonomy on employee motivation and on organizational performance is included in the forthcoming book by J. G. March and H. A. Simon, *Organizations*. In the latter work the generality of some hypotheses about autonomy under varying environmental conditions is considered.

22. H. A. Simon discusses the ambiguity of traditional propositions about centralization and decentralization, for example, in *Administrative Behavior* (New York, 1957) pp. 234-240.

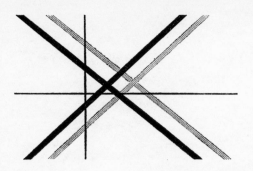

part V

RESEARCH FRONTIERS

"Present conceptions of the relevant variables allow only crude bases for differentiation. . . . The mere statement of administration in comparative terms focuses attention on these weaknesses of our present conceptual equipment." (p. 9).

The following chapters represent attempts to add to our conceptual schemes. Rather than reporting and analyzing the results of delimited empirical projects, they have a more speculative character. Here the attempt is to formulate some questions about administration in comparative terms, and then to reflect against those questions the research reports and theoretical discussions which have been made available by others.

One of the significant aspects of Chapter 11 is that Hammond starts outside the context of administration, finds an explanation for human behavior of a non-administrative sort, and then notes that the necessary conditions for that behavior also exist in administrative settings. By thus focusing attention on an aspect of administration which has been neglected, Chapter 11 illustrates the importance of interplay between administrative science and the broader aspects of the social sciences.

Frontiers have few landmarks, inadequate maps, no road signs. The test of the particular paths taken in the next three chapters will be whether they generate further research which adds significantly to knowledge of administration. Other promising paths will be discovered, but Part V demonstrates that there are research frontiers, that it is possible to begin exploring them, and that the comparative approach is a useful one for this purpose.

chapter 10

Technology, Organization, and Administration

James D. Thompson and Frederick L. Bates

Large-scale organizations have evolved to achieve goals which are
beyond the capacities of the individual or the small group. They make
possible the application of many and diverse skills and resources to
complex systems of producing goods and services. Large-scale organizations, therefore, are particularly adapted to complicated *technologies,*
that is, to those sets of man-machine activities which together produce a
desired good or service.[1]

As scientific knowledge has led to increasingly complicated technologies, large-scale organizations have multiplied; they have become
necessary in new fields, and they have changed their characteristics.
Medical care affords a striking illustration, for in this area the technology has been revolutionized within a generation. From reliance on
a few simple home remedies, passed from generation to generation, and
ultimate resource to a general practitioner with standard prescriptions
for standard symptoms, health-care practice in Western cultures has
moved to a much more specialized, more highly divided technology.
The diagnostic equipment and procedures used by the physician are
no longer simply constructed and exercised, and prescriptions are no
longer blended from a small list of basic powders and essences easily
stocked by any local pharmacist. The "simple" treatment of a virus
infection, for example, now relies on a whole series of large-scale
organizations which perform research, produce pharmaceuticals, and
ship, store, and prepare medications. Certain conditions which once
required confinement of the patient to the home with nursing by other
(amateur) members of the family now call for confinement in the hos-

pital, where a battery of technical specialists, nurses, and dietitians can contribute specialized skills toward therapy.

The list of examples is endless, illustrating the point that the elaboration of technology usually means that activities which formerly were considered single units of effort are dissected and split into multiple units of effort, each of them specialized and highly developed. With this "elongation" of the technology comes increasing complexity of the social organization designed to operate it.

In the following paragraphs we will explore some of the ways in which technology, as a variable, may impinge on organization and on administration. We will develop the general proposition that the type of technology available and suitable to particular types of goals sets limits on the types of structures appropriate for organizations and that the functional emphases, the problems of greatest concern, and the processes of administration will vary as a result. For this exploratory effort, we will focus on four types of organizations: the mining enterprise, the manufacturing organization, the hospital, and the university. While these clearly do not exhaust the major types of organizations, they have sufficiently different goals and technologies to serve as illuminating examples.[2] The discussion necessarily will be general; we are seeking central tendencies. Each class of organization displays variations. This is particularly true in the field of manufacturing, and to make the discussion manageable we will conceive of a factory mass-producing a single line of products widely distributed to consumers. Moreover, references to technology will be based on present technology.

We will compare these types of organizations with respect to three broad functional areas of administration: the setting of objectives, or policy formulation; the management of resources (including people, authority structure, money, and materials); and execution.[3]

Determination of Objectives

Whatever the motives of its members—accumulating wealth, achieving fame, exercising power, and so on—an enterprise must in the long run produce something useful or acceptable to others in order to merit support. The determination of what the enterprise will seek to produce we will refer to as the determination of objectives or goals or, alternatively, as policy formulation.

The manufacturing enterprise may have difficulty in determining what particular demands of what potential customers it will attempt to satisfy, and this is especially true in dynamic and highly competitive markets. Unless the product is extremely costly, however, or costs vary greatly with variations in volume, the manufacturing enterprise may test its decision through pilot operations. In any event the acceptance of the product is rather quickly and accurately reflected in sales figures or ultimately in profit figures, and reappraisal of decisions regarding objectives can therefore be rapid. If reappraisal leads to a redefinition of objectives, capital goods including machinery and raw materials can often be adapted to a new purpose or be sold, so that the manufacturing enterprise may be able to convert effectively from one objective to another; the technology may be relatively flexible. Finally, policy determination in the manufacturing enterprise is largely a matter for top administrators.

The mine is less flexible. It possesses highly specialized equipment and property rights which for the most part cannot be converted to other major objectives. The objectives of the mine may be adjusted to the extent that it may offer new sizes, grades, packaging, or delivery arrangements and hence may cater to a new market, but those responsible for the mining enterprise would find it difficult to get it out of mining and into a different industry—or even to shift from the mining of coal to the mining of a different mineral. The scope of alternative objectives thus appears to be less for those enterprises with heavy, specialized capital investments.

In both the university and the hospital the general or abstract purpose of the enterprise is relatively fixed. But in both cases there is wide latitude for interpretation of the general into more specific objectives. Because knowledge is so specialized the members of the university must decide what it will teach, and as new areas of knowledge develop or split off, they must decide anew. Here the product is intangible, and reappraisal of the policy decision is difficult and drawn out. Furthermore, because of the heterogeneity of university objectives and departments, top administrative officers can reappraise decisions only in gross or general terms; professional members specialized in the particular subject can claim greater qualification to judge. The university president is also highly dependent on that professional staff to interpret and implement a new educational policy. Hence, in a real sense, power to determine or veto objectives in the university is widely diffused.

The hospital, likewise, is highly dependent in the matter of objectives on the decisions of its professional medical members, who are the obvious authorities on health matters and who in the final analysis must implement the policy they believe in. Any shift in emphasis, for example, from treatment of the ill to maintenance of health can become effective only through the persuasion and conviction of professional members.

Thus in both the university and the hospital the general goal of the organization specifies an area of activity instead of a specific activity and therefore is subject to wide differences in specific interpretations. Since the technology employed by both types of organizations is relatively flexible as compared to that of the factory or the mine, goals may be revised or adjusted more easily to the technological resources available.

It appears, therefore, that the following variables are of particular importance as conditions affecting policy formulation:

(1) *Degree of concreteness of the goal*, as expressed in the product. This is a matter of tangibility and is verbally expressed by such questions as the precision with which the product can be described, the specificity with which it can be identified, and the extent to which it can be measured and evaluated.

(2) *Adaptability of the technology* associated with the goal. Here the question is the extent to which the appropriate machines, knowledge, skills, and raw materials can be used for other products.

While these definitions have not been operationalized, they seem to be adequate for our exploratory purposes, and we can advance the following hypotheses regarding these two variables and their relationships to policy formulation:

(1) If the product is concrete, such as mined material, and the technology unadaptable, the major concerns over policy will be the possibility that the environment may reject or dispense with the product. This is happening now in the case of the tuberculosis hospital, for example.

(2) If the product is concrete or tangible and the technology adaptable, the major concerns over policy will be when to shift to new products and which of the possible alternative uses of the technology present the most favorable opportunities. For example, should the watch manufacturer shift to cosmetic jewelry, to armament mechanisms, or to still another product calling for the machinery and skills at his disposal?

(3) If the product is abstract and the technology adaptable, the organization again has great adaptability to its environment, and the major policy-formulation problem will be achieving agreement on goals and on the appropriate application of technologies in pursuit of them. The modern university, for example, seems torn between emphasis on applied and on traditional studies; the National Foundation for Infantile

Paralysis is seeking new causes to support, having all but achieved its original purpose.

(4) If the product is abstract but the technology unadaptable, environmental redefinition of goals presents a serious threat to the organization, since the technology can be adapted to redefined goals only within limits. The administrative problem here is to "educate" or influence relevant parts of the environment to accept those products which are possible with existing technology. Political parties and fundamentalist churches seem to be facing this problem in modern America.

Management of Resources

Every enterprise has problems of acquiring and employing people, finances, materials, and authority. The difficulties of management are not necessarily equal in each of these four resource areas, however, and the amount of attention given to each probably varies from enterprise to enterprise as well as within one enterprise at different stages of its development. Likewise, the content of those activities which serve to manage any one resource varies, as the following paragraphs will illustrate.

MANAGEMENT OF MANPOWER

The factory and the mine, as enterprises operating on physical objectives, have relatively few problems of personnel selection below the management level, since the operational activities are either standardized or are settled by experience, and the training of operators is not overly difficult. There may be a high degree of functional differentiation in the factory, but this differentiation tends to be based on the machine rather than on the operator; operation of a complicated machine may be so simplified and repetitive that individuals are relatively interchangeable. Hierarchical distinctions tend to be shaded or gradual, with normal skill and experience qualifying the operator for advancement. Vacancies, therefore, can be filled from below. Since machinery is so important, a major personnel-management problem is to ensure safety in its operation.

Because many members of the general population are potentially qualified as members of the factory or the mine and because training to entrance-level standards is quick, expansion of activities may be undertaken on relatively short notice. Long-range forecasting of personnel needs may be an important factor in factory location, but "personnel-development" or training programs can be confined largely to preparation for future executive or supervisory positions. The large percentage of operative personnel, coupled with an open hierarchy, provides the factory enterprise with opportunity to screen members on the job and hence to locate future supervisory or executive talents. This is less likely in the mine, where the division between those working above and below ground is rather sharp, and mobility between these categories is low. In the mine, moreover, flexibility of daily operations is necessary because of the lack of control over the natural environment from which the material is taken. This front-line flexibility requires the exercise of judgment, and hence experience is a major basis for functional and hierarchical differentiation.

Both the hospital and the university must rely heavily on professionally trained people. In the case of the hospital, moreover, the situation is complicated by the fact that some of the key professionals are not employees of the hospital, in the sense of being on the payroll. They are not, therefore, recruited as employees. This is true also for many supporting activities which are performed by a voluntary "staff." Functional differentiation is extreme in both the hospital and the university, and the intensity of training required for each special area is so great that interchangeability is virtually unknown. There is sharp differentiation between student, clerical, and professional ranks in the university as well as little opportunity within a given university for a member to move from one level to another. Similar distinctions exist between patient, nurse, and doctor levels in the hospital. The length and cost of medical training mean that for practical purposes members cannot move from one category to a higher category; experience and seniority have nothing to do with a nurse's becoming a doctor.

The long periods of training required for professional competence in universities and hospitals mean that recruitment of professionals is not easy. On-the-job training may enhance the member's value within his specialty, but it is not a major means of obtaining replacements for vacancies in upper-level jobs. Moreover, while professional recognition or licensing presumably guarantees a minimum level of competence, there are many shades of ability above that minimum which are not easily judged until the individual member has already been established in the enterprise.

Thus in the modern factory and mine the technology relies largely on mechanical facilities supported by "know-how" which grows out of familiarity with the mechanical operation. But in the hospital and university, even complicated mechanical devices play second fiddle to professional expertise which is wrapped up in the human being and which grows out of long exposure to academic and abstract systems of thought.

These differences are reflected in recruitment, allocation, and training of personnel.

MANAGEMENT OF AUTHORITY STRUCTURE

In the factory, authority may be highly centralized or, conversely, the discretion of individual operators may be severely circumscribed, since activities are relatively routine and engineering standards such as quality controls can be used extensively. Particularly where various sub-assembly products feed into a final assembly line, central direction of the speed of operations and of the size, quality, or color mix is essential. The factory also has problems in maintaining a recognized position of authority for the supervisor, since experience tends to be a major basis for supervisory selection and the "boss" was formerly "one of us."

The mine, too, is predominantly staffed by "blue-collar" members, but the lack of standardization of the environment, together with distance and communication difficulties, requires a more decentralized day-to-day operation, with greater discretion lodged in the mine team and the supervisor. Constant danger, coupled with discomfort and darkness, makes members of the mining team somewhat reluctant to accept authoritative communications from executives above ground, and the mining enterprise probably would run into severe resistance if it attempted to set up and enforce rigid, disciplinary communications. Instead, authority or the exercise of discretion tends to be based on familiarity with the problem, and hence it is lodged in the most experienced member of the work team.

In the university, traditionally dominated by professional persons, authority on educational matters must be highly decentralized, since knowledge rather than title or seniority is recognized as the basis for authority—as reflected in "academic freedom"—and knowledge is highly specialized. Discretion in academic activities is controlled less by university executives than by professional peers of the faculty member. Student members of the university are more subject to centralized authority, but this is limited by a tradition that faculty members determine academic or educational policies, and anything which affects the student can be construed as an educational matter.

The authority structure of the modern hospital is an even more complicated matter. Since treatment of patients is not easily standardized, judgment must be exercised frequently by those with greatest knowledge of the case. The professional physician has the greatest knowledge about the ailment or disease, but on the other hand the nurse who is with the patient much more often may believe she has more knowledge of the patient. The social distance between physician and nurse is great, however, and the exercise of authority by the physician tends to be resented by the nurse (or vice versa) unless a strong informal organization bridges the two ranks. The bridging of this gap may be helped by the fact that both the nurse and the doctor know that the nurse cannot really threaten the doctor's position either in the hospital or in the larger community.

Thus it appears that in the mine and the factory, which rely heavily on mechanical aspects of the technology, authority is allocated primarily as control over the mechanical operation and takes the form of authority over people to the extent that behavior must be disciplined to the requirements of the mechanical operation. In the hospital and university, however, the heavy reliance on human (professional) abilities means that authority is exercised primarily with reference to people. Lacking the mechanical referent to bolster authoritative behavior, the university and hospital must depend to a much greater extent upon agreement or consensus, backed up by professional ethics and standards.

MATERIALS MANAGEMENT

The factory is concerned with acquiring and changing things, and there is emphasis, therefore, on moving inventory and on plant and machinery. Achieving volume and quality at low cost usually requires routinization of operations, and this in turn requires standardization of raw materials. Because a steady flow of standardized raw materials is so important to the factory and often constitutes a rather high portion of costs, purchasing, inventory, and transportation procedures attract a large amount of attention in day-to-day operations. The emphasis on precision scheduling and on predictability of production means that equipment failure may seriously cripple an entire operation, and preventive maintenance receives much time and thought. Control over use of materials can be approached in the factory through measurement of spoilage or waste. Since standardization is high, deviation can be measured readily. Hence responsibility for materials management can be widely diffused in the factory.

In the mining enterprise, rights to deposits replace plant as a major concern, and preventive maintenance and steps to control the sources of the mineral against flooding, cave-ins, and so on are particularly important. These can be standardized only in a rough way, and therefore judgment must be exercised frequently. Furthermore, maximum "winning" of material must be balanced against risk to personnel and to the remaining deposits. Machinery is cumbersome and difficult to move, hence effective placement is important. Purchasing is not the major matter in the mine that it is in the factory, but shipping is extremely important, since storage facilities can be depleted rapidly by the bulky product, and breakdown of transportation facilities can lead to shutdown of operations. Materials management in the mine is by and large a matter for supervisory and executive personnel rather than for operators.

Both the hospital and the university have important interests in plant, since both deal with people (who are "bulky") and both must provide space and facilities for a variety of human needs, including sleeping, eating, and recreation. Management frequently involves decisions as to the allocation of activities to various parts of the physical plant as shifts occur in technological procedures or in work loads.

Since in the university symbolic materials are major aids to the student and instructor, the collection, storage, and issuance of books requires constant attention. These materials, moreover, are far from standardized and are highly specialized, so that judgment regarding new materials must be exercised constantly and must be made frequently by the instructor concerned. Again, because symbolic materials are easily lost, stolen, or damaged, rigorous procedures must be established to maintain inventories.

The hospital has additional complications, since many of its expendable materials are highly specialized, easily confused, and perishable and since the hospital must be prepared for any of a variety of possible emergencies. Improper storage or errors in labeling medicines can be extremely costly, and the hospital often must rely on the health team to exercise care and discretion in these matters. Professional standards, reinforced by dread of being the cause of human suffering or loss of life, facilitate this decentralization of responsibility. Nevertheless the hospital provides a number of security routines, including the keeping of complete accounts of the disposal of certain materials and restriction on the identity of persons who can withdraw or use them.

MANAGEMENT OF MONEY

During periods of economic stability, at least, the manufacturing firm may be able to estimate its money needs rather accurately. Since its inventories and other assets are largely tangible, it can obtain needed money by frank exchange of the product for cash, by pledging assets as collateral, or by sale of an interest in the firm. Hence frequently the question of acquisition of money becomes one of seeking the most favorable terms, and large errors in such decisions can be detected relatively rapidly. During growth periods, however, investment matters may become more complicated, involving broader and less easily established alternatives and considerable risk. Expenditure of available money can be allocated within the manufacturing enterprise on the basis of expected return on yield and can be controlled by budgetary and accounting procedures, since standardization and predictability are relatively great. While neither allocation nor control are foolproof, such procedures are effective in the factory, and operating members can be held responsible for costs.

The mining enterprise can estimate its needs for money less precisely, since the cost of winning coal or ore is never perfectly known in advance, and disaster or geological fault may abruptly increase costs. Acquisition of money is again more difficult; reserves are less easily pledged as collateral than are the easily accessible inventories of the manufacturing firm. Allocation of available money may be budgeted on the basis of periodic estimates, but the technological requirements for flexibility may require frequent change of these programs. Formal control over the expenditure of money remains rather centralized, since the miner tends to be more safety conscious than cost conscious; and because mining operations call for judgment by the mining team, economic use of costly resources is not easily ensured.

For the university the determination of need is not difficult on the face of it, since enrollments and other costs can be fairly well forecast. But the intangibility of the product means that whether enough money has been raised is always a moot question. Acquisition, especially for the privately financed university, is a constant problem because those who most directly benefit from university activities usually are not able to pay the total costs for their training, and it is difficult to demonstrate graphically to potential contributors the indirect benefits they receive from the university's activities. Financial support rests largely on appeal, not trade.

Allocation of money is a time-consuming activity in the university. It cannot be accomplished by a few central officers because the various departments of a university are so specialized that there are few standards for evaluating the strength of their claims to scarce money. Control of expenditures through budgeting and accounting practices is relatively easy, although it tends to be accomplished only through administrative policing, since professional members of the university tend to place knowledge values above cost values.

Monetary needs of the hospital can be determined reasonably well; although work loads may vary widely from day to day or week to week, general trends can be predicted and irregularities averaged out. Acquisition of needed funds, however, presents another and more important problem, for the hospital in our culture is expected to render service on the basis of health needs rather than on ability to pay, and recovery of expenses often has been a drawn-out procedure. As far as operating costs are concerned, hospitalization insurance is relieving this problem, but capital funds still are difficult to acquire.[4] Allocation of funds may depend partly on budget procedures, but changes in work loads or new technological developments may require frequent revision. Control over the use of funds is accomplished largely by centralized handling of purchasing, but professional norms of service sometimes conflict with cost-reduction norms, and professional personnel tend to feel that cost drives interfere with their activities. Control over expenditure of items which eventually are translated into monetary terms is therefore somewhat difficult. Waste and spoilage are not easily checked.

Implications of Change for Resource Management

From the foregoing section, it appears that an important variable distinguishing various types of organizations is the extent to which the technology is lodged in human as contrasted with non-human resources. For the sake of simplicity we will refer to this variable as the *ratio of mechanization to professionalization.* Reflecting this variable against *the adaptability of the technology,* discussed earlier, it is possible to hypothesize the following:

(1) If the technology of an organization has a high ratio of mechanization and is readily adaptable, the major resource problem involved in a change of product is likely to center around properly standardized raw materials.

(2) If the technology of an organization has a high ratio of mechanization but is not adaptable, the problem will be to avoid technological obsolescence; major resource concerns will involve materials and money and the maintenance of fluidity by amassing financial reserves.

(3) If the technology has a low ratio of mechanization but the human abilities are easily refocused on new products, the major problems are likely to be those involved in execution, to be discussed below.

(4) If the technology has a low ratio of mechanization and at the same time is not easily adapted to other goals, personnel-management problems are likely to come to the fore, with emphasis on replacing and retraining members of the organization.

Execution

The problem of welding an enterprise into an integrated whole varies with the amount and kinds of differentiation of its parts and with the kinds of relationships which the technological process requires; that is, different kinds of heterogeneity call for different ways of homogenizing. The technology appropriate to a particular purpose not only determines in an important way the extent and type of differentiation but also determines the amount of coordination and cooperation required and the locus of responsibility for these.

The manufacturing enterprise, for example, may have major need for sequential interdependence, with each work team or section depending on others only for the timely and satisfactory completion of certain prior operations. Coordination required by this type of interdependence can be achieved largely by work scheduling and controls over the flow of materials and the quality of operations. In the factory, then, coordination between individual members of the work team may be the responsibility of an on-the-spot supervisor, but the linking together of various functional activities can be achieved largely by executives at relatively centralized points in the enterprise.

Mining involves separation or removal of minerals from their environment, and mining operations are therefore subject to unpredictable environmental changes—water seepage, geological faults, cave-ins, gas pockets, and so forth. Routinization is not easily achieved, and even with mechanized equipment environmental changes may make schedules inapplicable. The judgment of the miner is therefore indispensable, and the communication difficulties introduced by the above-ground and below-ground dichotomy increase the importance of the miner's reliability. Because day-to-day activities are somewhat unpredictable, relationships among members of the mining team can be specified only abstractly; specific relationships must be worked out on the spot, spatial requirements prevent close constant supervision, and coordination therefore is highly dependent on the informal organization.

Routinization of many aspects of hospital activity is essential, both to prevent dangerous omissions or oversights and to provide some predictability as the basis for carrying on when crises occur. On the other hand, each medical case is considered unique, and hence considerable flexibility (based on professional judgment) is required. To a much greater extent than in the factory, the hospital has need for collateral coordination, with the nurse, doctor, laboratory technician, dietitian, and so on integrating their activities simultaneously around the needs of the patient. In these cases central executives may act to facilitate coordination, but in the final analysis it must come largely through the cooperative efforts of operating individuals. Moreover, while there is ordinarily a certain rhythm in the amount and type of attention required during each twenty-four-hour period, the patient is an around-the-clock charge and requires periodic attention. Hence communication between shifts is vital, and there is considerable attention given to accurate posting of elaborate records. Nevertheless the specialized and complicated nature of medical technology means that records and charts cannot convey everything of importance, and informal organization of the therapy team is essential.

In the university routinization of a superficial sort is easily achieved. Hours of class meetings, systems of examinations and grading, and so forth usually are standardized. But in teaching matters routinization is not easily achieved because the imparting of knowledge remains a matter of judgment. The ability of the instructor to inspire and motivate the student cannot be centralized, and the integration of extracurricular activities can be centralized only partially. The instructor is free to maintain that he and only he can determine what his students should know and how they should proceed to acquire that knowledge about his special area of competence. Routinization tends, therefore, to be by discipline or topic rather than university-wide, and standardization is accomplished more by professional codes and standards than by administrative directive. Traditionally there is little interdependence between faculty members; although it is recognized that each deals with only "part" of the student, the integration of these part activities has been up to the student or is accomplished through informal interaction among faculty members and students. Faculty members typically are "not interested" in administrative matters except to escape interference by administrators, but the faculty may involve itself in many matters outside the classroom under the guise of "educational policy," since the development of the "whole" student is believed to result from his total experience in the university setting.

Under the more standardized conditions of the manufacturing firm, and to a lesser extent the mine, coordination can be planned and controlled relatively effectively from the center. In the less standardized, more professional fields, this is less likely to be the case—but at the same time more types of supporting activities usually are required. In the hospital and university these include feeding, housing, providing recreation, and providing opportunities for spiritual or religious expression, and so on.

177

Thus while responsibility for the integration of primary operations is relatively diffuse in professional-type enterprises, central executives tend to have a greater variety of activities and departments to integrate. Generally, it would seem, the greater the differentiation of an enterprise into identifiable parts, the greater is the need for fitting those parts together. Add to this the fact that human beings set themselves apart from one another on bases other than those officially arranged by administrators—on such bases as sex, age, ethnic origin, religion, style of living, political views, professional or union affiliations, and so on, and one perceives that the heterogeneity of the modern enterprise can be amazing.

Every criterion for differentiation of functions or hierarchy presents a possible or potential basis for cleavage and conflict—for the withholding of cooperation. Hence the more functional or hierarchical distinctions there are within the enterprise, the greater the problems of integration. Since systems low in mechanization of the technology and high in professionalization tend to be more clearly differentiated in this respect, it is in this kind of system that coordination problems are greatest.

Furthermore, it is in the enterprises where human differentiation is greatest that collateral types of coordination are most required, and hence interaction between people of various categories is the more intense. This interaction among people who are different or who have been led to believe they are different means that interpersonal frictions or tensions are to be expected. And yet it is in these same enterprises that interpersonal interaction must carry much of the burden for necessary coordination. In the hospital and the university, then, leadership in the form of emphasizing objectives and of stressing such factors as common devotion to a cause loom more important than they do in the manufacturing enterprise or the mine. And while resource management is important in the hospital and the university, the problems this presents are less demanding on the administrator than are those of executing.

The following hypotheses can now be advanced, based on the variable *ratio of mechanization* as it is related to the executing function of administration:

(1) If the technology has a high ratio of mechanization, executing problems are likely to be of an engineering nature since specialization is largely in the machine, the bases for human differentiation are small, and the human "zones of indifference" are great.

(2) If the technology has a low ratio of mechanization, however, the coordination and integration of human activities will be a major administrative concern. Members of the organization differentiate among themselves as specialists, a distinction leading to problems of

status and authority relationships. Any change in technology is likely to upset established relationships among members. Furthermore, if the goal is abstract, there is likely to be disagreement over the interpretation of the goal in terms of products; the human "zones of indifference" are small.[5]

Conclusions

The foregoing paragraphs have attempted to illustrate some of the differences that various goals—and appropriate technologies—can make for organization and administration. At one level of analysis, all large organizations have similar problems, but at a more detailed level of analysis, these problems become variables.

We have attempted to show that the following three variables are important enough to deserve extended research: (1) abstractness of the goal, as expressed in the product, (2) adaptability of the technology, and (3) ratio of mechanization to professionalization of the technology. We may perhaps underscore our argument that the general relationships between technology, organization, and administration provide important areas for study by advancing a final set of more general propositions:

(1) An organization overly identified with a particular technology may lose its opportunity to produce a particular product as more effective technologies are adopted by other organizations pursuing the same goal. This proposition simply applies the concept of "trained incapacity" to the organizational level rather than the personal level.[6]

(2) As a technology becomes more specialized, it appears that the organization's flexibility in shifting from one goal to another is curtailed. The corporation desiring to withdraw from a given industry, for example, no longer rearranges its resources once applied to that industry, but rather sells a division or subsidiary as a unit to another corporation.

(3) As a technology becomes more complicated, entry of a new organization into a field becomes more difficult. Entrance seems to occur usually in the case of (a) an existing organization with tremendous resources, shifting part of those into a new field, or (b) the formation of a new enterprise at a time when a new technology is appearing; by avoiding problems of relearning and reequipping itself, the new organization may be able to exploit a new technology more advantageously than an established organization.

(4) As a technology becomes elongated, any particular organization will tend to have less control over the total technological process, to be more dependent on other organizations for prior or subsequent opera-

179

tions in the total process (for resources and so on). This, again, tends to reduce flexibility in deciding goals and managing resources. The increased dependence on specialists, for example, means greater reliance on pretraining of personnel by organizations specializing in that training, such as universities and institutes.

(5) The organization adapting to new technology—as most are doing constantly—will be faced with "new" resource-management problems which established procedures and strategies will not always handle satisfactorily. Hence improvisation and constant learning will be characteristic of such organizations.

(6) Technological development, by requiring more specialization of personnel and equipment, adds to the heterogeneity of an organization. Related skills and knowledge formerly lodged in one person or one group are split. While such divisive developments undoubtedly allow for greater precision within an area of activity, they also intensify the need for, and concern over, integration of the several activities.

(7) Increasing technological complication is accompanied by the proliferation of professional and technical societies and associations, each with its unique values and code of ethics. Hence there is more likelihood for organizational members to owe loyalty or allegiance to a profession as well as to the organization, greater opportunity for the demands of the organization to conflict with those of the profession, and at the same time a greater opportunity for the individual employee to enforce demands on the organization by invoking sanctions from the profession.[7] Finally, the proliferation of specialization provides additional bases for organizational members to differentiate among themselves and hence for cleavage to develop.

Footnotes

1. We are thus using the term *technology* in its broad sense as a system of techniques. Similar usage is made by E. D. Chapple and C. S. Coon, who say: "Our present purpose is to show how different peoples combine their various techniques into total adjustments (to their environments), which we shall call technologies" (*Principles of Anthropology* [New York, 1942], p. 223).

2. A number of valuable studies throw light on these four kinds of organizations. While our gross examination here is highly simplified and is not necessarily an accurate reflection of any of these studies, we are indebted to the following: On mining: J. F. Scott and R. P. Linton, *Three Studies in Management* (London, 1952); A. W. Gouldner, *Patterns of Industrial Bureaucracy* (Glencoe, Illinois, 1954). On the factory: E. Jaques, *The Changing Culture of a Factory* (London, 1951); H. Ronken and P. R. Lawrence, *Administering Changes* (Boston, 1954); and Scott and Linton, cited above. On the hospital: A. H. Stanton and M. S. Schwartz, *The Mental Hospital* (New York, 1954); T. Burling, E. M. Lentz, and R. N. Wilson, *The Give and Take in Hospitals* (New York, 1956). On the univer-

sity: L. Wilson, *The Academic Man* (New York, 1942); F. Znaniecki, *The Social Role of the Man of Knowledge* (New York, 1940).

3. This framework is taken from E. H. Litchfield, Notes on a General Theory of Administration, *Administrative Science Quarterly*, 1 (1956), 3-29.

4. This is evidenced by the fact that fund-raising organizations have grown up to provide money-gathering services primarily for hospitals, churches, and colleges.

5. The concept "zone of indifference" was advanced by Chester I. Barnard, *The Functions of the Executive* (Cambridge, Mass., 1938), pp. 167 ff. See also Herbert A. Simon, *Administrative Behavior* (New York, 1945), pp. 11 ff. Simon prefers the term "zone of acceptance."

6. This is a restatement of Thorstein Veblen's concept. For a penetrating discussion of this and similar concepts at the personal level, see R. K. Merton, "Bureaucratic Structure and Personality," in his *Social Theory and Social Structure* (Glencoe, Illinois, 1949), pp. 151-160.

7. The organization may also resort to the reverse of this procedure.

An original article prepared especially for this volume.

chapter 11

The Functions of Indirection in Communication

Peter B. Hammond

Introduction

In the literature on administrative communication emphasis is on directness, clarity, and the maintenance of a "two-way" communication flow within the organizational hierarchy. The proper understanding of communication, however, depends upon an awareness of the distinction between what is ideal and what is real. Observation of actual organizational behavior indicates that much significant communication within an organization may, in fact, occur by indirect means.

The term *indirection* may be used to describe all forms of verbal expression and social interaction which achieve by circuitousness or evasion the minimization of the potential conflict inherent in most social relationships. However, it is used here to refer only to those forms which may be regarded as being employed purposefully. As such, it is a mode of communication and interaction which is negatively sanctioned in American culture and must be relied on covertly. When detected it is defined pejoratively as devious or "under-handed." As a departure from the idealized norm it is usually assumed by students of administration to be a matter for correction rather than analysis.

This essay, however, will approach indirection in communication on the assumption that it frequently is a necessary aspect of behavior in organizational contexts, and has positive psychological and sociological functions both for individuals and for the organizations of which they are a part. Following a discussion of some possible functions of indirection, several cases, taken from non-Western societies in which indirection is highly institutionalized, will be examined. As indirection

183

is explicitly recognized and elaborated in these societies it is readily observable. These examples will be used in an attempt to identify certain characteristics of social structure which may be correlated with reliance on indirection. It will then be suggested, with illustrations, that these same characteristics of social structure are to be found in American bureaucracy. Here also, it will be contended that indirection in communication frequently appears, despite its negative sanctioning.

Functions of Indirection

Social relationships frequently elicit ambivalent responses from their participants. Containing both positive and negative elements, they are likely to give their participants "mixed feelings," such as hostility and friendliness, toward one another. Such ambivalence may be characterized in a number of ways. If the positive and negative aspects are of approximately equal strength the ambivalence may be considered "sharp." If the relationship is important to the participants, the ambivalence may also be "intense."

Sharpness and intensity are not necessarily correlated, but when they coincide in a particular relationship, the relationship itself may be destroyed either by overt aggression or by complete withdrawal. To protect itself, the social system must provide alternative, more moderate, mechanisms for tension reduction and conflict resolution. Indirection in communication is such a mechanism.

Ethnographic studies are rich in examples of indirection.[1] Institutionalized *joking* and *avoidance* are two of its most characteristic forms. Among many non-Western peoples a joking relationship is found between two persons or two groups in which each is expected to tease or make fun of the other and neither is expected to take offense. Such a relationship frequently exists between in-laws who are required to behave cooperatively toward one another despite a conflict of interests. Joking relationships are often accompanied by avoidance relationships. These also exist between persons who stand to benefit by cooperation but would risk the expression of overt aggression if they were to interact face-to-face. Avoidance takes the place of joking when differences in age or status of the participants make joking inappropriate. In avoidance relationships the potential for overt aggression is minimized by mutual evasion of interpersonal contact; when circumstances bring such people together custom may either require that they ignore one another completely or limit communication to a rigidly prescribed exchange of polite salutations. All necessary communication between them is taken care of through an intermediary.

The functions of either form of indirection in such relationships, for (a) the reduction of tension through catharsis and (b) the evasion of tension through avoidance have been recognized. There are, however, two additional functions of indirection which have so far been largely ignored. They are (c) provision of a means of maintaining communication and (d) preservation of the positive elements of the relationship.

Among anthropologists, only Radcliffe-Brown approached explicit recognition of the function of indirection to preserve the positive aspects of a relationship when he described joking as a method of reifying an ambivalent relationship containing both "conjunctive" and "disjunctive" elements.[2] But his acknowledgment of the cathartic function of joking is brief and he ignores the fact that it provides a means of communicating the cause of displeasure without the listener taking offense, thus providing him with an opportunity to rectify his disturbing behavior in order that the relationship be preserved.

Indirection in Three Cultures

In order to substantiate these further propositions on the multiple functions of indirection in communication, examples of three differing forms of indirection will be taken from three differing cultures: intertribal joking (*ubutani*) between the Nyakyusa and the Hehe;[3] circuitousness in the system of tax assessment among the Fons;[4] and the verbal communication aspect of the mother-in-law avoidance relationship among the Mossi.[5]

INTERTRIBAL JOKING IN TANGANYIKA

Institutionalized joking accompanied by mock physical aggression is an important characteristic of communication between the Nyakyusa and the Hehe of Tanganyika. Formerly the two tribes were enemies. Now, under British rule, they are frequently required to work together in peace. The balance between the historical tradition of hostility and the present mutually recognized necessity to cooperate with one another is maintained in part by institutionalized joking. Custom prescribes that neither group take offense at the insults of the other.[6] Wilson states this is readily observable among workers. Moreau describes this joking as follows: "The joking itself is usually referred to by the Africans under two heads: *tukana* (curse, abuse, revile, insult, call bad names) and *danganya* (elude, delude, deceive, defraud, cheat, beguile, impose upon, belie). . . . So as far as I can gather the joking may be done in public with no restriction of place or time."[7]

The negative aspects of the relationship between workers—tensions resulting from traditional enmity—may be reduced through the catharsis of aggressive joking. If the aggression results from a specific annoyance its cause may be communicated and the behavior causing it rectified. Thus the positive aspect of the relationship—cooperation—may be preserved.

CIRCUITOUSNESS IN TAX ASSESSMENTS IN DAHOMEY

The Fons of Dahomey rely on a different form of verbal indirection in dealing with the problem of tax assessments. The development of overt conflict between the representative of the Dahomean king and the citizenry was always a potential whenever revenues were to be levied. No man was asked directly what he possessed in material goods, the extent of his harvests, or how many individuals comprised his household.

Herskovits writes that ". . . Dahomean kings eschewed the method of direct enquiry . . . according to native logic, a tax based on information derived from direct questioning about the number of palm trees, or sheep, or goats a man possessed, or the number of hoes he manufactured, or the number of animals a hunter killed, or the loads a porter carried, would naively ignore the motive for falsification . . ."[8] By an intricate system of devious enquiry the king's emissaries determined the real economic status of every citizen before the levy was imposed. No sources of revenue were overlooked.[9]

Here indirection in communication functioned not to reduce conflict by catharsis, but to minimize it by evasion. By avoidance the positive elements of the relationship between king and commoner were preserved and the peace of the social context was maintained.

MOTHER-IN-LAW AVOIDANCE IN UPPER VOLTA

In the institutionalized avoidance characteristic of the mother-in-law relationship found among the Mossi of the Voltaic Republic the possibility of conflict is reduced by the evasion of face-to-face interaction. When contact cannot be avoided communication is limited to the formalized exchange of polite salutations.

A man regards his mother-in-law as his most valuable ally in his relationship with both his wife and his wife's kinsmen. If he remains on good terms with her, she can be relied on to support him both in disputes with his other in-laws and with his wife herself. Yet there exists in the relationship a strong potential for conflict: over marriage presents, for example, or over his wife's economic or sexual responsibilities. To preserve these valuable aspects of the relationship the possibility of the overt expression of aggression must be minimized. This they accomplish by confining their verbal interaction to formal greetings. If they meet, they must kneel ceremoniously, face past each other and, with eyes averted, recite a series of rigidly prescribed salutations. Each then rises and departs. This avoidance is paralleled by a joking relationship with the wife's younger siblings which permits the inoffensive expression of hostile feelings which might otherwise be repressed. If a man needs his mother-in-law's assistance, or wants to ask her advice, he sends a friend to convey the request for him. She, in turn, will send a messenger with her reply.

Here again, reliance on indirection in communication is seen to minimize the possibility of conflict, the negative aspect of the relationship, by avoidance. Its positive aspect is preserved by the maintenance of indirect contact and communication.

Structural Correlates of Indirection

Having thus briefly indicated what the functions of indirection in communication may be, an effort can now be made to correlate reliance on indirection with certain structural characteristics common to the three social contexts described. Despite the differing cultural contexts from which those examples were drawn, the social structures in each case were characterized by (1) "functional diffuseness," and (2) "particularistic criteria."

A *functionally diffuse* relationship may be described as one in which peoples' rights and obligations to one another are diverse, covering several types of situations, and vaguely defined. For example, in some cultures, including our own, the relationship between husband and wife is typically diffuse, including responsibility for providing satisfactions for diverse social, economic, and emotional needs.

The phrase *particularistic criteria* implies that each party to the relationship behaves in certain ways because of *who* the other party is, not merely because of what he does. In our society, for example, the traffic policeman is expected to treat all violators alike, regardless of who they are. If he gives tickets to whites but not to Negroes, to men but not to women, or to Republicans but not to Democrats, he is employing particularistic criteria.[10]

187

In each of the cases of indirection cited earlier, the social context was characterized to some degree by both these characteristics, functional diffuseness and particularistic criteria.

The work relationship of the Hehe and Nyakyusa is diffused, requiring cooperation in many aspects of job performance, and the maintenance of peace in the social and recreational facilities they are required to share. Both their rivalry and their cooperation are particularistically determined; their traditional enmity by their tribal affiliation, and cooperation by the requirements of a job for which there are few alternatives.

Among the Fons the social, political, and religious interdependence between king and commoner is diffused. It involves a multiplicity of mutually advantageous reciprocal rights and obligations so interrelated that many would suffer from an open manifestation of conflict. The relationship is particularistically determined by a class system from which they cannot escape.

With the Mossi the relationship between a man and his mother-in-law is diffused. It links both kin groups in a beneficial relationship of social and economic cooperation. The relationship is particularistic, being determined by kinship affiliation.

In each instance reliance on one form or another of indirection in communication was correlated with a structural context characterized by the complexity, or functional diffuseness of relationships which were also governed by "particularistic" criteria. Thus it appears that in a diffuse relationship, both the participants and their associates are involved in a multiplicity of vaguely defined rights and obligations. Dissatisfaction with a specific aspect of the relationship does not negate the continuing satisfactions to be derived from its other aspects. The relationship is valuable to the associates of the participants as well. It is not desirable that a specific grievance should be permitted to cause a complete rupture of the relationship, hence both overt aggression and complete withdrawal must be avoided and an alternative means of tension reduction provided. Indirection in communication frequently provides this means.

When functional diffuseness is combined with particularistic criteria, reliance on indirection becomes still more useful. Particularism implies the relative absence of social alternatives, which makes withdrawal and overt aggression even more dysfunctional as mechanisms for tension reduction, and increases still further the usefulness of indirection as a means of tension reduction *within* the context of a relationship for which it would be difficult to find an alternative.

Indirection in American Bureaucracy

Bureaucracy usually is considered a prime example of a social system employing universalistic rather than particularistic criteria, and relying on functional specificity rather than diffuseness. Clients are supposed to be treated universalistically and members are to be recruited that way. Favoritism, nepotism, and discrimination violate the spirit of bureaucracy. Job positions are highly specialized, and jurisdiction and authority are delimited to the specific area of specialization.

There is an important distinction to be made, however, between bureaucracy as it relates to the larger society and bureaucracy as its members are related to one another. The bureaucracy may *recruit* members according to universalistic criteria, but this does not prevent reliance on particularistic criteria between members, once they are admitted.

Official job descriptions may be very specific in terms of *production* processes. But bureaucracies are more complex than that. They require their members to act on *organizational* problems as well as production matters. Thus job descriptions and position classifications frequently do not reflect the many-faceted interdependence of organizational members.

In the following paragraphs the presence of diffuseness and particularism will be illustrated in two well-known types of bureaucratic relationships, where reliance on indirection in communication also appears.[11]

THE SUPERIOR-SUBORDINATE RELATIONSHIP

The superior-subordinate relationship found in any hierarchical organization tends to be functionally diffuse and to be governed by particularistic criteria, in spite of organizational doctrine to the contrary. The superior is a source of production decisions and directives, while the subordinate is a source of production, and, often, of production information. But in addition, the superior usually is a source of organization rewards. Often the subordinate is a source of psychological rewards. Many additional roles may be incorporated into the relationship, such as that of teacher-pupil, friend, or ally in conflicts with other parts of the organization.

The relationship is also likely to be governed in part by particularistic criteria. Persons frequently find their superiors or subordinates assigned to them. Consequently they must behave officially toward one another in terms of their respective assigned status, not on the basis of personal choice or preference.

189

Diffuseness and particularism are reinforced in the superior-subordinate relationship by power and status differentials. Subordinates, especially, are inhibited from directly expressing aggressive responses to frustrating aspects of the job situation. Because of differences in status, aggressive joking, which, among equals, might serve both as a cathartic and as a means of communicating causes of tension cannot be relied upon. Nor is avoidance a solution, for their ascribed roles within the work situation may force them into contact with one another. Formalized politeness or the equally formalized "informality," typical of the American organizational myth of equality, may be relied on to evade the overt expression of aggression. But evasion of aggression alone does not serve to reduce tension.

Just as with the Mossi, where institutionalized avoidance was accompanied by joking relationships with *other* individuals within the social system, joking or grumbling among peers may have a cathartic function. But this alone does not serve to communicate the cause of grievance to the superior so that it may be rectified. Thus the conditions causing the initial tension are likely to persist.

A study of executive staff meetings in two Air Force Wings is illustrative of the function of indirection in the superior-subordinate relationship.[12] In the low production Wing, the Commander personally presented his production plan to the group. Fearful of criticizing their superior in his presence, the men refrained from raising objections until after the meetings, and their potentially useful suggestions were lost. In the high production Wing, the Commander called on a subordinate to present the production plan. He then called on others for suggestions, which often resulted in modifications of what *then* became the Commander's plan. The result was a more efficient utilization of the critical faculties of the men in the Wing. The resultant reduction of tension through the expression of dissatisfaction contributed to the maintenance of the positive, cooperative, aspects of the superior-subordinate relationship between the Commander and his men.

In the Wing where reliance on indirection in communication was facilitated, conflict could be reduced satisfactorily. In the Wing in which no provision was made for indirection, and where withdrawal was not a realistic alternative, the tension appeared to result in persistent dissatisfaction and lower efficiency.

THE STAFF-LINE RELATIONSHIP

The relationship of "line" and "staff," equally characteristic of American bureaucracy, affords another example of relations which are both functionally diffuse and particularistic. The problems of mediating the conflicting interests and aspirations of line and staff persist as an administrative dilemma.

The term "line" is used here in its general sense to refer to those organizational positions which hold ultimate responsibility for production or output of an organization's manifest product or service. In this often-quoted version the line organization is said to hold exclusive authority over production processes. The term "staff" then refers to those organizational positions which are provided to advise, consult, trouble-shoot, and generally serve the line. The staff organization in this version is described as having research and advisory roles. This is illustrated in a study of three factories by Melville Dalton.[13] The official expectation that advice given out of specialized expertise would automatically be incorporated into the commands made by line officials was complicated by the fact that the relationships were, in reality, more diffused, involving many-faceted interdependence. For example, to justify their existence, staff members felt compelled to fight the "line" for acceptance of their contributions. At the same time, staff promotion to higher staff offices was dependent on line approval, a condition which staff members assumed was dependent on maintaining friendly relations with those in line positions.

Staff-line relationships also are particularistic. Jones is assigned as staff officer to Brown; within the organization Jones may not select his clients freely nor can Brown freely select his advisors on a daily basis.[14] Since alternate relationships cannot easily be found, the potential for overt expression of conflict must be minimized *within* the relationship. Thus, the line-staff relationship appears to contain those structural characteristics of functional diffuseness and particularism which seem conducive to reliance on indirect communication.

THE COMBINATION OF STAFF-LINE AND SUPERIOR-SUBORDINATE RELATIONSHIPS

The fact that staff-line relationships are usually found in a context of superior-subordinate relationships adds to organizational complexity and contributes still further to the importance of indirection in communication as a means of reducing tension and maintaining communication. Dalton reports cultivation of line officers by staff as a means of getting the line officers to make favorable reports or pass on favorable images of staff officers to their staff superiors.[15]

Direct reporting of success by a staff officer to his superior might be discounted and he would risk being labelled a braggart. However, when a third party outside staff channels reports a staff success, it may be given greater credence. The converse of this may also occur. A line officer may communicate indirectly with his superior through a person holding a staff relationship to the superior. The importance of knowing a "third party" who has access to one's superior is frequently noted by participants in bureaucracies.[16]

But despite the positive functions of such a means of communication, indirection is negatively sanctioned in our culture. The individual making use of it must be adroit in order to avoid the accusation of deviousness.

Conclusion

This paper was intended to open an area for research, not to produce final conclusions, and certainly not to provide prescriptions for action.

Although indirection in communication has been observed in a variety of both non-Western and Western, or "tribal" and bureaucratic, settings its psychological and sociological functions have so far been inadequately examined.

Joking, avoidance, and reliance on intermediaries are only some of the forms which indirection may take. Further documentation is necessary in order to enlarge the gamut of all possible forms of this behavior. Very little is known of the way indirection is learned in a society like our own which places negative sanctions on anything but the most open and direct approach to communication.

If further evidence supports the hypothesis that functional diffuseness and particularism are the primary structural characteristics eliciting indirection, the range of relationships having those characteristics remains to be identified. It is doubtful, for example, that line-staff and superior-subordinate relationships are the only bureaucratic relationships possessing them. This analysis has purposefully taken as examples highly idealized models of the relationships described. As the realities of these and similar relationships are better understood, it may be possible to elaborate both a more orderly and a more subtle typology.

It has been contended that indirection in communication will not be adequately understood so long as it is explained in terms of cultural tradition alone, or considered simply as a deviation from "proper" behavior and a matter for correction. Wherever indirection in communication is found it should be examined in terms of its psychological and sociological functions for both individuals and the social systems in which they participate. Finally, it is contended that indirection may have ceased to be a behavioral phenomenon pertinent only to the work of the anthropologist, and that it may be time to recognize it as a significant aspect of contemporary bureaucratic behavior worthy of further research.

Summary

Indirection in communication was described as a means of minimizing potential conflict in complex relationships, by (1) reduction of tension through catharsis; (2) evasion of tension through avoidance; (3) communication of the cause of tension, thereby permitting its removal, and (4) preservation of the positive elements of the relationship.

Indirection was first examined in the context of three non-Western social systems, where it was both highly elaborated and socially approved. In each instance reliance on indirection was correlated with relationships which (1) contained a diversified set of rights and obligations, and (2) behavior which was determined by *who* the participants were as well as what they did.

It was then suggested that American bureaucracies regularly establish relationships having these characteristics. This suggestion was illustrated by line-staff and superior-subordinate relationships. In these relationships, also, reliance on several varieties of indirection in communication was noted.

Footnotes

1. A. R. Radcliffe-Brown, "On Joking Relationships," *Africa*, 13, (1940), 95-210; A. R. Radcliffe-Brown, "A Further Note on Joking Relationships," *Africa*, 19, (1949), 133-140; D. F. Thompson, "The Joking Relationships and Organized Obscenity in Northwest Queensland," *American Anthropologist*, 37, (1935), 460-490; A. I. Richards, "Reciprocal Clan Relationships Among the Bemba of Northern Rhodesia," *Man*, 47, (1927), 222; Denise Paulme, "Parenté à Plaisanteries et Alliance par le Sang en Afrique Occidentale," *Africa*, 14, (1943), 386-400; J. F. Pedler, "Joking Relationships in East Africa," *Africa*, 13, (1940), 170; F. Eggan (ed.), *Social Anthropology of North American Indian Tribes*, Chicago: University of Chicago Press, 1937, pp. 75-81; H. Labouret, "La Parenté à Plaisanteries en Afrique Occidentale," *Africa*, 2, (1929), 244; H. Junod, *The Life of a South African Tribe* (Vol. 1), London: MacMillan Book Co., 1928.

2. Radcliffe-Brown, *op cit.*, 1940, p. 197.

3. M. Wilson, "Joking Relationships in Central Africa," *Man*, 57, (1957), 111-112; and R. E. Moreau, "Joking Relationships in Tanganyika," *Africa*, 14, (1943), 386-400.

4. M. J. Herskovits, *Dahomey, An Ancient West African Kingdom*, (2 Vols.) New York: J. J. Augustin, 1938.

5. Data derived from writer's unpublished field materials on the Mossi of the Yatenga in the Voltaic Republic.

6. Wilson, *op. cit.*, p. 112.

7. Moreau, *op. cit.*, p. 391.

8. Herskovits, *op. cit.*, Vol. 2, p. 74.

9. Herskovits, *op. cit.*, Vol. 1, pp. 107-134. A parallel use of indirection in acquiring information, but in quite different contexts, has been suggested under the term "sounding out." See James D. Thompson and William J. McEwen, "Organizational Goals and Environment," *American Sociological Review*, 23, (February, 1958) 30-31.

10. Most recently this term has been used in relation to the problem of membership *recruitment*. However, as it is being used here, it refers to any kind of social relationship in which the quality of interaction is affected by who the persons are. For further discussion of these terms see Talcott Parsons, "The Professions and Social Structure," in *Essays in Sociological Theory, Pure and Applied,* Glencoe, Ill.; The Free Press, 1950, pp. 185-199; and Marion J. Levy, "Some Sources of the Vulnerability of the Structures of Relatively Non-Industrialized Societies to Those of Highly Industrialized Societies," in *The Progress of Underdeveloped Areas,* Bert Hoselitz, (ed.) Chicago: University of Chicago Press, 1952, pp. 113-125.

11. Studies of the functions of indirection within the bureaucratic context have been both rare and brief. See, for example, P. Brodney, "The Joking Relationship in Industry," *Human Relations,* 10 (1957), 179-87; and L. Despres, "A Function of Bilateral Kinship Patterns in New England Industry," *Human Organization,* 17, (1958), 15-22.

12. James D. Thompson, *The Organization of Executive Action,* Chapel Hill, North Carolina: Institute for Research in Social Science, University of North Carolina, 1953 (mimeographed).

13. Melville Dalton, "Conflicts Between Staff and Line Managerial Officers," *American Sociological Review*, 15, (June, 1950), 342-351.

14. That the universalistic criteria of impersonality was not a realistic one in this situation is suggested by another comment by Dalton who concluded that full and frank communication was impeded by a fear of veiled personal reprisal, which he attributed to "a disbelief in the possibility of bureaucratic impersonality," Dalton, *op. cit.*, p. 351.

15. *Op. cit.*, p. 350.

16. Some functional aspects of alternative or competing channels of communication in bureaucracies has recently been noted in another context by Andrew Gunder Frank. See his "Goal Ambiguity and Conflicting Standards: An Approach to the Study of Organization," *Human Organization,* 17, (1958-59), 8-13.

An original article prepared especially for this volume.

chapter 12

Strategies, Structures, and Processes of
Organizational Decision

James D. Thompson and Arthur Tuden

Despite the apparent importance of decision-making for theories of administration and the considerable attention recently devoted to the topic, present models and knowledge of decision-making have generated few hypotheses about administration, and they have not been adequately linked with organizational models.

A major deficiency of most decision models has been that they are economically logical models seeking to describe maximization processes. These *econo-logical* models have utility as criteria against which to reflect behavior, but they have contributed little toward the explanation or prediction of behavior.

Simon has achieved a major break-through with his "satisficing" model.[1] This is much more than the mere substitution of one word or one concept for another, for Simon's model is a *psycho-logical* model designed to describe and predict behavior. Its full significance seems not yet to be widely recognized.

This psychological model of decision-making is essentially one dealing with individual human beings. It applies equally to purposive choices of a personal or an organizational nature. Its generalizability is, however, both a source of power and of limitation, for it does not deal explicitly with the particular phenomena which surround the making of decisions in organizational contexts.

As a companion to the psychological model, therefore, we wish to develop *sociological* models. We believe they will point to important decision-making behavior which has been observed in organizations

195

but which is neither described nor predicted by econological or psychological models.

We will attempt to show (1) that there are several types of decisions to be made in and on behalf of collective enterprises, (2) that each type of decision calls for a different strategy or approach, (3) that there are several varieties of organizational structures which facilitate these several strategies, and (4) that the resulting behavior defines variations in decision processes. It has been our purpose to construct models which are neither culture-bound nor discipline-bound, containing no evaluative or normative elements.

Working Definitions

"Choice" from among alternatives seems to be the end-point of decision-making, but the term "decision" will not be confined simply to ultimate choice. Rather, "decision" will refer to those activities which contribute to choice, including recognizing or delimiting and evaluating alternatives as well as the final selection. Thus an individual may have responsibility for making a final choice on behalf of an organization, but if others help him delimit or evaluate alternatives we will not describe that individual as *the* decider.[2]

The term "decision" in this paper should also be understood to refer to organizational decisions. Personal decisions, i.e., choices presumed by an individual to have consequences only for himself, are excluded.[3] Likewise, unconscious choices or habits are not within the scope of this paper.

The term "decision unit" will be used to refer to that individual or group within an organization which has power, responsibility, or authority to choose, on a particular issue, for the organization. To illustrate, in American jurisprudence, "the court" may be the appropriate organization, but the power to decide certain issues is assigned to a single presiding judge as the decision unit; other issues are assigned to a jury as the decision unit; still others are assigned to a panel of justices as the decision unit.

Types of Decision Issues

The notion of differing types of issues calling for decisions is not new. More than a decade ago Simon distinguished ethical from factual decisions[4] but no one seems to have extended his analysis. More recently there has been considerable discussion of decision-making under the differential conditions of certainty, risk, and uncertainty.[5] Dorwin Cartwright has suggested distinguishing among judgment, preference-ranking, and "actual decision-making" (which he defines as commitment to action).[6] There have, however, been few attempts to build typologies of issues or decisions.

A typology of issues will enable the sorting out of (a) those aspects of decision situations which *confront* decision units from (b) those actions which decision units may take in such situations.

The main elements of decision—found both in the econological and psychological models available—seem to be three: (1) alternative courses of action, (2) differential consequences of the several alternatives (means), and (3) evaluation of the potential outcomes on some scale of desirability (ends).[7]

We will work with two of those three variables, dropping "alternative courses of action," since by definition a unit called upon to decide is aware of at least one pair of alternatives. Before working with the remaining two variables, however, we wish to redefine them slightly in order to achieve greater generalizability.

The notion of "consequences of alternative courses of action" assumes only a concern with present and future, not with past actions. Yet it seems reasonable, for example, to conceive of the trial jury as a decision unit which works backward from one present fact, e.g., a corpus delicti, to choose one of several possible past actions which may account for the present fact. This sequence may also characterize certain decisions in scientific research and in audits or inspections. The notion of *causation*, as applied to several alternatives, seems to us to subsume both questions of present and future states and questions of past actions which may explain present states.

We would also like to avoid some of the possible implications of such terms as desirability scale, which is inanimate, and to substitute for them some term with more explicit behavioral overtones. For this purpose we will speak of *preferences about outcomes*. In conceiving of our major variables as *causation* and *preferences*, we have gained a certain flexibility without losing the value of previous work on economic models. The means-ends approach falls within our scheme, but we have the added advantage of being able to include other approaches too.

Since we are dealing with organizations—social systems—it cannot be taken for granted that causation will be "known" as soon as a decision issue appears, nor can it be assumed that the organization is certain of its preferences regarding the several alternatives apparent. Often the organization's decision unit cannot simply choose, but must act to determine what its knowledge or beliefs are regarding cause-

197

and-effect relationships, and what its preferences are about the postulated effects.

Now, if the two variables *causation* and *preferences* are reflected against the additional question of whether there is *agreement or consensus within the decision unit* about those two matters, it is possible to construct a four-fold typology of decision issues.

	PREFERENCES ABOUT POSSIBLE OUTCOMES	
	AGREEMENT	DISAGREEMENT
BELIEFS ABOUT CAUSATION AGREEMENT	COMPUTATION	COMPROMISE
DISAGREEMENT	JUDGMENT	INSPIRATION

The labels in the four cells—computation, judgment, compromise, and inspiration—are descriptive of four *strategies* which we believe are appropriate for the four types of decision issues. In the following section we will elaborate on those strategies, and connect them with certain types of social structures. For the time being we will deal only with "pure" cases.

Pure Strategies and Structures

Decision by Computation. Where there is agreement regarding both causation and preference, i.e., where a preference hierarchy is understood and where knowledge is available or believed to be available, decision-making is a technical or mechanical matter. In its extreme form, this situation requires no genuine choice, since the problem-solution appears as common sense.[8]

But in many instances, the appropriate techniques for equating cause-effect knowledge with known preferences are quite complicated. The data may be so voluminous for example, that only an electronic calculator can make sense of them. Likewise, the particular sequences of action involved in the techniques may be hard to master and difficult to carry out, so that only the highly trained specialist can arrive at an appropriate choice. In either event, the strategy for decision is straightforward analysis, and we term this decision by computation.

A Structure for Computation. Assuming for the moment complete freedom to build an organization which will face *only* computation issues, and that our guiding norms are economy of effort and efficiency of performance, what kind of organization shall we build?

This will be an organization of specialists, one for each kind of computation problem we can anticipate, and we want to introduce four constraints or rules to: (1) prohibit our specialists from making decisions in issues lying outside their spheres of expert competence, (2) bind each specialist to the organization's preference scale, (3) route all pertinent information to each specialist, and (4) route every issue to the appropriate specialist.

The organization which we have just built contains the heart of what Max Weber described as the "pure type" of bureaucracy. This bureaucratic model is clearly expressed in the "formal" or "official" structure of the great majority of business firms, governmental agencies, and military units. For each of these, presumably, preferences can be stated with some clarity. Members are appointed to positions only so long as they embrace those preferences. Moreover, bureaucracy is formulated on the assumption that rules or procedures can be established for classes of cases or problems, and that the events which will call for organizational decisions are repetitive or serial events for which expert competence can be developed.[9] Candidates for these positions are expected to hold licenses or degrees indicating successful completion of training for the specialized positions, or to pass tests.

It is in these organizations that the concept and practice of "delegation" seems most widespread, and that decision units officially are comprised of single individuals. Expert specialization means that the organization can enjoy the economy of assigning problems to individuals or their electronic counterparts.

Decision by Majority Judgment. Where causation is uncertain or disputed, although preferences are clearly known and shared, decision-making takes on new difficulties. Lacking in acceptable "proof" of the merits of alternatives, the organization must rely on judgment.[10] Triangulation illustrates this simply and clearly. Each member of the three-man team is presumed competent by virtue of his training and his equipment to make a judgment, but because none has indisputable and complete evidence, none is permitted to make the decision alone, and no member may outvote or override the judgment made by other members. But triangulation is a special case of the more general problem—special because each judge focuses on the same empirical phenomenon from his own special vantage point. More frequent, perhaps, is the case where there is not only differential perception but also differential interpretation, and this is most clearly illustrated by the voting situation in which the collective judgment determines the decision. We will refer to this strategy of organizational decision as one of majority judgment.

A Structure for Majority Judgment. What kind of organization shall we build as an ideal one to handle only judgmental problems? This is to be an organization of wise and knowing men, operating according to constraints or rules which: (1) require fidelity to the group's preference hierarchy, (2) require all members to participate in each decision, (3) route pertinent information about causation to each member, (4) give each member equal influence over the final choice, and (5) designate as ultimate choice that alternative favored by the largest group of judges—the majority.

What we have just described may be labelled, for lack of a better term, a *collegium.* This concept has been used in ecclesiastical literature to refer to a self-governing voluntary group, with authority vested in the members.[11] Whatever this type of organization is labelled, the social science literature does not seem to contain formal models of it, as it does for bureaucracy.

Nevertheless, this type of organization is described in case studies of "voluntary associations" and in the constitutions and by-laws of many organizations, including many American universities and trade unions. All of these not only take steps to "get out the vote," but incorporate into their by-laws provisions requiring a quorum for the transaction of official business. Direct elections of governmental officials approximate the collegial situation, with each literate citizen-of-age presumed to have equal competence and influence at the polls.

Governing boards of directors or trustees are also established on the collegial principal, with the requirement of a quorum in order for judgments to be binding.[12]

Decision by Compromise. On occasion there may be agreement by all parties as to the expected consequences or causes of available alternatives, but lack of consensus over preferences toward such "facts." Neither computation nor collective judgment is "appropriate" for this type of issue, for the blunt fact is that if one preference is satisfied, another is denied. An organization facing this situation may fall apart through schism, civil war, or disinterest, unless some common item or point can be found on the several extant preference scales. It can be illustrated by imagining an organization composed of two factions. For faction A, the preference scale runs 1, 2, and 3, while for faction B, the scale is 4, 5, and 6. In this case, in order for either faction to obtain at least an acceptable solution the other must be denied all satisfaction, and this presages the end of the organization. If the preference scales run 1, 2, and 3, in that order, and 3, 4, and 5, both factions can attain a modicum of satisfaction by choosing 3. The appropriate strategy where causation is conceded but preferences are in dispute thus appears to be one which will arrive at the common preference. We will refer to this strategy as decision by compromise.

A *Structure for Compromise.* Now the task is to construct an ideal organization to handle compromise types of issues economically and efficiently.

Whereas computation problems call for the smallest possible decision unit, and collective judgment for the widest possible participation, compromise seems to require a decision unit of intermediate size. What we want is a structure to facilitate bargaining, and since this involves detailed and subtle exploration of the several factional preference scales, the decision unit must be small enough to permit sustained and often delicate interchange. On the other hand, there is the requirement that all factions—or certainly all important factions—be involved in the decision. This leads, we think, to the *representative body* as the appropriate structure.

For this purpose, we will build rules or constraints into our organization to: (1) require that each faction hold as its *top* priority preference the desire to reach agreement, i.e., to continue the association, (2) ensure that each faction be represented in the decision unit, (3) give each faction veto power, and (4) give each faction all pertinent, available information about causation.

The United Nations Security Council approximates this type of decision unit, if we assume that the member nations represent all important blocs. Federations often provide the representative structure for boards of directors. The American Congress appears to fit this pattern, with the "veto" requirement relaxed because of the size of the body. It is possible to conceive of the Congress as an arena for bargaining and compromise, rather than judgment, with the vote considered merely a mechanical device for measuring at any point in time the current state of negotiations.[13]

The representative decision unit, operating toward compromise, is also seen, though less formally, in many loosely organized societies in the form of "consensus decision-making" by councils of tribal chiefs or elders.[14] In these instances power is relatively diffused, so that a "veto" of an alternative by any one member of the decision unit prevents the choice of that alternative. While not necessarily elected, members of the decision unit have to maintain followings and thus may be considered representatives. This is clearly brought out in the studies cited.

The American trial jury for capital cases can also be seen as an attempt to ensure bargaining or weighing of the evidence against the conflicting preferences of freeing the innocent and punishing the guilty. The jury situation differs from many other compromise situations in that each member of the unit is presumed to be an advocate of *both* of the competing values (rather than an advocate of one factional position) who "bargains with himself." The requirement of unanimity for the jury seeks to remove the decision from the area of majority judgment to one of arriving at a choice endorsable by all members of the decision unit.

Decision by Inspiration. The fourth and in our typology the final type of issue is one in which there is disagreement both as to causation and as to preferences. This is, of course, a most dangerous situation for any group to be in; certainly by definition and probably in fact the group in this situation is nearing disintegration. While this situation seems to be far removed from the usual discussions of decision-making, we believe it has empirical as well as theoretical relevance.

The most likely action in this situation, we suspect, is the decision not to face the issue. Organizations which appear to be slow to sieze opportunities or to respond to environmental events may, on close inspection, be organizations which contain disagreement as to both preferences and causation. To the extent that the organization in this predicament can avoid an issue, it may at least maintain itself as an organization. If it is forced to choose, however, the organization is likely to dissolve—unless some innovation can be introduced.

Anthropologists have recorded on numerous occasions institutionalized means of gaining inspiration by referring "insoluable" problems to supernatural forces, and it is no secret that responsible public officials in "less superstious" nations call on Divine Guidance when they must make momentous decisions for which there is no precedent and the consequences are highly uncertain. A related device is for the group to rely on a *charismatic* leader.

As Weber pointed out,[15] the charismatic leader is thought by his followers to have solutions or at least the wisdom to find them. Frequently he offers a new set of ideals or preferences which rally unity out of diversity, by shifting attention. Pointing to a real or fancied threat from outside is one ancient device for this.

The 1958 election of deGaulle and adoption of the new French communante seems to reflect the charismatic or inspirational type of situation.[16] But it also seems possible for individuals in nominal positions of leadership to attain and articulate enough imagination to create a new vision or image and thereby pull together a disintegrating organization. This seems consistent with the conclusion of Karl Deutsch and his colleagues as to the importance of innovation and invention in bringing about political integration.[17] Whatever the particular form of leadership exercised, we believe that decisions of this type—where there has been dissensus about both causation and preferences—are *decisions by inspiration.*

A Structure for Inspiration. It is difficult to conceive of an ideal structure for decision by inspiration, for the thinking of the social scientist is oriented toward pattern and organization, while the situation we face here is one of randomness and disorganization. If these situations occur it probably is seldom by design. Nevertheless, an attempt to deliberately construct such a situation might be instructive for the student of organization.

What we are trying to build now has been labelled by Durkheim as a state of *anomie,* normlessness, or deregulation.[18] As a rough approximation, anomie occurs when former goals or values have lost their meaning or significance or when such goals appear unobtainable with the means available. Thus, our problem is to create a situation of chaos, but to do so with an aggregation of persons who in some sense can be considered to constitute a group or collectivity. We will therefore call for the following constraints: (1) the individuals or groups must be interdependent and thus have some incentive for collective problem-solving,[19] (2) there must be a multiplicity of preference scales and therefore of factions, with each faction of approximately equal strength, (3) more information must be introduced than can be processed, and it must be routed through multiple communication channels,[20] and (4) each member must have access to the major communication networks, in case inspiration strikes.

While it is doubtful if empirical cases of organizational anomie are deliberately created, there seems to be evidence that the more carefully structured organizations do sometimes find themselves in a state of anomie. The routed military organization, for example, is characterized by de-emphasis of military values and an abundance of rumors, contradictory information, and loss of contact or faith in nominal leaders.

Anomie and inspiration probably appear in less stark form in formal organizations, for the most part. Befuddled administrators of organizations caught up in forces which are not understood may and sometimes do rely on decision by inspiration in one of two forms: (a) imitation of more prestigeful and successful organizations, or (b) importation of prestigeful and authoritative management consultants to tell them what they should want and how to go after it.

In each of these illustrations the effect is to convert the *anomic* situation into something resembling a computational situation, and to rely upon a decision unit composed of one individual, as in the case of bureaucracy. The basis for designating the "expert" differs, of course. But the production of a new vision, image, or belief, is basically a creative kind of activity and it is doubtful if either voting or bargaining structures are likely to produce it.

Designation of Decision Units. Our argument to this point, regarding types of pure issues, pure strategies, and pure structures, can be diagrammed thus:

		PREFERENCES ABOUT POSSIBLE OUTCOMES	
		AGREEMENT	NON-AGREEMENT
BELIEFS ABOUT CAUSATION	AGREEMENT	COMPUTATION IN BUREAUCRATIC STRUCTURE	BARGAINING IN REPRESENTATIVE STRUCTURE
	NON-AGREEMENT	MAJORITY JUDGMENT IN COLLEGIAL STRUCTURE	INSPIRATION IN "ANOMIC STRUCTURE"

Note what this suggests about differences in composition of decision units. For a computation issue, the "ideal" decision unit consists of an individual, acting on behalf of the entire organization. For the voting type of issue, the decision unit is made up of the entire membership. In the compromise situation, a group of representatives or delegates constitute the ideal decision unit. In the inspiration situation, the individual again becomes the most appropriate decision unit.

This typology has some distinct parallels to the work of March, Simon and Guetzkow who discuss four major processes: (1) problem-solving, (2) persuasion, (3) bargaining, and (4) "politics." These four processes are treated, however, simply as processes whereby organizations resolve conflict, which seems to us to be only one aspect of organizational decision phenomena. Moreover, they quickly collapse the four process categories into two: analytic and bargaining.[21]

It seems ironic that the only discipline whose focus has traditionally spanned all four types of situations has been the least productive of decision models.[22] Political science typically has dealt with three branches of government—executive (or bureaucratic); legislative (or bargaining); and judiciary (or collegial). Its interest in statesmen, great men, and leaders seems to cover the fourth (anomic or inspirational) situation.

Mixed Situations

There are a variety of reasons why the purity of our illustrations may be relatively infrequent.[23] A major proposition of this essay is that usually an organization adopts one of the four strategies—computation, collective judgment, compromise, or inspiration—as its dominant strategy, and bases its structure on that strategy.

To the extent that this is true, we can expect or predict several kinds of organizational difficulties which will be presented to administrators when the organization faces issues or problems which do not fit the formal neatness of our pure types.[24] We can also expect difficulties if the appropriate constraints are not present within the particular decision unit. Finally, we can predict that problems will arise if an issue calling for one strategy is presented to a decision unit built to exercise a different kind of strategy.

CONFUSION OF ISSUES

The difficulties of means-ends distinctions are as real for operating organizations as for scientific observers. Psychological time perspectives have much to do with whether a particular issue is seen as one of means or ends. Despite the fact that social systems of various kinds generally are expected by members to persist through time, their members may attach different valences to varying periods of the future. The holder of the short-run viewpoint may see an issue as one of preferences, while the long-run adherent sees the issue as one of causation.

In a dynamic and complex organization, moreover, the range of possible outcomes widens rapidly as the time-span is extended.[25] If this is true, then members of an organization probably are less inclined to grant the competence of experts for long-run decisions, even when they would grant the ability of the same experts for short-run matters.

Thus different members of an organization or of its decision unit may respond to the same stimulus in varying ways, some seeing it as a matter for computation, others as a judgment matter, and still others as requiring bargaining.

ABSENCE OF STRUCTURAL CONSTRAINTS

One constraint common to all of the pure structures described earlier, except for the case where the decision unit is an individual, was that each judge, each bargainer, each faction, had equal power to influence the choice. While this usually is a formal specification for such units as trial juries, legislatures, or boards, we know that such units in fact exhibit inequality of membership. Strodtbeck, for example, reports that sex and social status affect the amount of participation of jury members in the decision process, the perceptions that fellow jurors have of their competence as jurors, and the degree to which they influence the outcome.[26] Such factors as party loyalty and party discipline, seniority, political skills, and the endorsement of pressure groups may affect the legislator's ability to make his voice heard as loudly as the next one. Within bureaucracies there are well-known inequalities between offices and divisions which formally are equal, and such scholars as Dalton have documented some of the reasons why computational experts may temper their computations with other considerations.[27]

Another constraint common to all but the anomic structure was that each participant in the decision unit have access to all available, pertinent information about causation. In fact, despite all of the attention given to communication in modern organizations, the condition called for by this constraint is at best approximated but seldom achieved. Colleagues of the expert in a bureaucracy, then, may grant the competence and good intentions of an official, but refuse to honor his decision on grounds that he did not know the local or "real" situation. Well informed minorities may control the collegial body whose other members are ill-informed, and "private information" obtained by one faction may make a mockery of the compromise situation.

This listing is intended to be illustrative rather than exhaustive. Relaxation of other constraints, peculiar to particular structures, will be discussed below.

INAPPROPRIATE DECISION UNITS

If organizations were completely pliable, it would be a relatively simple thing to assign each problem to a decision unit designed especially for it. But, of course, organizations would cease to be organizations if they were completely pliable. Regularity, pattern and structure are inescapable.

Presumably the basic structures which prescribe the standing or regular decision units of organizations are established because they are expected to be appropriate for the *typical* problems those organizations will face. In some organizations, at least, precedent and tradition lead members to expect that *all* decisions will be made by the decision units and processes established for typical decisions. This undoubtedly will vary with the history of the organization and with the social and cultural attitudes surrounding it. In our own society and decade, it is not unusual to hear officials of bureaucracies complain that committee participation (on judgment problems) interferes with their work—by which they seem to mean expert computation in their own offices. On the other hand, we frequently hear university faculty members, conditioned to expect collegial decisions, complain when department heads or deans make purely computational decisions.[28] There are also situations, particularly in certain types of military units, when members are dismayed if leaders so much as ask their opinions. For some in the military organization, the commander must be an expert and every issue must be a computational one.

Thus the attitudes and expectations of members may make it difficult for organizations to create *ad hoc* or alternative decision units to deal with problems for which basic, traditional structures are ill-suited.

Another important source of structural rigidity is the shifting nature of human knowledge. Types of problems which at one time are identified by members of a group as appropriate for judgment may at another time be defined as computational problems, as the group changes its beliefs about cause-and-effect relations. We will have more to say about an opposite trend below, but the dominant "scientific" trend on the American scene in recent years has been to remove more and more items from the sphere of opinion to demonstrable "certainty."

Thus problems which once called for voting or inspirational strategies have become problems for computation or bargaining, and traditional structures are threatened. The city manager movement threatens both the party organization and the council by redefining certain types of problems as no longer subject to bargaining or voting but as appropriate for expert computation. The increasing scope of required expertise forces the American Congress to establish bureacratic agencies to make decisions which once were prerogatives of the legislature—and Congress then becomes jealous of its own creations.

EXPANSION TENDENCIES IN DECISION ISSUES

Decision issues appear to be broader, more complex, and more time-consuming as we move from computation issues to voting to bargaining issues. There is reason to believe that, left to their own devices, members of social systems tend to expand decision issues. In a revealing summary of community issues and the course of their disposition, Coleman[29] notes a tendency for transformation of issues from specific to general, and from disagreement to antagonism. Bales also notes in small problem-solving groups, that interpersonal tensions mount as the decision process moves from orientation to evaluation to control.[30]

As knowledge becomes increasingly pluralistic, in the sense that new specialized logics are developed, the bureaucracy encompasses not one but several sets of beliefs about appropriate means to organizational ends. Thus the competence of the single expert becomes doubted and members define issues as calling for judgment rather than computation. If, for example, the expert can be forced to admit that his is but a professional opinion—a tactic in jury trials—the way is cleared to insist that others be consulted and a balance of judgments obtained. This has also been a common practice in communities where public health experts have decided to introduce fluoride into the public water supply.[31]

It is clear that in the past several decades, American corporations have shown a proliferation of specialized staff agencies, each with its own logic for maximizing a particular function or procedure. As the beliefs about causation have thus become increasingly pluralistic, there has been a plea for the development of "generalists," but also there seems to have been a corresponding increase in the use of decision units appropriate to judgmental issues.[32] Committees, conferences, staff meetings, and "clearance" procedures have not only proliferated but have been dignified on wall charts—at least to the extent of dotted lines.

With problems which appear to call for judgment, the heat of debate can lead proponents of the several alternatives to overstate their cases and discount missing information; often it also leads them to refer to more general but extraneous organization preferences as a means of finding moral justification for the selection of the alternative they endorse. When this occurs, the issue is no longer one of judgment regarding causation, but becomes one of dispute over (relevant) ends and thus subject to compromise.

The issue which seems a natural for bargaining may verge on the anomic, since it frequently generates difficulties in the identification and exploration of causation. Inherently emphasizing preference conflict, the bargaining structure leads its members to discount causation theories endorsed by opponents and to overemphasize their own. This hampers the effort to get the "facts" and where preferences already are at issue, disputes over facts create anomic situations. Moreover, if one faction is adamant or unwilling to "bargain fairly," there is a tendency for the other faction or factions to seek to expand the issue into a larger, more general category, and to threaten the adamant faction with trouble on unrelated matters. This too, tends toward anomie.

Administration and Decision-Making

We can now offer the general proposition that an important role for administration is to *manage* the decision *process*, as distinct from *making the decision*. We are not suggesting that administrators do one to the exclusion of the other, but if issues are not automatically crystallized, the ideal structural constraints are not automatically present, or appropriate decision units are not automatically selected, it may fall to administrators to take action which will facilitate decisions.

The following discussion is not offered as exhaustive, but as illustrative of the potential utility of considering administrative roles with respect to the decision process. [33]

Where a time dimension is not clearly implied by the nature of the issue, one role of administration is to delineate by fiction or otherwise, such a time dimension. This facilitates the sorting out of means from ends, by the decision unit, and thus tends to contain the issue from expanding into a more complex one.

When there are many alternatives available, a role of administration is to provide machinery for elimination of all but a few. This can be particularly important when an issue is assigned to a voting unit, which seems to be able to operate effectively only on binary problems. At one level of generality this is an important role for Congressional committees. [34] At a more general level of analysis this is the function of political parties in the two party system; the necessary compromises of platform and candidates are achieved before the issue is put to the electorate. By way of contrast, in multi-party France the function of compromising a plurality of interests devolved on the legislature more than on intraparty processes, and was an important factor in the lack of effectiveness of the Fourth Republic. [35]

In the bargaining situation the important role of administration may be to obtain initial mutual commitment to reaching agreement, and to maintain this commitment as taking priority over factional preferences. This approach may guard the issue from expanding into one of anomie, for as Dubin points out, mutual commitment to the necessity for reaching agreement in effect moves the issue in the direction of judgment and voting. [36] One method of handling the bargaining issue, and seemingly an indispensable one when the preference scales do not contain common items, is to place the particular issue in a larger context. This can be done by "horse-trading," thus assuring the losing faction on the present issue of priority treatment on a future issue. [37]

Another role of administration which seems to be important under certain conditions is that of crystalling consensus about preferences. Ambiguity in a decision situation may result in lack of knowledge, on the part of members of a decision unit, of the similarities of their preferences. When this is the case, an administrator who can sense the agreement and articulate it may play a vital part in organizational decision. In this connection it appears that timing may be as important as sensitivity to cues. Keesing and Keesing, observing formal group deliberation in Samoa, note that a senior elite person may choose to speak early if he wants to give guidance to the discussion *or knows that prior informal consultations have made clear a unanimous stand,* but that usually he will let others carry the active roles, making his pronouncements after the debate has pretty well run its course.[38]

A final suggestion regarding possible roles of administrators in facilitating organizational decision-making concerns the extremely complicated kinds of issues that frequently face administrators of "loose" organizations. We have in mind such social systems as the community (as viewed by a mayor, council, or manager); the school district (as viewed by the superintendent or board), or the bloc of nations (as viewed by their diplomats and officials). We refer to these as "loose" organizations because only a portion of the relevant "members" are directly subject to the hierarchy of authority. In the legal sense, that is, some of the groups are not "members," although in the behavioral sense they are.[39]

When such organizations face important and complicated issues, we believe, it may become necessary for administrators to redefine the issue into a series of issues, each assigned to an appropriate decision unit. It may also be that there are patterns in the sequence in which the series is handled. For example, in order to achieve a "community decision" on a fluoridation or school bond issue, it may be necessary to *first* get agreement and commitment of the powerful elements on preferences. This might be done "informally" in the smokefilled room, by compromise, and it might include the important choice as to whether to tackle the issue at all. After that decision is made, the *second* step might be to frame a judgmental issue for presentation to an electorate. Finally, within the limits of the majority decision, specialists can be presented with such issues as the proper equipment for fluoridation or the most appropriate timing for bond issues.

We feel rather safe in predicting that there is a cumulative effect in this sequence. Weakness in the first step probably forecasts trouble in succeeding steps, and so on.

It seems apparent that in terms of time and effort, issues increase in "cost" in the same order in which they increase in breadth; computation is the quickest and simplest and involves the fewest members; judgment by voting membership is slower and diverts the energies of many; and bargaining usually is a drawn out energy-consuming process.

Organizations operate in environmental contexts and hence cannot always take a leisurely approach in making decisions. The actions of competitors or of potential collaborators and clientele frequently place time deadlines on issues. Moreover, the interrelatedness of the parts of large organizations may mean that delay at one point suspends activities at others, and when costs must be reckoned closely this fact exerts serious pressures to have issues settled promptly.[40]

Thus if an issue can be defined in more than one way, responsible officials may be tempted to define it in an easier, faster and less frustrating way, i.e., as calling for computation rather than judgment, or as appropriate for voting rather than bargaining.[41] In some cases the pressures of time, or habit, may lead administrators to force issues into molds which are patently inappropriate.

TIMING OF CHOICE AND CONSENSUS

Except in situations where force can be brought to bear on members, it appears that consensus or acceptance of both means and ends is necessary for effective organizational action.

The four types of issues posited above are successively "broader" in the sense that they incorporate into the issue itself the necessity of finding or building consensus. It is only in the simplest type—computation—that consensus on means and ends exists prior to the decision. The judgment issue involves finding a cause and effect hypothesis about which a majority can agree. The bargaining issue involves finding a preference on which consensus can be established. The anomic situation requires the creation of both preferences and causation-beliefs acceptable to a majority.

If the fact or the fiction of consensus is not present at the time a choice is made—and this may frequently be the case when rapid decisions are necessary—the required consensus must be achieved following choice. The hypothesis here is that for organizational decisions to be implemented effectively both consensus and choice are necessary. If for reasons of expediency, choice is made *before* consensus is achieved, the burden of achieving consensus *following* choice remains.

This hypothesis, if accurate, has important implications not only for decision-making but for the larger administrative process of which decision is a part.

Conclusion

We have attempted to develop a format for studying decision processes in organizations, by identifying four major types of decision issues and pairing them with four major strategies for arriving at decisions. For each strategy, we have suggested, there is an appropriate structure. Obviously there are many combinations and permutations of issues, strategies, and structures, but we believe that the format suggested points to a limited number of such arrangements, and that patterns can be found in them. We hope we have shown that this approach to organizational decision processes has important implications for theory and application.

What has been presented here can be considered no more than a first approximation. The empirical evidence along these lines has not been collected systematically, and further conceptual development undoubtedly will be necessary. It is possible, for example, that added leverage can be gained by distinguishing between "lack of agreement" and "disagreement," and thus developing a nine-fold typology of issues.[42] This format could also be extended into an analysis of how decisions are blocked or prevented. Such an extension should tell us something about the important area of belligerent behavior in or between organizations, and it should also provide a useful test of the models presented here.

Whatever the eventual results, we hope we have made the case for development of sociological models of decision processes, which can be joined with the psychological "satisficing" model to their mutual advantage.

Footnotes

1. Herbert A. Simon. "A Behavioral Model of Rational Choice." *Quarterly Journal of Economics*, February, 1955; reprinted in Simon, *Models of Man*, New York: John Wiley & Sons, 1957.

2. For the notion of "composite decisions" see Herbert A. Simon, *Administrative Behavior*, New York: Macmillan, 1957. See also R. Tannenbaum and F. Massarik, "Participation by Subordinates in the Managerial Decision Making Process," *Canadian Journal of Economics and Political Science*, August, 1950.

3. This distinction is made by Chester I. Barnard, *Functions of the Executive*, Cambridge: Harvard University Press, 1936.

4. Simon, *Administrative Behavior*, (first edition), 1945.

5. For examples, see the collection of papers edited by M. J. Bowman, *Expectations, Uncertainty and Business Behavior*, New York: Social Science Research Council, 1958; and R. D. Luce and H. Raiffa, *Games and Decisions*, New York: John Wiley & Sons, 1957.

6. In Bowman, *op. cit.*

7. We believe this is not inconsistent with the statements of such diverse writers as Simon, *Models of Man* (*op. cit.*); Irwin D. J. Bross, *Design for Decision*, New York: The Macmillan Co., 1953; Richard C. Snyder in Roland Young (ed.) *Approaches to the Study of Politics*, Evanston: Northwestern University Press, 1958; Jacob Marschak in Paul Lazarsfeld (ed.), *Mathematical Thinking in the Social Sciences*, Glencoe, Illinois: The Free Press, 1954; and Bernard Berelson in Berelson, Paul F. Lazarsfeld and William McPhee, *Voting*, Chicago: University of Chicago Press, 1954.

8. Simon notes that what he terms "programmed" choice situations sometimes elicit behavior which suggests that the choice has been made in advance. In these cases, he says, there is a well-established procedure that leads through a series of steps to a determinate decision. He also stresses that programmed decisions may involve a very great amount of computation before a choice is actually made. See his paper in Bowman, *op. cit.*

9. Bowman, in *Expectations, Uncertainty, and Business Behavior, op. cit.*, commenting on the papers read at the conferences, notes that only two authors focus on cases involving nonseriability. She comments that "Neglect of the higher degrees of uncertainty (or nonseriability) was undoubtedly deliberate in some instances, reflecting the hypothesis that businessmen ignore parameters about which they cannot at least make reasonably informed guesses, and that they commonly avoid taking actions the outcomes of which are characterized by extreme uncertainty. . . . However, problems involving the more extreme degrees of uncertainty were probably by-passed for another reason, the obvious difficulty of dealing with them systematically." p. 5.

10. See Leon Festinger's important distinction between "social reality" and "external reality" as bases for the validation of opinions of group members. Festinger, "Informal Social Communication," *Psychological Review*, 1950, pp. 271-292.

11. Max Weber discussed the "colleagiality" or collegial system, but used the term more loosely than we propose to do here. See Hans Gerth and C. Wright Mills, *From Max Weber: Essays in Sociology*, New York, Oxford University Press, 1946, pp. 236-244.

12. The typical conception of the corporation as pyramidal in form, with ultimate authority peaking in the office of the president, is thus misleading. It would be more descriptive to think of the corporation as a wigwam, with a group at the top.

13. This view seems consistent with the findings of Stephen A. Bailey, *Congress Makes a Law*, New York: Columbia University Press, 1950; and E. Latham, *The Group Basis of Politics*, Ithaca: Cornell University Press, 1952. See also Latham in Heinz Eulau, S. Eldersveld and M. Janowitz (eds.) *Political Behavior*, Glencoe, Illinois: The Free Press, 1956.

14. For example, see F. M. and M. M. Keesing, *Elite Communication in Samoa*, Stanford: Stanford University Press, 1956; W. B. Miller, "Two Concepts of Authority," *American Anthropologist*, April, 1955 (Chapter 7 in the present

volume); and M. Nash, "Machine Age Maya: The Industrialization of a Guatemalan Community," *American Anthropologist*, Part 2, April, 1958.

15. Gerth and Mills, *op. cit.*

16. Although nominally a choice by vote, the majority approached unanimity, and it seems that voters were not asked to judge his ability to solve such specific problems as the war in Africa, but rather were asked to impute to him and endorse qualities of omnipotence.

17. Deutsch, et al. *Political Community and the North Atlantic Area*, Princeton: Princeton University Press, 1957. They say: ". . . our studies of the more promising strategies of integration have left us strongly impressed with the importance of political innovation and invention. Many of the decisive advances in bringing about political integration involved the making of political decisions in a manner such that improbable or original measures were adopted rather than their more obvious or probable alternatives. Many of the central institutions of amalgamated security communities thus were original and highly improbable at the time they were adopted. The American Articles of Confederation, the Federal constitution—. . . none of these has any close counterpart in the 18th century politics or law. . . . It seems worth adding that a number of amalgamated political communities were wrecked precisely as a consequence of decisions which were highly probable at the time and place at which they were made." p. 114.

18. Emile Durkheim, *Suicide*, transl. by J. A. Spaulding and George Simpson, Glencoe, Illinois: The Free Press, 1951. See also Robert K. Merton, *Social Theory and Social Structure*, Glencoe, Illinois: The Free Press, 1957, Chapters 4 and 5.

19. This does not guarantee, of course, that the various factions will remain members of the organization, for we have not ruled out the possibility that they will exploit other resources as substitutes for those provided by the organizations.

20. Dissensus over causation might be achieved by *withholding* pertinent information about cause and effect, but this is not foolproof because organization members can invent *fictions* to fill in the missing gaps. Dubin describes organization fictions as ways of dealing with the unknown, and suggests that fictions can provide the ideological goals and purposes necessary to an organization, as well as beliefs regarding the efficacy of available means. See "Organization Fictions" in Robert Dubin (ed.) *Human Relations in Administration*, New York: Prentice-Hall, 1951.

21. See James G. March and Herbert A. Simon, with the collaboration of Harold Guetzkow, *Organizations*, New York: John Wiley, 1958.

22. Recent exceptions to this generalization include Snyder, *op. cit.*, and Morton Kaplan, *System and Process in International Relations*, New York: John Wiley, 1957. Kaplan identified chain-of-command decision-making units; persuasive decision-making units; and veto decision-making units.

23. On the other hand we have no proof that the pure examples are rare. Millions of organizational decisions of a computational nature, for example, probably are made every day in bureaucracies. The mixed situations may be more noticeable and memorable because of the difficulties they pose rather than because they are more frequent.

24. It also has implications for personnel recruitment processes, but we will not deal with that matter in this paper.

25. This is suggested by the decision trees of decision theorists. See Luce and Raiffa, *Games and Decisions, op. cit.*

26. F. L. Strodtbeck, Rita M. James and C. Hawkins, "Social Status in Jury Deliberations," *American Sociological Review*, December, 1957. Similar observations have been made in the hospital setting by A. H. Stanton and M. S. Schwartz, *The Mental Hospital*, New York: Basic Books, 1954.

27. Melville Dalton, "Conflicts Between Staff and Line Managerial Officers," in *American Sociological Review*, June, 1950.

28. This often is *expressed* by questioning their competence.

29. James S. Coleman, *Community Conflict*, Glencoe, Illinois: The Free Press, 1957.

30. Robert F. Bales, "The Equilibrium Problem in Small Groups," in Talcott Parsons, Robert F. Bales, and Edward A. Shils, *Working Papers in the Theory of Action*, Glencoe, Illinois: The Free Press, 1953.

31. See Coleman, *op. cit.*

32. For a report on the increasing use of committees for key decisions on new products, on personnel policy, production volume, and long-range planning, see "Committees: Their Role in Management Today," *Management Review*, October, 1957.

33. For a similar conclusion, though approached differently, see Philip Selznick, *Leadership in Administration*, Evanston, Illinois: Row Peterson and Co., 1957.
    N. W. Chamberlain, in a study of the corporate decision-making process as applied to the transfer of employees, notes the distinction between deciding and managing the decision process, and offers a number of stimulating hypotheses. See Chamberlain, *Management in Motion*, New Haven, Connecticut: Labor and Management Center, Yale University, 1950.

34. See Latham, *Group Basis of Politics, op. cit.*

35. For an analysis of this see Duncan MacRae, "Factors in the French Vote," *American Journal of Sociology*, November, 1958.

36. Suggested by his analysis of union-management relations. See "Power and Union-Management Relations," *Administrative Science Quarterly*, June, 1957.
    Bernard Berelson makes a related point. Surveying political voting research he writes, ". . . it would seem to be at least likely that the *same* avowed principles underlie political positions at every point on the continuum from left to right. . . . Democratic theorists have pointed out what is so often overlooked because too visible, namely, that an effective democracy must rest upon a body of political and moral consensus. . . . In this circumstance, a seeming consensus which is accepted at its face value is far better than no consensus—and a seeming consensus is sometimes reflected in loyalty to the same symbols even though they carry different meanings. A sense of homogeneity is often an efficient substitute for the fact of homogeneity. . . . What this means, then, is that the selection of means to reach agreed-upon ends is more likely to divide the electorate than the selection of the ends themselves." See Berelson in Heinz Eulau, S. J. Eldersveld, and M. Janowitz (eds.) *Political Behavior*, Glencoe, Illinois: The Free Press, 1956, p. 110.

37. The important role of the larger context in facilitating decisions was suggested to us by Professor Bela Gold, School of Business Administration, University of Pittsburgh.

38. *Elite Communication in Samoa, op. cit.*

39. Such "loose" organizations are found in industry, too. For an instructive analysis of this, see Valentine F. Ridgway, "Administration of Manufacturer-Dealer Systems," *Administrative Science Quarterly*, March, 1957.

40. Rose Laub Coser, comparing medical and surgical wards in a hospital, finds that the emergency nature of the surgical setting results in decision-making by fiat, whereas the more tentative, diagnostic atmosphere in the medical ward results in decision-making by deliberation and consensus. See Coser, "Authority and Decision-Making in a Hospital: A Comparative Analysis," *American Sociological Review*, February, 1958, (Chapter 8 in the present volume).

41. March, Simon, and Guetzkow see this tendency. They write: "Because of these consequences of bargaining, we predict that the organizational hierarchy will perceive (and react to) all conflict as though it were in fact individual rather than intergroup conflict. More specifically, we predict that almost all disputes in the organization will be defined as problems in analysis, that the initial reaction to conflict will be problem-solving and persuasion, that such reactions will persist even when they appear to be inappropriate, that there will be a greater explicit emphasis on common goals where they do not exist than where they do, and that bargaining (when it occurs) will frequently be concealed within an analytic framework." (In *Organizations, op. cit.*, p. 131.)

Lipset, surveying political sociology, writes: "Inherent in bureaucratic structures is a tendency to reduce conflicts to administrative decisions by experts; and thus over time bureaucratization facilitates the removing of issues from the political arena." In Robert K. Merton, Leonard Broom, and Leonard S. Cottrell, Jr., (eds.) *Sociology Today*, New York: Basic Books, 1958, p. 102.

42. Suggested by Professor Frederick L. Bates, Department of Sociology, Louisana State University, in private communication.

index

Performance, 35, 65, 99; motivation of, 60; quality of, 60, 61, 64

Personal relations. *See* Interpersonal relations and relationships

Personnel, 8, 56, 57, 134, 135, 143; allocation, 171; background of, 39, 57, 62, 82; clerical, 87; managerial, 81; needs, 167; potential, 63; problems, 74; rank, 72; recruitment, 45, 74, 89, 90, 169-71, 189, 214 (n. 24); selection, 169; supervisory, 22, 81, 83, 86-90, 152, 171; technical, 90; training, *see* Training; unlicensed, 46; welfare of, 90. *See also* Staff, personnel

Persuasion, 168, 204

Planning, 42, 66 (n. 7), 73, 110, 132, 139, 150, 159

Policy-making, 6, 72, 91 (n. 8), 166-68

Political integration, 203

Political organization, 93

Political science, 12, 204

Political units, size of, 95

Power, 28, 29, 30, 32, 34, 35, 36, 69, 94, 100, 113, 126, 127, 135, 196, 201; contingent, 103, 104; defined, 19-20; differential, 25, 190; hierarchy, *see* Hierarchy, power, *and* Power, structure; illegitimate, 19; locus of, 25, 37, 101; nucleus, 35; perceived, 29; royal, 97; prerogatives, 103; rankings, 24; structure, 19-20, 23, 28-30, 32, 35; supernatural, 103-8, 110, 111, 112, 202

Preference, 197, 198, 200-3, 205, 208, 210; conflicting, 202; hierarchy, 200; scales, 201, 203, 209

Prestige, 44, 99, 104, 125, 128

Process, administrative. *See* Administrative processes

"Product differentiation." *See* Market, activity

Production, 32, 36; levels, 32, 34, 36; workers, 19

Products, 134

Professional: associations, 180; demands, 73; ethics, 172, 180; fields, 178; groups, ix; licensing, 170; personnel, 168, 170, 171; specialization, 167

Professionalization, 63, 178

Provincialism, institutional, x

Psychological model. *See* Models, psychological

Psychology, 12

Public administration, x, 15 (n. 6); theory of, 3, 4

Punishment. *See* Sanction

Purposes, organizational. *See* Organizational, purposes, *and* Goals

Q

Quality of work, 65

Quorum, 200

R

Recruitment, personnel. *See* Personnel, recruitment

Regulatory agencies and groups, 144, 146

Relations and relationships: authority, 178, 179; avoidance, 184; bureaucratic, 189; cause and effect, *see* Causation; dependency, 112; environmental, 117; functionally diffuse, 187; interpersonal, *see* Interpersonal relations and relationships, *and* Interaction; joking, 184-87 *passim;* kin, 112, 186-88; line-staff, 192; management, 151, 169, 175; primary, 65; service, 125; social, 183-84; status, 178-79; superior-subordinate, 190, 192; tribal, 93

Representatives, 201, 204. *See also* Delegate system

Research frontiers, 165

Research goals, 72, 76

Research method, 20, 21, 24, 26, 27, 36 (n. 4), 37 (n. 6-9), 39-40, 57-62, 74-75, 82-84, 119, 132-34, 141, 154, 160, 161 (n. 8-10)

Resources, 143, 149, 154, 166, 169, 175, 178-80

Responsibility, 21, 22, 40, 64, 72, 135, 136, 138, 157, 196

Rewards and punishments. *See* Sanctions

RICHARDSON, STEPHEN A., 17, 39 ff.

Role, 23, 35, 37, 53, 56, 58, 108, 113, 122, 189; administrator's, 15 (n. 8), 23, 50, 210; behavior, 119; conceptions, 55, 58, 60-63, 65; conflict, 73;

COMPARATIVE STUDIES IN ADMINISTRATION

*was composed in Linotype Caledonia with Craw Modern display.
Designed by John O'Connor, the book was printed
on White Saturn Book Paper by the William G. Johnston Company
and bound by William F. Zahrndt and Sons, Incorporated
for the University of Pittsburgh Press*